EXPLORING THE WEST

by Herman J. Viola

Smithsonian Books Washington, D.C.

Trade distribution by
Harry N. Abrams, Inc., New York

THE SMITHSONIAN INSTITUTION
Secretary Robert McC. Adams
Assistant Secretary for Public Service
  Ralph Rinzler
Director, Smithsonian Institution Press
  Felix C. Lowe

SMITHSONIAN BOOKS
Editor-in-Chief Patricia Gallagher
Administrative Assistant Anne P. Naruta
Senior Editor Alexis Doster III
Editors Amy Donovan, Joe Goodwin
Assistant Editor John F. Ross
Research Bryan D. Kennedy
Senior Picture Editor Nancy Strader
Picture Editor Frances C. Rowsell
Assistant Picture Editor R. Jenny Takacs
Picture Research Carrie E. Bruns
Picture Assistant Louisa Woodville
Copy Editor Eileen McWilliam
Production Editor Patricia Upchurch
Production Consultant Irv Garfield
Business Manager Stephen J. Bergstrom
Marketing Manager Gail Grella
Marketing Consultant William H. Kelty
Design Phil Jordan & Associates
Separations The Lanman Companies
Typography Harlowe Typography, Inc.
Printing W.A. Krueger Company

The author and the editors of *Exploring the West* gratefully acknowledge their debt to William H. Goetzmann, whose lifetime of research and writing on the exploration of the American West has blazed the trail for all who follow. Dr. Goetzmann's publications include *Exploration & Empire: The Explorer and the Scientist in the Winning of the American West*, for which he won a 1967 Pulitzer Prize; *Army Exploration in the American West, 1803–1863*; *The West of the Imagination* (with William N. Goetzmann), which accompanied a PBS series of the same name; *New Lands, New Men: America and the Second Great Age of Discovery*; and *Looking Far North: The Harriman Expedition to Alaska, 1899* (with Kay Sloan).

Manufactured in the United States of America
First Edition
5 4 3 2 1

Page 1: *Louis—Rocky Mountain Trapper*, by Alfred Jacob Miller; pages 2–3: String Lake, Jackson Hole, Grand Teton National Park; pages 4–5: Bull elk battle on a frosty meadow in Yellowstone National Park during fall rut; pages 6–7: *Encampment in the Teton Country*, by John Mix Stanley; page 8: Pen and ink sketch by Titian R. Peale of an Indian on horseback; pages 10–11: Scientists at campsite in the Yellowstone on Ferdinand V. Hayden's geological explorations of 1871–72; page 12: Sunset on the Colorado River.

Library of Congress Cataloging-in-Publication Data

Viola, Herman J.
  Exploring the West.

  Includes index.
  1. United States—Exploring expeditions.
2. West (U.S.)—Description and travel.
I. Smithsonian Books (Publisher) II. Title.
F591.V56 1988   978'.02   87-28515
ISBN 0-89599-021-0 (alk. paper)
ISBN 0-8109-0889-1 (Abrams : alk. paper)

CONTENTS

INTRODUCTION

America was born with an "exploring spirit." Indeed, the United States came into being during a distinctly new age of worldwide scientific exploration and discovery. Only exploration of the geography of the vast North American continent and contact with its many different ecological systems and multitudes of native peoples could lay a foundation for truly characterizing America and its peoples.

In this process of North American continental exploration, the West assumed almost mythical proportions as a land of larger-than-life. Informed people knew it was vast—a country of endless plains, high mountains, deserts, and even rivers that led, some argued, to lost cities and long-hidden empires. These rivers, like the Mississippi, the Platte, the Columbia, the Colorado, and the Yukon, seemed to lead to "the back of beyond," and the United States was weaned, if not born, out of this mystery—a mystery only the intrepid explorer could solve.

From the very beginning, the federal government played a large role in the exploration of the West. Now, Herman Viola makes this even clearer, if it was not already dramatized by his extraordinary exhibition in November of 1985, "Magnificent Voyagers: The U.S. Exploring Expedition, 1838–1842."

It was during the research for this exhibition that Dr. Viola and his colleagues at the Smithsonian became aware of the U.S. government's very large role in North American exploration. It is this role, especially as seen from the Smithsonian, that forms the primary narrative thread of this book. Jefferson's enormous personal role in the exploration of the West is highlighted in some detail—detail that takes us beyond the textbook observation that he purchased something called "Louisiana" from the French. Further, Dr. Viola has illustrated the contributions of the U.S. Army's Corps of Topographical Engineers in surveying and mapping the trans-Mississippi West.

In large matters of science, however, the Topographical Engineers and even the naval explorers soon began to owe a large debt to the new Smithsonian Institution. Dr. Viola's close-up description of the activities of Smithsonian assistant secretary Spencer Fullerton Baird in aiding the cause of exploration really forms the heart of this book.

Viola concludes this stirring, beautifully illustrated account of western exploration by discussing three explorers of Alaska: Robert Kennicott, William Healey Dall, and Edward H. Harriman. Kennicott came at Alaska from the Yukon, or Canadian, side. Dall worked to explore for a round-the-world telegraph line, while Harriman, with a Noah's Ark of "scientifics," including the gentle John Burroughs and the acerbic John Muir, spent a summer exploring Alaska's coastline aboard the good ship *George W. Elder.* Dr. Viola ends his book with Harriman's remark, "I don't give a damn if I never see any more scenery!"

A long time ago now I concluded my preface to *Exploration & Empire: The Explorer and the Scientist in the Winning of the American West* by urging others to follow up on what, after all, had been only a historical reconnaissance of western exploration. Since then a number of scholars and writers have improved my trail and, I hope, have partaken of the spirit of adventure that I felt along with the explorers out there in the unknown. In the "Magnificent Voyagers" exhibition, and now in this beautiful book, it is abundantly clear that the Smithsonian Institution continues to imbibe and communicate this spirit of scientific adventure.

William H. Goetzmann
Dickson, Allen & Anderson Centennial Professor
in American Studies and History
The University of Texas at Austin

Already the gateway to the West for fur trappers, traders, and explorers, the city of St. Louis rises over the Mississippi River in this 1832 painting. French fur trader Pierre Laclède and his stepson Auguste Chouteau founded a settlement here in 1764, and it was not long before St. Louis became the fur trade capital of the West.

JEFFERSON'S VISION

Thomas Jefferson, the grand architect of Manifest Destiny, never ventured farther west than Harper's Ferry, West Virginia. Yet he determined the westward course of America's territorial expansion as surely as he had earlier charted her route to political independence. Without question, our nation's phenomenal growth was due to his vision, his pragmatism, and, perhaps most important, his scientific curiosity. Clearly, such trailblazers as Meriwether Lewis and William Clark were his "eyes" to behold the wonders of the West.

Scarcely had the American colonies achieved their independence than Jefferson first revealed his interest in the trans-Mississippi West. Alarmed at word that financial interests in London were planning expeditions to explore the Far West—a pretext for colonization, he suspected—Jefferson decided the new republic should sponsor its own expedition. "How would you like to lead such a party?" he asked Revolutionary War hero General George Rogers Clark in early 1783. Clark could not accept the challenge and the anticipated British exploration failed to materialize, but Jefferson did not drop the idea. Three years later, while in Paris, he encouraged John Ledyard of Connecticut to undertake a journey across Siberia. Had Russian authorities not stopped him about 200 miles from the Kamchatka peninsula, Ledyard might have traveled from the Pacific Coast eastward across the North American continent. In 1792 Jefferson tried again, urging the American Philosophical Society, of which he was vice president, to finance a transcontinental expedition conducted by French botanist André Michaux. Although the botanist's recall to France blocked the plan, there is an interesting footnote. An 18-year-old army officer named Meriwether Lewis learned of the expedition and petitioned Jefferson to be included in it.

It was only after he became President of the United States that Jefferson was able to push his ambitious plan to completion, having waited impatiently to do so for at least two decades. But now his vision included acquiring the West as well as exploring it, a turn of events made possible by Napoleon's need for funds to finance his wars of empire. "All eyes, all hopes, are now fixed on you," wrote Jefferson on January 13, 1803, urging James Monroe to become his special envoy to France. "On the event of this mission depends the future destinies of this republic."

Monroe's "mission" resulted in the Louisiana Purchase, one of the shrewdest real-estate transactions in American history. For $15 million, Monroe and Robert Livingston, the U.S. Minister to France, obtained the entire 830,000-square-mile tract of land claimed by France in North America. The American envoys had little knowledge of what they had purchased, and the French claimed ignorance as well. French Foreign Minister Talleyrand insisted that the United States take Louisiana as his

An 1801 portrait of Thomas Jefferson at Virginia's Natural Bridge, right, evokes both his love of the land and his fascination with natural history. Although he engineered the Louisiana Purchase in 1803— thus doubling the size of the Republic—and urged Congress to appropriate money for the Lewis and Clark expedition, Jefferson never traveled farther west than Harper's Ferry, opposite, which he described as "one of the most stupendous scenes in nature."

In January 1803, James Monroe sailed for Paris to assist U.S. Minister to France Robert Livingston in his attempt to buy the port of New Orleans. When Monroe arrived, Napoleon offered to sell all of Louisiana to the United States. Left, the seal and gold-washed skippet from the Louisiana Purchase document.

country had received it from Spain a few years earlier.

"I asked him how Spain meant to give them possession," Livingston later reported.

"I do not know," Talleyrand shrugged.

"Then you mean that we shall construe it our own way?" Livingston asked.

"I can give you no direction," Talleyrand responded. "You have made a noble bargain for yourselves and I suppose you will make the most of it."

And that is exactly what Jefferson had in mind. Even as his envoys were negotiating with Talleyrand, he had set in motion his plans for exploring the trans-Mississippi West. On January 18, 1803, he asked Congress for $2,500 to defray the costs of

what was to become the Lewis and Clark expedition. Under the guise of encouraging trade with the western Indians, Jefferson proposed sending an expedition up the Missouri River to some westward flowing stream—ideally the Columbia—which could then be used to reach the Pacific. Congress accepted his argument that the trek across the continent would have commercial value and authorized the use of army funds for salaries and rations. By doing so, it blessed scientific exploration under military auspices, setting a precedent for scores of other government explorers who followed.

Planning for the expedition had obviously begun long before then, perhaps even before Jefferson took the presidential oath of office. Why else did he invite Meriwether Lewis, now a captain

in the army, to become his secretary and aide two weeks before inauguration day? "Your knolege of the Western country, of the army and of all it's interests & relations has rendered it desireable for public as well as private purposes that you should be engaged in that office," wrote Jefferson. Lewis, whose ardor for exploration had obviously not diminished since 1792, eagerly accepted the offer and for the next two years lived at the President's House—as the White House was then called—and at Monticello. During that time, Jefferson and his protégé had ample time to discuss their long overdue expedition.

As co-commander of the expedition, Lewis selected William Clark, younger brother of General George Rogers Clark, who had declined the command in 1783. Lewis had served under

Clark in the army, knew his mettle, and trusted his judgment. Asking him to keep the expedition "inviolably secret," Lewis invited him to join the enterprise and share "it's fatiegues, it's dangers and it's honors." Clark needed no urging.

The extension of American commerce may have been Jefferson's official justification for the expedition, but, as is clear from his instructions to Lewis and Clark, an equally compelling objective was the acquisition of knowledge. The Corps of Discovery, as the expedition was named, was not merely to find a suitable route to the Pacific—or a "Northwest Passage"—to delineate the "face of the country." They were also to observe its "growth & vegetable productions"; record weather conditions; identify the wildlife, especially animals deemed to be "rare or extinct"; and befriend the western Indian tribes, learning as much as possible about their numbers, militancy, and way of life. All observations were "to be taken with great pains & accuracy, to be entered distinctly, & intelligibly for others as well as yourself." To protect against loss, Jefferson instructed them to make several copies of all notes, placing them "into the care of the most trustworthy of your attendants."

Jefferson had not left the gathering of scientific data to chance. Since Lewis was to be the expedition "scientist," Jefferson saw to it that he received training in virtually every branch of the natural sciences considered essential for conducting a successful exploration. As a result, Lewis spent an intense three months in the spring of 1803 receiving instruction from astronomer-surveyor Andrew Ellicott, botanist Benjamin S. Barton, anatomist Caspar Wistar, physician Benjamin Rush, and mathematician Robert Patterson. This hurried tutoring did not make Lewis a full-fledged scientist, of course, but it is doubtful whether anyone else in the country could have performed the investigative duties more competently. As historian Donald Jackson has pointed out, Jefferson's primary goal "was to get a few men to the Pacific and back, encumbered no more than necessary by equipment, and intelligent enough to recognize and collect . . . the natural resources of the region." Lewis and Clark did just that.

Besides fulfilling their obligations to science, the explorers also had to serve as American ambassadors of good will. Whenever they encountered Indian tribes, Lewis and Clark would hold a conference, distribute presents, and inform the astonished natives that they now owed allegiance to the United States instead of to France, Spain, or England. The most important of the gifts the Indians received were American flags and medals bearing an image of Jefferson or George Washington on one side and the symbols of peace and friendship—clasped hands and a crossed pipe and tomahawk—on the other. Lewis and Clark distributed as many as 100 of these "peace medals," which the Indians valued so greatly that they often carried them to their graves. Even today, these Jefferson medals are occasionally found in western burials that have been uncovered by archaeologists, road construction crews, or erosion.

By the time they left St. Louis on May 14, 1804, the two captains had assembled a group of about 26 soldiers as well as interpreters, Clark's slave, York, and his Newfoundland dog,

The Corps of Discovery, led by Meriwether Lewis, right, and William Clark, far right, traveled more than 7,000 miles on its epic western expedition. Carpenter Patrick Gass of the exploring party was the first to publish an account of the journey. His journal, seen below with Clark's compass, includes the engravings, left, which show, from top to bottom, "Captain Clark & his men building a line of Huts," "Captain Lewis shooting an Indian," "A Canoe striking on a Tree," and "Captain Clark and his men shooting Bears."

Scannon. Military ranks remained important throughout the expedition, for, despite its extraordinary character, it was an army operation with military discipline—including an occasional flogging—firmly enforced.

The Corps of Discovery traveled up the Missouri until, in late October 1804, they reached the Mandan Indian villages about 60 miles upstream from what is now Bismarck, North Dakota. They remained in their winter camp, known as Fort Mandan, until April. After sending couriers back to St. Louis with reports and natural history specimens, the captains and their company set out once again, traveling in six small canoes and two pirogues. "This little fleet altho' not quite so rispectable as those of Columbus or Capt. Cook," wrote Lewis the night before leaving Fort Mandan, "were still viewed by us with as much pleasure as those deservedly famed adventurers ever beheld theirs; and I dare say with quite as much anxiety for their safety and preservation."

"Rispectable" or not, the expedition secured a place in history for Lewis and Clark. Toiling to the headwaters of the Missouri, they crossed the rugged Bitterroot Mountains and then descended the Columbia River to the Pacific where, in a dramatic moment, Clark carved the following words on a massive spruce: "Capt. William Clark December 3rd 1805. By land. from U. States in 1804 and 1805." Finding no trading vessels on the coast that could carry them to civilization, the explorers spent a miserable winter in a crude camp and then returned overland to St. Louis, arriving on September 23, 1806.

By any standard, their enterprise had been as successful as it was monumental. The first white men to cross this vast land, they had not only survived, they had thrived. Though they had encountered every hazard from hostile Indians to aggressive grizzly bears, only one of their number had died (probably from a ruptured appendix). They had walked, ridden horseback, paddled canoes, and poled barges; they had crossed seemingly endless prairies, scaled mountains, and braved torrential waters. Thanks to the evenhanded discipline of their two captains, the explorers had overcome every obstacle, met every challenge. No other 19th-century expedition to the Far West would be so free of blunders.

One reason for the expedition's success was the harmony of its members, even though—in keeping with the melting-pot character of the country they represented—they were an unusual ethnic mélange. Several were of mixed Indian and white blood, most were of English or Scotch-Irish descent, and one had been born in Germany. York was black. A giant of a man, he was a strong swimmer and a superior hunter. He also amazed the Indians, who came from miles away to see "Great Medicine," as they called him, and to rub his skin to see if the color would wipe away.

At Fort Mandan, the explorers had added to their numbers the French trapper Toussaint Charbonneau and his Shoshone wife, Sacajawea, who soon gave birth to a son they named Jean Baptiste—although he was known to the explorers as Pompey or "Pomp." Pomp was later educated in St. Louis at Clark's expense. Pomp's father had the dubious distinction of possess-

ing one of the West's most extensive collections of Indian-made pornographic pipe bowls, a fact documented in oils by artist George Catlin. Sacajawea rendered valuable service to the expedition by interpreting and by identifying plants and animals.

One of the most useful members of the party proved to be Private Pierre Cruzatte, part French and part Omaha Indian. An interpreter and musician, he somehow managed to protect his violin through all the hazards, and its lively tunes did much for morale. "Such as were able to shake a foot amused themselves in dancing on the green to the music of the violin which Cruzatte plays extremely well," Clark wrote. The violin also fascinated visiting Indians; as Cruzatte played and the men danced, the delighted Indians would remain entranced "until a late hour."

Cruzatte may have been an excellent fiddler, but, suffering from poor eyesight, he was a liability with a gun. Near the end of the expedition, he mistook Lewis for a wounded elk and shot him through the buttocks. The wound was painful but not life-threatening, and proved of little consequence—except to Lewis.

The expedition achieved all of its scientific objectives. Lewis and Clark compiled exhaustive and accurate information about the regions they visited, laboriously recording observations about flora and fauna, native inhabitants, and natural resources and climate. They determined the true course of the Upper Missouri and its major tributaries, proved that a navigable waterway did not connect the Mississippi and Columbia rivers, and made the first real contributions to understanding the topography of the Far West. Although Jefferson and others had

Lewis and Clark collected and brought back to the East numerous plant and animal specimens, Indian artifacts, and other objects, many of which have been lost to history. The Indian handicrafts shown here are from the Smithsonian and were collected by artist George Catlin, who devoted his life to studying and painting American Indian culture. Catlin may have obtained some of these objects around 1830 from William Clark, then serving as superintendent for Indian affairs in Missouri Territory.

believed that only a narrow, easily crossed mountain range stood between the United States and the Pacific Coast, Lewis and Clark encountered two formidable mountain systems—the Rockies and the Cascades.

In addition to their maps of western topography, the explorers returned with incredible amounts of scientific information. They discovered and described hundreds of species of fish, reptiles, mammals, birds, plants, and trees. Among mammals alone, they are credited with discovering the pronghorn antelope, bighorn sheep, mountain beaver, prairie dog, mountain goat, grizzly bear, coyote, mule deer, and various species of rabbits, squirrels, foxes, and wolves. Not only did they ship back or carry with them skins, bones, and horns, but they also sent live animals to Jefferson—four magpies, a sharp-tailed grouse, and a prairie dog. That Lewis and Clark shipped these specimens is remarkable enough; that the prairie dog and one magpie survived is even more so, considering their 4,000-mile trip from the plains of Dakota to the banks of the Potomac. It took almost four months. During that time, the bewildered creatures traveled by barge, ship, and wagon.

Imagine the surprise of the servant at the executive mansion who welcomed that shipment! Jefferson was at Monticello when the menagerie arrived, but his majordomo wasted no time in telling him: "I have just received . . . a barrel and 4 boxes, and a kind of cage in which there is a little animal resembling the squirrel, and in the other a bird resembling the magpie of Europe." These souvenirs from the West, he advised Jefferson, he had

placed in the room "where Monsieur receives his callers."

Unfortunately, American science and government were no better prepared to receive the collections of the Lewis and Clark expedition than Jefferson's domestic staff. Little thought was given to safeguarding their reports, journals, maps, and natural history specimens. In truth, however, the intellectual and institutional channels for adequate scientific analysis and preservation did not yet exist. Almost a decade went by before Nicholas Biddle's narrative account of the expedition, drawn from Clark's journals, was published.

Dr. Barton, Lewis's botanical mentor, agreed to write up the natural history findings, but then failed to do so. When he died in 1815, a friend wrote Jefferson that Barton had "left such an immense heap of papers, and in such disorder."

The botanical specimens in Barton's hands did not come to light again until 1896, when they were found—somewhat the worse for wear—in a forgotten cranny at the American Philosophical Society. Jefferson planted some of the seeds brought back by the expedition and sent others to interested amateur botanists. He retained a few Indian artifacts and zoological trophies, such as horns, which he displayed at Monticello, and shipped the rest of the specimens, including the magpie and prairie dog (which lived for about a year) to his friend Charles Willson Peale for his museum in Philadelphia.

Peale, like Jefferson, was universal in his interests, and he believed ardently in the potential of museums for public enlightenment. He had often expressed to Jefferson his hope for a

Lewis and Clark gave peace medals, such as the Jefferson medal whose two sides are shown at left, to chiefs of various tribes. The Mandan buffalo robe, above, with painted scenes of the Mandans and Minnetarees fighting the Sioux and Arikara, was collected by Lewis and Clark and presented to President Jefferson.

national museum in the nation's capital that would incorporate his collections. It was an idea 50 years ahead of its time. When Peale's museum closed in 1846, the collections were dispersed. Thus, it is almost impossible today to identify more than a handful of items from the Lewis and Clark expedition.

Although Jeffersonian America could not do well by the scientific fruits of the expedition, the President did not overlook his obligations to the men who had made it possible. Each received a grant of land, including Lewis and Clark, who also received public office. Lewis was appointed governor of Louisiana Territory, Clark that territory's superintendent of Indian affairs.

For three years Lewis and Clark had acted almost as one, but their lives afterwards could not have been more different. Temperamentally unsuited for his administrative post, Lewis was soon wallowing in a swamp of petty bureaucrats, jealous subordinates, and questionable financial transactions. Hoping to clear his

name and reputation, he left for Washington, arriving at Fort Pickering at the Chickasaw Bluffs—today Memphis, Tennessee—in what the fort's commander described as a "state of mental derangement." Just over three weeks later, Lewis shot himself at a roadside inn. He died on October 10, 1809, only three years after his triumphant return from the Far West. Although some claimed their friend had been murdered, Jefferson and Clark did not think so. "Governor Lewis had, from early life, been subject to hypochondriac affections," admitted Jefferson, who had witnessed his "sensible depressions of mind" during the two years the intense young man had been his secretary. Upon hearing the news, Clark said simply, "I fear the weight of his mind has overcome him."

Clark's subsequent life was as full and rewarding as Lewis's was brief and tragic. In addition to serving as governor of Missouri Territory, he continued to superintend Indian affairs for

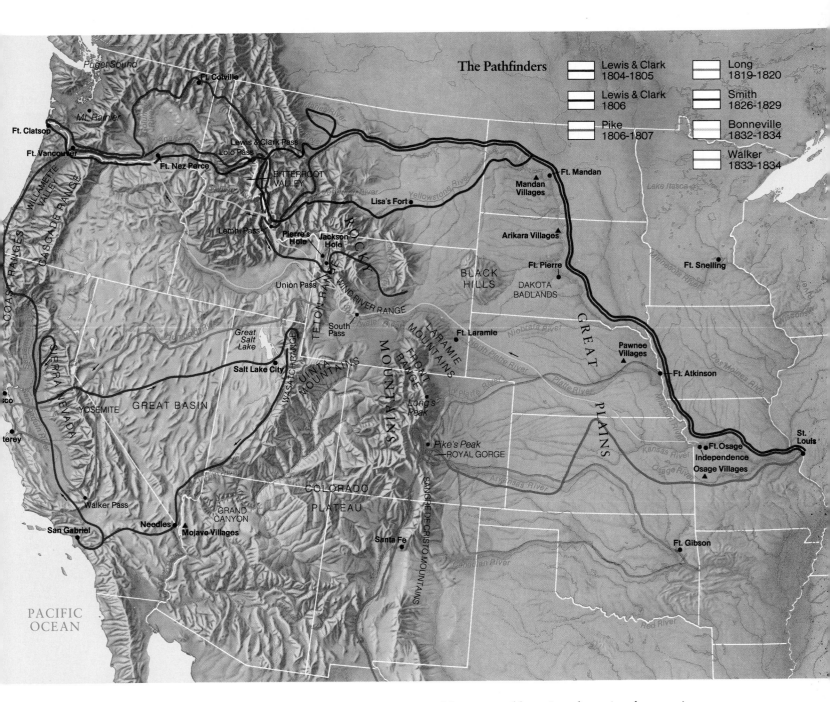

The Pathfinders

Lewis & Clark 1804-1805	Long 1819-1820
Lewis & Clark 1806	Smith 1826-1829
Pike 1806-1807	Bonneville 1832-1834
	Walker 1833-1834

Seeking more of the "verry palitable and tender" meat of a whale that had washed ashore just south of the salt-making camp, Clark set out with 12 men and (after her entreaties) Sacajawea for "the great waters" at what is today Cannon Beach on the Oregon coast, left. When they arrived, however, they *found that local Indians had already taken "every Valuable part" of the whale, leaving only the skeleton behind. Clark then traded with the Indians for a few gallons of whale oil and 300 pounds of blubber.*

some 30 years, and he enjoyed a national reputation as an authority on Indians and the West. An endless stream of government officials, adventurers, and would-be explorers came to him in St. Louis for advice and encouragement before venturing forth themselves into the land whose secrets he had been the first to uncover. He died at 69 on September 1, 1838, while at the home of his son, Meriwether Lewis Clark.

The Lewis and Clark expedition had given Jefferson the opportunity to enlist government support for science for the first time and also provided the basis for America's later claim to the Far West. Never was the importance of the expedition lost on Jefferson. "The work we are now doing," he wrote while Lewis and Clark were still wending their way across the continent, "is, I trust, done for posterity, in such a way that they need not repeat it. . . . We shall delineate with correctness the great arteries of this great country: those who come after us will extend the ramifications as they become acquainted with them, and fill up the canvas we begin."

Indeed, even before Lewis and Clark returned, Jefferson had begun the work of filling up the canvas, planning a series of expeditions into Louisiana designed to unlock the secrets of the trans-Mississippi West as well as determine the southwestern boundaries of his recent purchase. One would ascend the Red River to its source and investigate the headwaters of the Arkansas, another would explore the Platte and Kansas rivers, and a third would travel the Des Moines and the Minnesota rivers.

Only the first of these, however, was actually carried out—and this only after a trial run up the Ouachita River, a tributary of the Red, in October 1804. Led by William Dunbar, a noted scientist familiar with the Mississippi Valley, and George Hunter, a Philadelphia chemist, the journey was planned in such a way as to avoid a possible conflict with hostile Osage Indians and what would be a certain confrontation with Spanish authorities. These were reluctant to give up their historic if tenuous hegemony over the southern part of the continent, originally traversed nearly 200 years before by explorers and conquerors Hernando de Soto and Francisco Vásquez de Coronado. To foil any possible U.S. ambitions in the area, the Spanish had issued a proclamation prohibiting an expedition up the Red. Traveling as far north as Hot Springs in what is now central Arkansas, the three-month Ouachita River expedition became the first major scientific probe of Louisiana.

Jefferson persisted in his plans for Southwest exploration and finally succeeded in launching a Red River expedition, this one led by surveyor and astronomer Thomas Freeman. Consisting of 24 men and two flat-bottomed barges, the party left Fort Adams in Mississippi Territory on April 19, 1806. After 600 miles of backbreaking effort, the expedition was aborted by a sizable Spanish force, which ordered the Americans to turn back. Common sense prevailed, and Freeman reluctantly retreated.

Jefferson had better luck with exploration in the North. The choice of commander this time was Lieutenant Zebulon Montgomery Pike, a young officer destined to have his name forever linked with western exploration. Son of a career army officer, Pike sought glory on the battlefield. "You will hear of my fame or my death," he boasted during the War of 1812. Instead, he achieved immortality because "Pike's Peak"—a mountain he neither named nor climbed—became both the symbol and goal of a restless nation.

"Pike's Peak or Bust," the motto scrawled on countless wagon covers during the great westward migration, would have been an appropriate legend for Pike's coat-of-arms, for few who followed his path to the Rockies—and got "busted"—met with worse luck. He was a poor explorer with a knack for getting lost, and an even poorer judge of character. His patron was the notorious General James Wilkinson, and thus Pike became embroiled in the Aaron Burr-Wilkinson conspiracy.

Pike had first made his mark in August 1805, when he left St. Louis with 20 men and a keelboat full of supplies to locate the source of the Mississippi River. The effort was poorly planned and ill-timed. Upon reaching Little Falls in what is now Minnesota, he left half of his men behind and pressed forward by sled to Leech Lake, which he proudly but erroneously identified as the Mississippi's source. Hardly had he completed his report when he received orders to lead another, more challenging expedition to seek out the headwaters of the Arkansas and Red rivers to the southwest.

The orders came from Wilkinson, the crafty and opportunistic governor of Louisiana Territory. Although the full truth about Wilkinson may never be told, enough is known to cast suspicion on all his actions. For years he accepted money from the Spanish Crown in return for information on American military movements, which as governor and commander of southern troops he was often in a position to control. He was deeply involved with Aaron Burr in a scheme to carve out an empire on the southwestern frontier. Whether Pike was an unwitting tool of Wilkinson or a co-conspirator remains a mystery. Regardless, the circumstances of Pike's second expedition have all the ingredients of an espionage thriller.

His name forever linked to a mountain he neither climbed nor named, Lieutenant Zebulon M. Pike was the first official American explorer to traverse what is today Colorado and to note the "sandy deserts" of the western prairies.

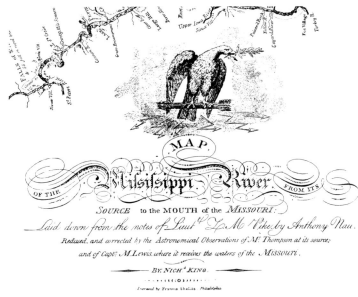

MAP OF THE Missisippi River FROM ITS SOURCE to the MOUTH of the MISSOURI:

Laid down from the notes of Lieut. Z. M. Pike, by Anthony Nau.

Reduced, and corrected by the Astronomical Observations of M. Thompson at its source;

and of Capt. M. Lewis, where it receives the waters of the MISSOURI.

BY NICH. KING.

Engraved by Francis Shallus, Philadelphia.

On August 9, 1805, Pike set out with 20 soldiers in a 70-foot keelboat to explore the headwaters of the Mississippi River. Pike did not find the river's true source, but his journal and map, a detail of which is shown at left, offered the first real cartographic portrayal of the Mississippi's upper regions. The following year, he led an expedition into the Southwest and, after a bitter winter trek through the Sangre de Cristo Mountains, was arrested in Spanish territory by a Spanish patrol and taken to Santa Fe, above.

Exploring the region in 1807, Pike described the sand dunes in what is today Great Sand Dunes National Monument in southern Colorado as looking like a "sea in a storm (except as to color)." The dunes, the tallest in North America, reach a height of almost 700 feet.

Whatever his hidden agenda may have been, Pike's legitimate instructions were more than enough to keep him busy. In addition to conveying 51 Osage Indians—captured by the Potawatomi several months earlier—back to their villages, arranging peace with the tribe, establishing friendly relations with its Pawnee and Comanche neighbors, and then exploring the Arkansas and Red rivers, he was to note the region's geography, geology, and biology. All this was to be done without alarming or offending the Spanish residents, a tall order since Wilkinson had warned the Spanish authorities that Pike was headed their way. To assist him, Pike had the questionable services of 18 enlisted men, who had accompanied him on his previous trip and whom he described as a "Dam'd set of Rascels"; General Wilkinson's son, a lieutenant in the army; an interpreter; and a civilian doctor named John Hamilton Robinson, who was apparently on a special spy mission for Wilkinson.

Pike left Fort Bellefontaine, 14 miles above St. Louis, on July 15, 1806. Five weeks of poling up the Missouri and Osage rivers brought the explorers and their Osage Indian contingent to the Grand Osage village, where they received a tumultuous welcome. The enthusiasm was short-lived, however, and, after days of negotiation, the Osages reluctantly traded them 15 worn-out horses as pack animals. Pike and his men, accompanied by 30 warriors and chiefs, set out on September 3, the first United States explorers to venture across the southern Great Plains. In a week they covered only 90 miles of rough, rocky terrain that left them all with "blistered and very sore" feet.

Upon reaching the first Pawnee village, Pike learned that a large Spanish cavalry patrol had been in the area searching for him and "had made a great impression on the minds of the young men." Perhaps this explains why the Pawnees were less than cordial and at times militant towards the small band of American explorers. After two weeks at the Pawnee villages, Pike and his company marched south across the plains of what is today Kansas until they reached the Arkansas River, at which point he sent Lieutenant Wilkinson and a small party downriver and back east. Poorly equipped for their task, the group managed to reach the Mississippi after a 73-day struggle, becoming the first Americans to cross the region between the Kansas and the mouth of the Arkansas. Pike, meanwhile, had been following the Arkansas upstream to its source, but he was also seeking the path of the Spaniards who had been looking for him. He did this, he later reported, in hopes of finding a convenient route to Santa Fe, but historians believe it indicates he had more in mind than reaching the source of the Red River.

As Pike continued to work his way west, he became increasingly disenchanted with the country, despite encountering large herds of game. The landscape reminded him of the African deserts, and he predicted that eventually the region would become an American Sahara, worthless for the agriculture of his time. Such a prospect, he thought, was not entirely unpleasant, as the region could then serve as a buffer between American and Spanish territory, a no man's land populated by roving bands of Indians and wild animals. "I believe that there are buffalo, elk, and deer sufficient on the banks of the Arkansas

alone, if used without waste, to feed all the savages in the United States territory one century." This inhospitable terrain could also serve as a barrier to westward expansion because it would force American citizens—"so prone to rambling"—to "limit their extent on the west, to the borders of the Missouri and Mississippi." Pike's observation launched the myth of the "Great American Desert," which, reinforced a decade later by Stephen H. Long, persisted until after the Civil War.

As Pike was crossing his "sandy deserts," he noticed a distant mountain, which looked like "a small blue cloud." A short time later, his party crested a hill and saw laid out before it the grand panorama of the southern Rockies, a sight that inspired his men—"with one accord"—to give "three *cheers* to the *Mexican mountains*." Pike decided to scale the magnificent peak that had caught his attention, but much like John C. Frémont more than 35 years later he badly misjudged the difficulty of the task.

Distances in such clear, dry air were deceptive, and 10 days of hard traveling passed before they camped near what is now Pueblo, Colorado. Then Pike and three men, clad in light cotton overalls and no stockings, set out on what they thought would be a hike of a few hours' duration. On the morning of the fourth day after this hopeful beginning, after a camp without food, water, or blankets, the little group reached a minor summit and discovered, to their intense frustration, that the mountain's real summit was still miles away and as high again as the one they had climbed. So barren and icy did it appear that Pike concluded, "no human being could have ascended to its pinical."

Major Stephen H. Long, *opposite, led the scientific contingent that accompanied the ill-fated Yellowstone Expedition of 1819, whose steamboats were the first to ply the waters of the Missouri River. Long and his explorers traveled in the* Western Engineer, *seen at left in a sketch by Titian R. Peale, as far as Council Bluffs, where artist Samuel Seymour painted Long in council with Pawnee Indians, above. The expedition as such was then abandoned, and Long was ordered instead to explore across the plains to the Rocky Mountains.*

Son of portraitist and avid naturalist Charles Willson Peale, 19-year-old Titian R. Peale served as assistant naturalist and painter on Long's expedition up the Missouri and to the West and produced some of the first pictures of western fauna, including his bison bulls, right, and his pronghorn antelopes, opposite.

That was the closest Pike came to the peak that bears his name. Still, the explorers could appreciate "the sublimity of the prospects below. The unbounded prairie was overhung with clouds, which appeared like the ocean in a storm; wave piled on wave and foaming, whilst the sky was perfectly clear where we were." The temperature was 22 degrees Fahrenheit. Returning to an intermediate camp they discovered that animals had destroyed their provisions. "It began to snow . . . and we, all four, made a meal on one partridge, and a piece of deer's ribs, . . . the first we had eaten in that 48 hours."

From here Pike's expedition went from bad to worse. Upon passing Royal Gorge, the Grand Canyon of the Arkansas, Pike turned north in search of the Spanish patrol and found instead another substantial river, which he identified as the South Platte. Veering west, he came upon yet another river, which he believed to be the Red, and, thinking he was now headed home, proceeded to follow it downstream. Four long weeks later, in January 1807, he found himself on a singularly inauspicious morning hunt. Discouraged when he discovered his weapon was damaged, Pike soon despaired when a fall "broke her off by the breach." Then, as "the unbounded space of the prairies again presented themselves to my view," a mortified Pike realized he was back at Royal Gorge. His Red River had actually been the Arkansas. "This was my [28th] birth-day, and most fervently did

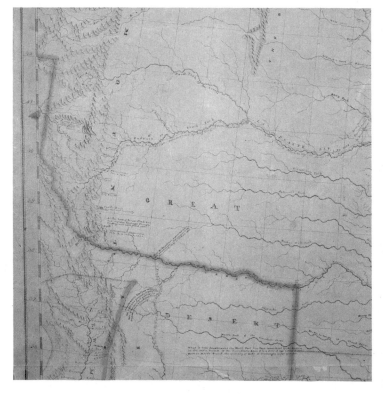

AMERICAN ANTELOPE.
Antilocapra Americana Ord.

View near the base of the Rocky Mountains

I hope never to pass another so miserably."

Yet more misery lay ahead, in the reality of a winter crossing of the Sangre de Cristo Mountains in what is now New Mexico and Colorado. This agonizing ordeal involved struggling through snowdrifts, withstanding intense cold, and going for days without food and for nights without sleep. Nine of his party of 13 men developed frozen feet, and eventually Pike made the heart-rending decision to leave behind those who could travel no farther. After two weeks, he found a pass that brought him into the San Luis Valley. On a sizable stream that he once again believed to be the Red River, Pike built a fort and sent five volunteers back to rescue those left in the mountains. Eventually all were saved, but not before the rescue party had returned with bones taken from the disintegrating feet of several still left behind, to lend urgency to their appeal for deliverance.

Meanwhile, on February 7, Dr. Robinson took his leave, claiming he had business in Santa Fe. His arrival there alerted the Spanish authorities, who sent out two men to find Pike's camp, which they readily did, perhaps directed by Robinson. They were followed nine days later by a much larger force, and Pike was politely informed that he was in Spanish territory. Instead of the Red River, Pike had found the Rio Grande. He and his men were escorted to Santa Fe, where his notes and papers were confiscated, then to Chihuahua, and finally by a long, circuitous route back across Texas to the American border post at Natchitoches on the Red River. This was the very spot Pike was supposed to have reached a year earlier from a different direction.

Even without his notes, Pike was able to recall a great deal of geographical, commercial, and military information, which appeared in a section of his report called "Observations on New Spain." Since at least 1,000 miles of his excursion in the hands of the Spanish authorities was through territory destined to become part of the United States, the data ultimately proved useful and pertinent.

Rather than returning to accolades such as those accorded Lewis and Clark, however, Pike found himself caught up in the scandal of the Burr conspiracy and fending off charges of collusion and duplicity. His staunch support of Wilkinson only served to make him more suspect, but nothing was ever proved against him, and many historians think Pike was guilty of little more than hero worship and gullibility. Nonetheless, the controversy hurt his reputation and kept him from promptly completing his report. Moreover, he had to reconstruct most of his journal from memory, leading his publisher to complain that no book "ever went to press under so many disadvantages." Fortunately, Pike's original notes and journals, held in Mexico for more than a century, were later returned to the United States and published in full by editor Donald Jackson. Pike's expedition may suffer in comparison to that of Lewis and Clark, Jackson wrote, but he and his men were second to none in courage and endurance.

When Jefferson left the presidency in 1809, the zeal for official exploration died out, not to be rekindled until the advent of Stephen Harriman Long after the War of 1812. If Jefferson is the father of western expeditions, then Long is their doting uncle, for he laid the bureaucratic foundation that subsequent government explorers used to such advantage. Whereas Jefferson had relied on enthusiastic army officers and amateurs as his scientific explorers, Long sought professionals. He also successfully urged the War Department to accept scientific data gathering as a legitimate corollary of military mapping and surveying. Yet despite the fact that he led five expeditions between 1816 and 1823 and covered an estimated 26,000 miles, probably more than any other government explorer, Long has been largely forgotten in the history of western exploration.

Born in 1784, Long seemed destined for a career as a school-teacher until his "mechanical ingenuity" brought him to the attention of the chief of army engineers, who hired him to work as an engineer on the defenses of New York Harbor during the War of 1812. This led to an appointment as an assistant professor of mathematics at West Point, where he so impressed his superiors that in 1816 he received a brevet commission as a major in the army's topographical engineer unit.

It was the ideal assignment for Long. His first important task was to select the site for a fort on Lake Peoria in Illinois, and he enjoyed this expedition so much that he proposed building a small steamboat for reconnoitering the main tributaries of the Mississippi and the Great Lakes. Instead of a steamboat, however, Long was presented with a six-oared skiff and the task of charting parts of the Mississippi and Wisconsin rivers.

These modest assignments may have answered the needs of military planners, but they only whetted Long's appetite for adventure. He wanted to lead a full-fledged scientific expedition. "Such an object," he wrote the chief of army engineers in October 1817, "would, I am confident, be of service to the Public, and at the same time lead to a very desirable issue as it respects myself."

In the spring of 1819 Long got his expedition. He was given charge of a group of scientists attached to the ill-fated "Yellowstone Expedition," a grandly conceived campaign to overawe the militant Indians of the Upper Missouri and intimidate British traders operating out of Canada by building a fort at the mouth of the Yellowstone River. Led by Colonel Henry W. Atkinson, the 1,000 troops of the Yellowstone Expedition boarded five steamboats, the first on the Missouri River. Unfortunately, the Missouri proved too shallow for these boats, forcing Atkinson to establish a winter camp at Council Bluffs, well short of his goal. There his men fell ill with scurvy and fever, ending any hopes of further operations in the spring. Congress, in the meantime, lost interest in the military expedition and terminated it.

Long and his scientists fared only a little better. His party included William Baldwin as physician and botanist, Dr. Thomas Say as zoologist, Augustus E. Jessup as geologist, Titian Ramsey Peale as assistant naturalist, Samuel Seymour as painter, and Lt. James Duncan Graham and Cadet William H. Swift as assistant topographers. Peale later distinguished himself as a naturalist on the Wilkes expedition, and Seymour, as a result of this expedition, is credited with being the first artist to sketch the Rocky Mountains. Long designed his own shallow-draft steamboat, the *Western Engineer*, to navigate the Missouri shoals and snags.

Still, problems continually hampered the work of the scientists. Say lost his horses and equipment to Pawnee raiders while collecting specimens on shore, and then he and Jessup fell ill, delaying the expedition until they were well enough to travel. Baldwin became so sick that he had to be left behind at Franklin,

a little community on the Missouri, where he died a few days later. His place was taken by Dr. Edwin James, who became the expedition's official chronicler. When the scientists joined Atkinson's troops in winter quarters at Council Bluffs, Long and Jessup took the opportunity to return to the East—Long to marry, Jessup to retire from exploring.

Congress, having decided to bring Atkinson and his troops back to St. Louis, sent the scientists in a new direction: overland across the prairies to the headwaters of the Red, Arkansas, and Platte rivers. "Detestable parsimony!" exclaimed Edwin James. "The only country but one in the world, that has not been reduced to an avowed or virtual bankruptcy; the country which has grown and is growing in wealth and prosperity beyond any

other and beyond all nations, too poor to pay a few gentlemen and soldiers for exploring its mighty rivers, and taking possession of the empires, which Providence has called it to govern."

Like it or not, the following spring the explorers headed west, following the Platte until they reached the Rocky Mountains. After locating Long's Peak, one of their few original discoveries, they proceeded southward towards the headwaters of the Arkansas, stopping along the way to allow Dr. James and two others to scale Pike's Peak, perhaps the first men to do so. Upon reaching Royal Gorge on the Arkansas, they divided into two groups. One, led by Captain John R. Bell, turned east to descend the Arkansas and accomplished little; the other, led by Long, went south in search of the Red River, struck the Cana-

After several unsuccessful attempts by different explorers to locate the source of the Mississippi River, Northwest frontier Indian agent and naturalist Henry R. Schoolcraft finally found it in 1832, and named it Lake Itasca from the Latin veritas ("truth") and caput ("head").

dian instead, and thereby clarified that aspect of western geography. But Long offset this contribution by reinforcing Pike's dismal impression of the southern plains, describing them as "almost wholly unfit for cultivation."

Unfortunately, most of the expedition's journals and scientific

One of the last of the great rendezvous—legendary annual gatherings at which trappers, fur traders, and Indians met to carouse and exchange goods—was pictured in 1837 by artist Alfred Jacob Miller. This youthful American had been engaged by Scottish soldier, adventurer, and heir to a peerage, William Drummond Stewart. Miller pictured

mountain man Jim Bridger, at lower left, in the steel cuirass and helmet that Stewart had brought him from his ancestral castle in Scotland. Although rendezvous continued until 1839, the Green River meeting of 1837 was regarded by participants as one of the wildest and best.

notes were stolen by three deserters from Bell's party on the lower Arkansas and were never recovered. Nevertheless, James's narrative of the exploration, published in 1823, incorporated Seymour's sketches, meteorological and astronomical data, Indian vocabularies, Long's topographical report, and maps.

The fifth and final expedition of Long's career as a scientific explorer focused on the Upper Mississippi. His orders from Secretary of War John C. Calhoun directed him to proceed up the Mississippi to Fort St. Anthony—today Fort Snelling—then to the mouth of the Minnesota River, up the Minnesota to the Red River of the North, up the Red to the 49th parallel, and then along the northern boundary to Lake Superior, returning home by way of the Great Lakes. His orders also included the by-now standard instructions to observe the region's topography, Indians, and natural resources.

Long's 1823 expedition was enlivened considerably by the addition of "the man with the red umbrella," as the Indians called him. Usually known as Giacomo Beltrami, this flamboyant Italian, an aristocratic former judge, was an archetypal romantic adventurer who always carried a parasol. Long did not fully appreciate him, and described him as an "Amateur traveler." Beltrami, in return, considered the major pompous and ill-mannered. "Major Long did not cut a very noble figure," the temperamental Italian later complained. "I forsaw all the disgusts and vexations I should have . . . to endure from littleness and jealousy."

Beltrami joined the expedition at Fort St. Anthony but, after friction with Long, struck out on his own to discover the true source of the Mississippi. He had not gotten very far before his two Chippewa guides, fearing a confrontation with their Sioux

enemies, deserted him. Thus, a somewhat bemused European with no wilderness experience found himself alone in the wilds of the Northwest, unable even to paddle a canoe. "It was absolutely indispensable for me to learn how to guide the canoe with the oar," he realized, but he found it easier to pull than paddle. "The fatigue I endured was extreme, and I preferred returning to my drag-rope [pulling the baggage-laden canoe] whenever the river permitted walking in it."

After considerable hardship, Giacomo Beltrami reached a small lake, which he named Julia and ecstatically but erroneously proclaimed to be the source of the Mississippi. This so pleased Beltrami, who fancied himself another Columbus, that in his memoirs he paid a tribute of sorts to Long. "I felt towards him a sort of gratitude for having by his disgusting manners only strengthened my determination to leave him, in order to discover the sources of the king of rivers; and it is partly to him that I am indebted for the fortunate success of my enterprise, as the Americans are for the jealousy which that success has excited in them."

Although easily dismissed as but one of many well-intentioned but impractical adventurers who roamed the American West, Beltrami's exploits are not entirely without merit. He assembled an impressive collection of Indian artifacts, for example, which today reside in a museum in Bergamo, Italy, his home town. Eccentric though he was, Beltrami's souvenirs are important ethnographic objects that predate similar items in the collections of the Smithsonian Institution. Fittingly, a county in Minnesota bears his name.

Henry R. Schoolcraft rightfully claims credit for determining the Mississippi's true source. A frontier scientist and Indian agent, he spent almost his entire life in the Old Northwest. As obsessed as Beltrami with the elusive source of the Mississippi, Schoolcraft tried at least three times to locate it—in 1820, 1830, and 1832. He made his final attempt in what was ostensibly a mission of mercy, undertaken to vaccinate the Indians in the region against smallpox and to attempt to curb the ongoing enmity between the Sioux and Chippewa. That he had other objectives in mind, however, is evident from his conversation with a missionary who accompanied his party of soldiers and government employees. Schoolcraft voiced concern that he did not have a splendid name for his anticipated discovery. "What," he asked, "are the Latin words for the headwaters or true source of a river?" The missionary had no idea, but he suggested *veritas* ("truth") and *caput* ("head"). These were classical enough for Schoolcraft. Dropping the first syllable of *veritas* and the last one of *caput*, he used what was left to form "itasca," the name he gave the lake when he found it on July 13, 1832. The Indians who lived there had called it Elk Lake, but Itasca it became and Itasca it remains today.

Long's last expedition closed out more than two decades of government exploration, but the vast interior of the trans-Mississippi West was still largely unknown and unmapped. Jefferson's dream of a series of systematic and comprehensive explorations had not fully materialized. Moreover, two government explorers—Pike and Long—had done much to dampen

Earliest of the great American fur traders, Louisiana-reared Manuel Lisa, right, pioneered the fur trade in the Upper Missouri River region. Dozens of trappers, among them the most famous mountain men, answered William H. Ashley's 1823 advertisement, above.

official enthusiasm about the West. If they were to be believed, it was not a fertile garden but a "Great American Desert."

Their discouraging assessments may have given a penurious Congress second thoughts about sending out more expeditions. They did not, however, deter the fur traders and mountain men, who by 1840 had penetrated every corner of the Far West, driven not by scientific curiosity but by the desire for wealth. In their pursuit of beaver, whose pelt was so highly prized in foreign markets, these reckless and fiercely independent nomads—folk heroes to some, lawless vagabonds to others—unlocked many of the secrets of the West. They followed its rivers, discovered its passes, climbed its mountains. Those who survived the tomahawk and scalping knife also played a key role in the official exploration of the West that took place when the beaver were gone. Men like Joseph Walker, Christopher "Kit" Carson, Thomas "Broken Hand" Fitzpatrick, and scores of their comrades provided invaluable service to government explorers as guides, hunters, and interpreters.

The trappers' rush to the Rockies was actually initiated by

Lewis and Clark, for they had not only found mountain rivers teeming with beaver, but had also blazed an easy trail. The first to follow it was Manuel Lisa, a Spanish trader from St. Louis who, in the spring of 1807, led a large party of trappers up the Missouri River and down the Yellowstone to the mouth of the Bighorn. Here he built a fort and launched the Missouri Fur Company, which dominated the Rocky Mountain fur trade for half a dozen years.

One of Lisa's most important recruits was John Colter, a member of the Lewis and Clark expedition who had elected to remain behind when his comrades returned to St. Louis. Alone and on foot, Colter prowled much of what today is Wyoming, Montana, and Idaho, becoming a legend in his own time as he sought new trapping areas for his employer. On his first great trek out from Lisa's Fort, he crossed the Continental Divide and stumbled upon a land of geysers and other natural wonders that became known as "Colter's Hell." He also traversed the Teton Range, witnessed the splendor of Jackson Hole, and was most likely the first white man to see the area that is today Yellowstone

At the 1837 rendezvous, Alfred Jacob Miller depicted Captain Joseph Walker and his Indian wife in A Bourgeois of the Rocky Mountains, *below.* Four years earlier Walker had concluded his historic journey as the chief guide of Captain Benjamin Bonneville's semi-official reconnaissance of a route through the southern Rockies to California. The trip was written up by Washington Irving and celebrated in this Pawnee Edition, *right.*

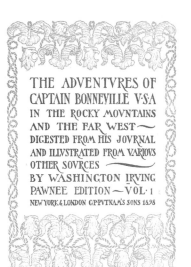

THE ADVENTVRES OF
CAPTAIN BONNEVILLE V·S·A
IN THE ROCKY MOVNTAINS
AND THE FAR WEST ~
DIGESTED FROM HIS JOVRNAL
AND ILLVSTRATED FROM VARIOVS
OTHER SOVRCES
BY WASHINGTON IRVING
PAWNEE EDITION ~ VOL· 1
NEW YORK & LONDON G·P·PVTNAM'S SONS 1898

The life of the fur trapper was often lonely, usually dangerous, and always hard. In Trappers' Tree by John Clymer, left, two trappers find scant shelter in a lean-to from a Rocky Mountain winter. Far-seeing eyes distinguish four great mountain men, below, left to right: Jim Bridger, Jim Baker, Jim Beckwourth, and Kit Carson. Alfred Jacob Miller captured the romantic essence of the wild, free life of the mountain men in Breakfast at Sunrise, 1858, right.

National Park. On subsequent outings he had a series of hair-breadth escapes from Blackfoot scalp hunters and vowed, "If God will only forgive me this time and let me off I will leave this country day after tomorrow—and be damned if I ever come into it again." A man of his word, he returned to St. Louis and to a pauper's death of jaundice in 1813.

Lisa's success encouraged competitors, the most successful being William Henry Ashley and Andrew Henry of St. Louis. In 1822 they formed a partnership and began advertising for "enterprising young men" willing to brave the western wilderness for an annual salary of $200. The names of many of those who answered their ads were destined to become legendary: Jim Bridger, William and Milton Sublette, Hugh Glass, Edward Rose, Jim Beckwourth, and Jedediah Smith. Most were illiterate, and a few, like Rose—a half-black, half-Cherokee river pirate—had already tasted adventure before signing on with Ashley and Henry.

Heartened by the response to their ads, the partners moved up the Missouri and built a fort and trading post. The next year, however, after 14 of his trappers were killed in battle with Arikara Indians living along the Missouri, Ashley deemed the river approach too dangerous. He began sending his men overland in small groups, staking them to a year's provisions in exchange for a part of their take in furs, which was to be collected at an annual rendezvous. This plan proved so successful that it soon became the mainstay of the fur trade. Henry retired in 1824, but Ashley continued the profitable business until the 1826 rendezvous, when he sold out to a partnership headed by Jedediah Smith. This group later sold out to the Rocky Mountain Fur Company, which was formed by still other veterans of the fur trade and New York financial interests.

Jedediah Smith was one of the most remarkable of the mountain men, compressing a lifetime of high adventure into a dozen years spent in the Far West. By the time he was 25, this Bible-carrying explorer had survived hand-to-paw combat with a grizzly bear and an attack by Indians, managing meanwhile to lead an expedition that explored the Wind River Range and crossed South Pass in the process. A skillful trapper—his single-season catch of 668 beaver pelts may well have been the record—he was an even more accomplished explorer.

In 1826, Smith went searching for the mythical Buenaventura River and became the first white man to traverse the land from the Rockies to California. He also was the first to cross the Great Basin, the first to cross the Sierra Nevadas from west to east, and the first to venture overland from southern California to the Pacific Northwest. Although he retired to St. Louis in 1830, he agreed to make one more trip. As he was leading a wagon train to Santa Fe, Comanche warriors ended his life. And so, at the age of 32, Jedediah Smith was gone. He had undoubtedly seen more of the West than any other man, but his journals were never published, and his vanished maps never recovered.

The giant of the fur trade, of course, was John Jacob Astor, the energetic German immigrant who parlayed the beaver into the financial empire of the American Fur Company. Astor differed from his competitors in his global vision, for whereas men like Lisa, Ashley, and Henry thought in terms of regional monopolies, Astor, like Jefferson and John Ledyard, envisioned the West Coast as merely a stop on the way to the markets of China and India. He therefore launched a two-pronged assault on the Pacific Northwest, sending a boat, the *Tonquin*, around Cape Horn to the Columbia River in September 1810 and an overland expedition across North America in the spring of 1811.

Soon after the *Tonquin* reached its destination, however, Astor's Pacific aspirations quite literally blew up. Sailing up the Northwest Coast in search of trade, the *Tonquin* was attacked by Indians, and most of the crew were massacred. The following day, as looters swarmed over the ship, a badly injured crewman managed to set fire to the powder magazine, killing himself and some 200 Indians on board.

Astor's overlanders fared somewhat better. Led by Wilson Price Hunt, the western crossing was the second great expedition to the Pacific Coast after Lewis and Clark. Although Hunt and his men suffered considerable hardship and privation—after eating their horses and dogs, they survived on skins, roots, and beaver paws—they proved it was possible to reach the Pacific by going over the central Rockies.

It was Hunt's associate, Robert Stuart, however, who made the major discovery of the Astorians. Heading east from Fort Astoria on June 29, 1812, Stuart blazed what was to become the Oregon Trail as he skirted the southern end of the Wind River Range and found the South Pass of the Rocky Mountains. A 20-mile-wide natural gateway consisting of a series of rising hills, South Pass transformed crossing the Continental Divide into an easy exercise that Frémont later likened to climbing Capitol Hill in Washington, D.C.

Not one to share potentially useful information with competitors, Astor kept Stuart's discovery under wraps for a long time. Indeed, South Pass remained his secret until finally, in his old age, he asked author Washington Irving to write *Astoria*. Since the account was written as a favor to the now retired fur baron, Irving had access to the American Fur Company's records and was able to chronicle the accomplishments as well as the disappointments of the Astorians.

Irving also immortalized another member of the fur trade family. This was Captain Benjamin Louis Eulalie Bonneville, a French-born army officer who received a leave of absence in 1831 to seek his fortune as a fur trader and explorer. Like Pike's, however, his real motives for going west remain somewhat clouded. Many historians believe that Bonneville had espionage as well as commerce in mind, for he carried official instructions from the War Department directing him to collect information on a variety of subjects other than the fur trade, including the geography, geology, and topography "of the Country within the limits of the Territories belonging to the United States, between our frontier, and the Pacific. . . ."

Given leave from the army for two years, Bonneville took five, using them to probe various parts of the West. Not much of a trapper himself, he had the good fortune to befriend and join forces with the veteran mountain man Joseph Rutherford Walker in the summer of 1833. Although much less well known

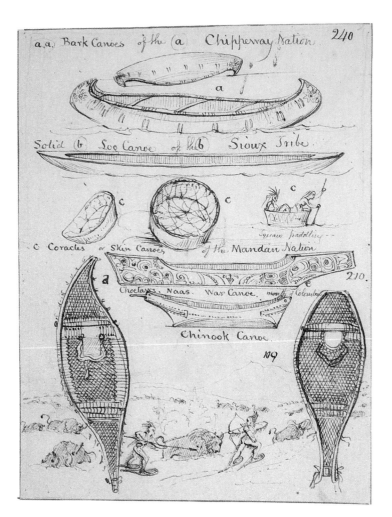

Completing as many as six sketches a day, George Catlin of Pennsylvania was the first artist to capture the intensity and vitality of Plains Indian life. His detailed sketches of Indian artifacts, above left, are among the valuable resources of students of that vanished culture. In a rare self-portrait, Catlin pictured himself at his craft among fascinated Mandans, above. An oil, left, depicts the area around the Big Bend of the Missouri near the mouth of the Platte, a stretch of the river Catlin traversed on the steamer Yellowstone in 1832.

PLATE. XLVI.

John James Audubon, perhaps the greatest of the early artist-naturalists to depict America's wildlife, is portrayed below in a painting by his son John Woodhouse Audubon. Audubon had just returned from a trip up the Missouri River as far as Fort Union to gather information for The Viviparous Quadrupeds of North America, *on which he collaborated with naturalist John Bachman. At right, Audubon's painting of beaver, whose glossy underfur—much in demand for the fashionable beaver hats of the time—lured scores of trappers into the wilderness. A collection of Auduboniana, left, includes two specimens of the now-extinct Carolina parakeet (upper left) and a manuscript in which Audubon and Bachman describe a new species of western fox.*

CASTOR FIBER AMERICANUS, LINN.
AMERICAN BEAVER.

than Jedediah Smith, Walker shares with him the distinction of being one of the greatest of their breed. He led expeditions on various errands throughout the West over a 41-year period, making many geographical discoveries. Despite numerous harrowing adventures, this taciturn captain died of old age, having, as far as is known, lost only one man from all the parties he led.

Commissioned by Bonneville to seek a trail to California, Walker and his men set out in July 1833, crossed the barren flat lands beyond Salt Lake, and followed the Humboldt River to the Sierras, which they crossed in a terrible 20-day trek into California, becoming the first white men to see what is now Yosemite National Park. They then proceeded to Monterey, where they were warmly received by the Mexican authorities. Setting out for home on January 13, 1834, they followed a different route back and found what became known as Walker Pass, the gateway through the southern Sierras, which became a major emigrant trail to California.

Except for his contributions to the cartography of the West—he may have been the first to represent the Great Basin on a map—Bonneville had little to show for his five-year experience. The army dropped him from its ranks for overstaying his leave but then restored him to service in time for the Mexican War. Were it not for Irving's romantic portrayal of this soldier-adventurer in *Scenes and Adventures in the Rocky Mountains*, published in 1837, Bonneville might well have vanished into obscurity.

Close on the heels of the mountain men and fur trappers fol-

lowed another group of explorers. Collectively, they could be
called naturalists, but in reality they were a disparate group of
artists, scientists, and other civilian enthusiasts. Although a few
were aristocrats like Giacomo Beltrami, most were impoverished
and eccentric zealots.

The artists are especially important to our story, for they
enabled a wide audience to visualize the American West. Best
known of the artist-explorers is George Catlin, who dedicated
himself to documenting Indian life and customs. Catlin's ambition was to visit "every nation of Indians on the Continent of
North America," and so, in 1830, after several years of painting
portraits in Philadelphia and Albany, he left for St. Louis, then
the hub of the American fur trade and the point of departure for
adventurers such as himself. For the next six years, he roamed
the West—from the High Plains to Lake Michigan and from
North Dakota to the Gulf of Mexico—in his relentless search
for Indian portraits and scenes.

Typical of the collaboration that often occurred between
civilian naturalists and the army was the permission given Catlin
in 1834 to accompany an expedition of dragoons to the southwestern plains. Led by Colonel Henry Leavenworth, the party

left Fort Gibson on the Arkansas River in late June, a reconnaissance mission with plans also to arrange a peace treaty with the
belligerent Comanche Indians. It was an extremely difficult trip
and ultimately a futile one. Several dragoons died—including
Leavenworth, who was replaced by Henry Dodge—and many
fell ill. Catlin himself suffered from the virulent fever, the result,
he surmised, of drinking contaminated water from stagnant
pools "in which the buffaloes had been lying and wallowing
like hogs in a mud-puddle." Despite his illness, Catlin not only
painted the first portraits of the militant Comanches, their Kiowa
allies, and the semisedentary Wichita, but also rendered some
of the earliest views of the wildlife and scenery in the Arkansas
River Valley.

In return for the army's protection, Catlin had offered observations "in the Sciences of Geology—Mineralogy—Botany and
Natural History, all of which have been my favourite studies."
He did collect fossils, horned lizards, and other natural phenomena, but after lugging them for several miles, the impatient artist
left them by the wayside, only to attempt other collections later.

Fortunately, Catlin demonstrated more self-discipline as an
artist than as a scientist. All told, he completed during his artistic

Trained as an engraver in his native Switzerland, Karl Bodmer accompanied German naturalist Prince Maximilian of Wied-Neuwied to America and then, starting in April 1833, journeyed with him more than 2,000 miles up the Missouri to the American Fur Company's remote trading post in Blackfoot Indian country near the river's headwaters. Bodmer worked industriously during the winter of 1833–34, producing magnificent paintings of the Missouri frontier and the Indians who lived there. His portraits of Mandan Indian life, *such as* View of the Mandan Village Mih-Tutta-Hang-Kusch, *opposite, depicted that culture only a few years before it was decimated by a smallpox epidemic.* Pehriska-Ruhpa (Two Ravens) Hidatsa Man, *left, bears striking testimony to Bodmer's masterful skill in portraying ethnological detail.*

career nearly 600 Indian paintings, which he exhibited in various cities both here and abroad. Although his hopes for riches failed to materialize, his wonderful gallery, including a significant array of Indian "curiosities," was eventually rescued by a wealthy manufacturer from Pennsylvania. His widow later gave this invaluable collection to the Smithsonian, to which the impoverished Catlin had long hoped to sell them.

Two other talented young artists, Karl Bodmer and Alfred Jacob Miller, also painted portraits of Indians and scenes of their unique way of life. Each of them spent an adventurous season touring the West, Miller traveling as far as the Rocky Mountains. Miller, furthermore, was the only white artist to picture firsthand the annual fur traders' rendezvous, although the golden era of the mountain man was already past its zenith when he saw and sketched it during 1837.

Most popular of the artists who painted western wildlife was John J. Audubon, a Frenchman by birth, who ranged North America from Labrador to Texas in his tireless quest for birds, mammals, and other animals to place before his easel. Although declining health prevented Audubon from making an extensive excursion into the Far West, he managed to complete his monumental study, *Birds of America*, by using the skins collected by other pioneering ornithologists such as John Kirk Townsend and Thomas Nuttall.

A protégé of Benjamin Smith Barton of Philadelphia and perhaps the most eccentric of the traveling naturalists, Nuttall accompanied Astorian Wilson Price Hunt's expedition of fur traders up the Missouri in 1811. A decade later he explored along the Arkansas and Red rivers, and in 1834–35 he traveled with Townsend to Oregon, California, and the Hawaiian Islands. Nuttall collected thousands of plant, animal, and fossil specimens, and studied the weather and the different Indian tribes. He would have been no help against hostile Indians, however, for he clogged his rifle with dirt by using it to dig up plants. Affectionately called "le fou" by his boatmen, the scholar was no less peculiar out of the wilderness in Cambridge, Massachusetts, where he was a professor of botany at Harvard. The only entrance to his second-floor residence there was by means of a rope ladder, which he rarely lowered for visitors.

One can scarcely overestimate the importance of these naturalist-explorers. Imagine, for example, how little we would know of the world of the Plains Indian before photography had it not been for Bodmer, Catlin, and Miller. And the early naturalists identified and described thousands of plant and animal species from the West that were new to science. We celebrate them today with, among many others, our Townsend's warbler and Nuttall's woodpecker. For the most part, however, these enthusiastic collectors lacked the means, temperament, and energy to organize major scientific expeditions. Moreover, their collections of specimens, often obtained at personal hazard and expense, were at risk. When the collectors died or became insolvent, their life work, usually little understood or appreciated, was often discarded or dispersed, although some—such as Catlin's paintings—found their way to universities, historical societies, or museums around the country and abroad.

Only the federal government had both motive and means to undertake truly systematic and comprehensive exploration. Jefferson had realized this and led the way, but, unfortunately, the leaders of government who followed him often lacked his vision and curiosity. The great canvas he had written about was eventually filled in, but it took the cooperation of many people and many branches of government, and perhaps even a smattering of divine providence. It also took the initiative and active collaboration of the Smithsonian Institution to ensure that the scientific fruits of further western exploration would not be lost to posterity.

MISSOURI BEAR.
Ursus horribilis: Ord.

T R Peale delin.

Specimens col. by Lt. Pike presented to C.W. Peale

In an 1822 self-portrait, opposite, Charles Willson Peale lifts the curtain on his Philadelphia museum, the first of its kind in the United States. His wide-ranging collections featured artifacts and natural history specimens from Lewis and Clark's and other expeditions to the American West, including two grizzly bears, above, which were taken as cubs by Lieutenant Zebulon M. Pike and presented originally to President Thomas Jefferson. Among those naturalists who were inspired to head west in part by the Peale Museum and its displays was botanist Thomas Nuttall, who collected the flowering dogwood, right, on a trip to Oregon in 1834.

The flagship Vincennes of the United States Exploring Expedition of 1838–42, commanded by Lieutenant Charles Wilkes, left, rests in Disappointment Bay, Antarctica, in this painting attributed to Wilkes. The Exploring Expedition sailed along 1,500 miles of the Antarctic coast and declared the great land mass to be a continent.

FROM SEA TO SHINING SEA

In background and temperament, the remarkable mid-19th-century explorers Charles Wilkes and John C. Frémont presented an interesting study in contrasts. A naval officer, Wilkes was a patrician by birth, while Frémont, an army officer, was the illegitimate son of an impoverished French refugee. Wilkes was arrogant and severe, Frémont charismatic and warm. And while Wilkes failed to secure powerful voices in Congress who could turn his vices into virtues, Frémont married the daughter of perhaps the Senate's greatest western booster and found many enthusiastic supporters among the other proponents of western expansion.

Their similarities were equally striking. Both became national figures as a result of their exploits as explorers. Both were fired with ambition and self-confidence, both harbored fragile egos. Although capable and intelligent, they were headstrong and willful, and each was to face court-martial during his career. Both were mapmakers and pathfinders, one by sea, the other by land. They both saw the Pacific Coast of North America—Wilkes by sailing around the world, Frémont by trekking across the continent—and both recognized its importance to the young nation.

These two great standard-bearers of Manifest Destiny may have walked with the gods, but they also shared the same setbacks, disappointments, and weaknesses that beset ordinary mortals. As Feral Egan, one of Frémont's many biographers, wrote, "the ultimate curse of being a national hero is that once the fires of acclaim go out, only the ashes of criticism remain." Both Frémont and Wilkes climbed the peaks of glory, but on more than one occasion they also descended into the valleys of disgrace and humiliation. As a result, despite remarkable achievements, they have only recently been restored to their rightful places in America's pantheon of heroes.

Charles Wilkes was only a lieutenant when in 1838 he was named to command the United States Exploring Expedition. Born on April 3, 1798, in New York City, he was the son of a prosperous businessman and the nephew of Elizabeth Seton, who was canonized in 1975 as the first American Roman Catholic saint. Although his father planned a banking career for him, Wilkes wanted to go to sea. When he was about 17 years old, he joined a ship bound for France as a cabin boy; three years later, he was appointed midshipman on board an American man-of-war. By the time he retired a half-century later, he was a rear admiral, having weathered two courts-martial and a reprimand for his audacity in the Civil War's celebrated *Trent* affair, so named for the British steamer from which Wilkes seized Confederate diplomatic agents James M. Mason and John Slidell. Not without reason was Wilkes known as "the Stormy Petrel."

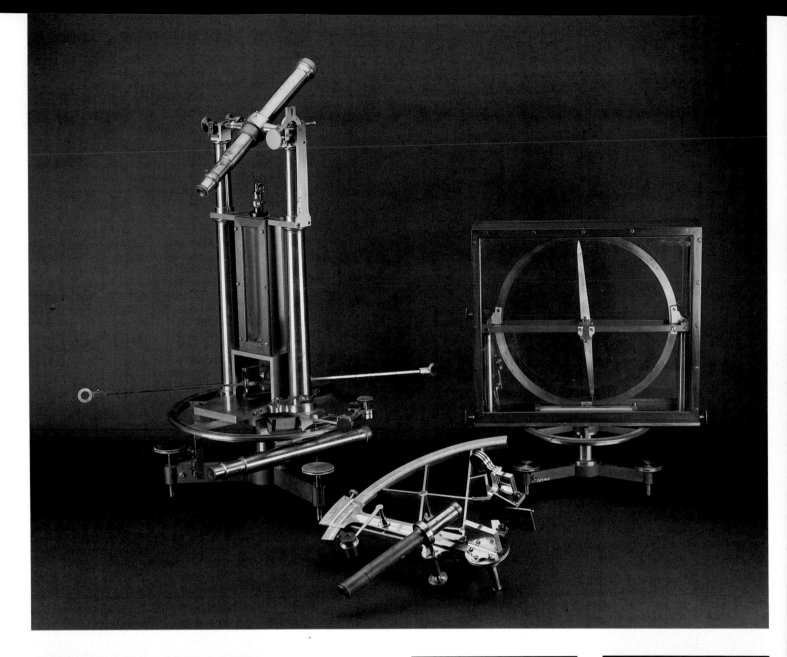

Scientific instruments like those above enabled Wilkes and his men to survey and chart islands and harbors around the world, as well as 800 miles of coastal and inland waterways of Oregon territory. The wooden globe, right, illustrates John Cleves Symmes, Jr.'s "holes-in-the-poles" theory, which, though not widely accepted, prompted New England sealing and whaling merchants to encourage Congress to sponsor a South Seas exploring expedition. Left, sailors as sketched by expedition artist Alfred T. Agate. Opposite, the title page and charts from the diary of armorer William Briscoe.

A silver nameplate, right, adorns the stock of expedition naturalist Titian R. Peale's double-barreled sporting rifle, which he used to obtain bird and mammal specimens. Places and dates etched in the plate mark occasions when the gun was fired against hostile natives. Peale's rifle is shown in full below in a display case from the Smithsonian's "Magnificent Voyagers" exhibition honoring the Wilkes expedition. Also featured are a harpoon gun with harpoon, a beaver trap (lower left), fishing apparatus (upper right), and artist Joseph Drayton's field drawings of fish and mollusks from South America.

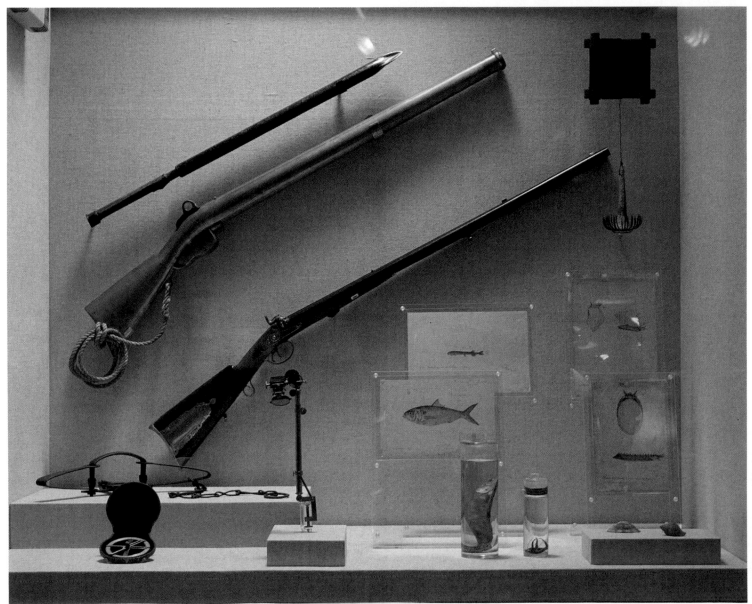

Despite his junior status in 1838 (of 40 lieutenants in the Navy at the time, 38 had seen more sea duty), Wilkes had scientific training and considerable surveying experience. Secretary of War Joel Poinsett's choice of the young officer to command the squadron proved to be wise, for Wilkes led the six small ships in what is recognized as one of the U.S. Navy's finest accomplishments in peacetime during the age of sail. In four challenging years, Wilkes's Exploring Expedition surveyed 280 islands, constructed 180 maps and charts, mapped 800 miles of the Oregon coast, and confirmed the existence of Antarctica as a continent. Furthermore, the Wilkes expedition helped to establish the U.S. Navy as well as America as a presence in the Pacific and in the world.

In addition to a full complement of naval officers and crewmen, the expedition included nine civilian naturalists and artists known as "scientifics," whose job it was to collect examples of flora and fauna from the places they visited. The scientifics provided the expedition its scholarly focus, and their appointment marked the first time in American history that civilian and naval personnel combined their talents and resources in a common effort. Young, enthusiastic, and talented, most of them were academically trained—in contrast to the wealthy amateurs who had previously dominated the natural sciences in America—and several went on to become giants in their fields. James Dwight Dana, the most gifted of the group and already the author of a major work on mineralogy, became one of the nation's most outstanding scientists. Artist and naturalist Titian Ramsey Peale, a member of the illustrious Peale family of Philadelphia, had traveled to the American West with the Long expedition two decades earlier.

It was Wilkes, however, who gave the Exploring Expedition its distinctive stamp. Aloof and resolute, he drove his men, his ships, and himself to the limits of endurance. His men thought him petty as well as harsh. At best, he was a most complex man. Dana commended Wilkes for his skill at charting, his daring, and his drive. No one, he thought, could have done better as leader of the expedition. On the other hand, he criticized him for "never praising his officers but always finding fault with them—and often very unjustly; especially when he had prejudices the screws came down rather severely."

Combining naval and scientific objectives was not always easy. Some officers derided the scientifics as "clam diggers" and "bug catchers"; others resented the numerous additional tasks they were required to perform, such as ferrying the scientifics from ship to shore so they could collect plants and animals from the islands the squadron surveyed. Even Wilkes, who took seriously the scientific objectives of the expedition, objected to the noxious odors that emanated from dissected creatures and prohibited their study below decks. Nonetheless, the two groups of men worked well enough together that the scientific and cartographic results of the voyage served as an excellent model for subsequent government-sponsored exploring expeditions.

Of the six ships that set sail from Hampton Roads, Virginia, in August 1838, only two—the flagship *Vincennes* and the *Porpoise*, a two-masted brig—completed the expedition. The *Sea Gull*, a small schooner, was lost with all hands off Cape Horn; the *Relief*, the Navy's first supply ship, was sent home because its lack of speed would have delayed the rest of the squadron; the *Peacock* foundered at the mouth of the Columbia River; and the *Flying Fish*, considered no longer seaworthy, was sold in Singapore during the return voyage.

By the time the squadron arrived in Honolulu in September

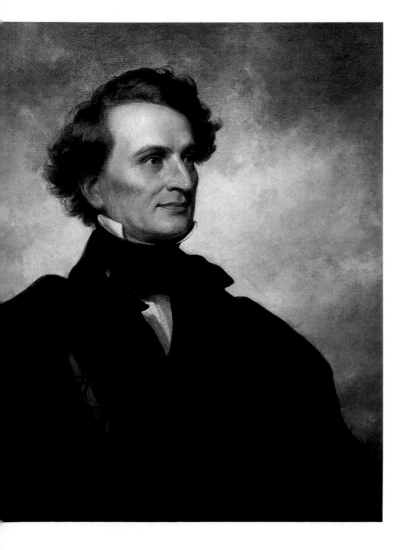

One of nine "scientifics" appointed to the expedition, eminent geologist James Dwight Dana was also an accomplished zoologist, and upon his return he produced Zoophytes *(1846) and the two-volume* Crustacea *(1852–53). The expedition's route among the many active volcanoes of the Pacific presented Dana with an unprecedented opportunity to study volcanism, and in 1849 he published* Geology, *the most enduring scientific contribution of the voyage.*

1840, exploring had lost much of its romance and glory. The "everlasting" expedition—as some were beginning to call it—was nearly a year behind schedule, and officers and men had grown heartily weary of surveying. Some 50 sailors, their enlistments expired, turned deaf ears to appeals to patriotism and offers of increased wages and shore leave and stomped away without a backward glance. "It was a sorrowful sight to see," lamented one of those who stayed, for "tha were some of the best men in the Expedition." To man his ships, Wilkes had to hire Hawaiians, returning them to the islands after his survey of the Oregon coast.

There was reason for discontent. The rigors of exploring and surveying in the waters of Antarctica had taxed men and ships beyond endurance. At one point, only three of the 18 sailors on board the *Flying Fish* were well enough to handle the frozen rigging and canvas. The others were so ill and miserable that death seemed a welcome alternative. Of the able-bodied seamen, one suffered from the "venereal" and another had feet so swollen he could wear only stockings. Then, from the relentless ice and cold of Antarctica, the explorers sailed to Fiji, which promised to be a tropical paradise. These islands presented a different set of terrors and challenges, however, including the very real prospect of being eaten by cannibals, a fate that had already befallen American sailors in those waters. Their worst fears were realized when natives on the Island of Malolo attacked the crew of a surveying launch and killed two officers, one of whom was Wilkes's nephew. It was the only time during their four-year adventure that their captain wept, his hard-bitten crewmen recalled. Wilkes retaliated by destroying two villages and killing more than 80 islanders in a brutal, hard-fought battle between club-wielding warriors and sailors armed with muskets and cutlass pistols.

The delightful climate and friendly people of Hawaii were a wonderful restorative of health and spirit, while the islands themselves were a scientific wonderland. Only the islands of Fiji could match them for botanical discoveries. The explorers also brought back at least a dozen specimens of the now-extinct honeyeater, the o'o, a native bird whose prized yellow underwing plumes the Hawaiians used in making their spectacular feather robes.

While Hawaii's splendid wildlife kept the scientifics occupied, the seamen conducted extensive surveys of her waters and volcanoes. In fact, the most dramatic event of the expedition's stay in Hawaii was a six-week scientific study of Mauna Loa on the island of Hawaii. Wilkes led a party of 16 expedition members and 200 porters, assembled on the authority of King Kamehameha III, in an arduous nine-day trip to the summit. Today, the ruins of the expedition's campsite on Mauna Loa are the only known physical remains of the U.S. Exploring Expedition in the Pacific.

The squadron's next major landfall was at the mouth of the Columbia River on the northwest coast of North America. From here, Wilkes and his men charted the coastal waterways from the Strait of Juan de Fuca, which today forms part of the U.S.-Canada border, to San Francisco, where they met up with

Tropical idyll, below, by Alfred T. Agate, depicts life in Hanapepe Valley on the island of Kauai. The 18-inch-high gourd container, right, similar to that carried by the Hawaiian in Agate's drawing, is enmeshed in woven fiber netting, which was suspended from the end of a carrying pole.

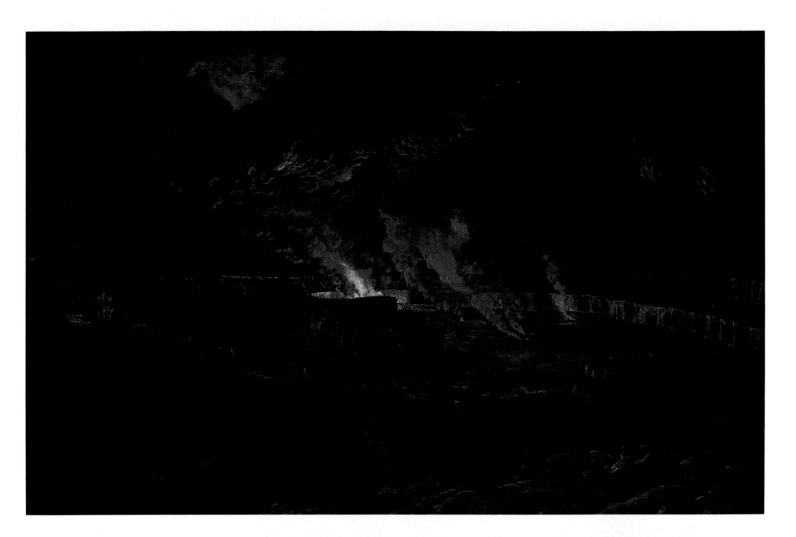

Titian Peale painted Kilauea by Night, *above, after visiting that volcano with Dana on the island of Hawaii in the fall of 1840. Expedition explorers studied both Kilauea and Mauna Loa on the Big Island. The treasure trove of botanical discoveries from the Hawaiian Islands included these specimens of* Wilkesia, *right, native only to the west side of Kauai and named for the squadron commander.*

Lieutenant George Emmons's overland party of officers and scientists from Fort Vancouver. The expedition's "Map of the Oregon Territory" proved to be a monumental contribution to the cartography of the American West. Issued in 1844, it was the first comprehensive map of the region north of the Sacramento River. Wilkes, not one to shrink from glory, boasted that this area had been virtually "incognite to the people of the United States" before his surveys, a boast that was supported by the Secretary of the Navy, who declared the map alone to be worth the cost of the entire expedition.

Scientifically, the Pacific Northwest offered a bewildering array of as yet undescribed rocks and other geologic features, which Dana and the other scientifics eagerly examined. Dana explored Saddle Mountain, south of Astoria, Oregon, collecting numerous fossil mollusks, but he was unable to examine firsthand the great volcanoes of the Cascade Range. Even from a distance, however, he realized from their shape that they differed from the volcanoes he had seen in Hawaii. He also correctly concluded that these were very recent volcanoes and that Mount St. Helens, at least, had been active within the past

few years. By the time he submitted his report, his suspicions had been confirmed by Frémont's notice of an 1842 eruption of Mount St. Helens.

Meanwhile, Wilkes had been conducting his own investigations. The United States may not have had any territorial ambitions in the Pacific at that time, but Oregon was a different matter. Expansionists both in and out of Congress had long since cast covetous eyes on the Oregon territory, a vast region on the Pacific Coast that today embraces Oregon, Washington, Idaho, and British Columbia. According to the treaties of 1818 and 1827, the territory was to be occupied jointly by the British and the Americans, whose claim was based on the discovery of the Columbia River in 1792, the Lewis and Clark expedition of 1804-06, and the Adams-Onis treaty with the Spanish in 1819. Nevertheless, it was the British who maintained de facto control of the region through the Hudson's Bay Company. By the time Wilkes's expedition arrived in 1841, 10 years of organized American emigration to Oregon had led the company to encourage immigration from Canada.

In his memoirs, Wilkes claimed that he would have con-

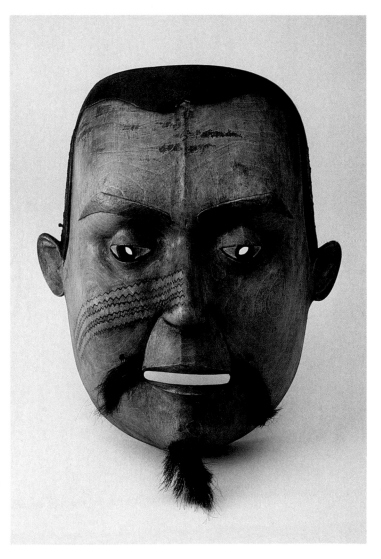

After arriving on the west coast of North America, the Wilkes expedition was presented with these wooden masks, opposite and left—carved by Pacific Northwest Indians—by employees of the Hudson's Bay Company near the mouth of the Columbia River. Below, a sailor struggles to measure the girth of a huge Sitka spruce or Douglas fir near Astoria, Oregon. The trees were identified only as pines in Wilkes's Narrative.

ducted his surveys regardless of British wishes, being "fully satisfied [that Oregon] . . . was to be full part and parcel of our country." However, he did nothing to raise the fears of the British Oregonians. Although the leading British official in the area, John McLoughlin, chief factor of Hudson's Bay, was suspicious of Wilkes, who had arrived without warning, he graciously extended the commander and his fellow explorers every courtesy. McLoughlin's friendship to the shipwrecked sailors from the *Peacock*, which included shelter, clothing, and food sold to them at cost, was reciprocated by Lieutenant William Hudson, the *Peacock*'s skipper, who sent the agent 40 sailors to help bring in the harvest.

Meanwhile, the overland party of explorers had gone up the Willamette Valley and then south to the Sacramento River and San Francisco Bay, where Wilkes met them with the *Vincennes* and the *Oregon*, a vessel he purchased to replace the *Peacock*. Of California, then still controlled by Mexico, Wilkes wrote: "It is very probable that this country will become united with Oregon, with which it will perhaps form a state that is destined to control the destinies of the Pacific." Although he expected that the United States would eventually acquire California, Wilkes nonetheless seemed to find the region of little interest. He prepared no special report on California and made no contact with Thomas Larkin, the American merchant who later led the American separatist movement. For Wilkes, direct intervention in pro-independence movements, like Frémont's during his exploration of California three years later, would have been unthinkable.

Despite some excitement in scientific circles at their findings, Wilkes and his explorers came home in 1842 to a seemingly uninterested public, an unfriendly Congress, and doubts about their achievements, especially those of their Antarctica exploration. Part of the problem was the Stormy Petrel himself, who by the end of the voyage had managed to alienate almost all of his officers, including one lieutenant who wrote, "Wilkes merits hanging, only that he deserved impaling, long, long ago."

Perhaps what hampered the success of the expedition more

Snow-crowned Mount Rainier, above, a 14,410-foot-high peak in the Cascade Range of the Pacific Northwest, inspired Joseph Drayton's painting, above left, during the expedi- *tion's stay in the region. Geologist James Dana studied these mountains from a distance and recognized in them a volcanism different from the kind he had witnessed in Hawaii.*

than anything else, however, was timing. Its accomplishments were almost immediately overshadowed by the exploits of John C. Frémont, the dashing and charming young army engineer considered by many the preeminent explorer of the American West in the 19th century. Strictly speaking, his nickname, the "Pathfinder," was a misnomer, since he traveled few trails unknown to his guides. Frémont's great contribution was to map the paths scientifically and to inspire people to follow them. As his wife, Jessie Benton Frémont, so aptly phrased it, "cities have risen on the ashes of his lonely campfires."

Frémont probably covered more of the West than any other explorer of the day, leading five expeditions across the plains between 1842 and 1853. Although his achievements were monumental, they also were controversial. Such eminent historians as Hubert Howe Bancroft and Bernard DeVoto dismissed him as an adventurer and filibusterer, criticized his conduct, and even questioned his character.

Undeterred by his humble origins, Frémont had grand aspirations and made excellent use of all opportunities that came his way. Born in Savannah, Georgia, in 1813, he attended the College of Charleston, but managed to get expelled just short of graduation for "incorrigible negligence."

No matter. Frémont's charm and his brilliance at mathematics had brought him to the attention of some of Charleston's leading citizens, among them Joel Poinsett, one of three patrons who helped shape his life. Poinsett had just returned from serving as ambassador to Mexico; later he was to become secretary of war and a principal figure behind the successful launching of the Wilkes expedition. Thanks to Poinsett, Frémont at age 20 became a mathematics instructor on a U.S. warship that had docked in Charleston before embarking on a cruise to South America. Upon Frémont's return from this voyage, Poinsett secured an appointment for him with the U.S. Topographical Corps, later the army's Corps of Topographical

AN EXPLORING EXPEDITION ON THE CANAL STREET PLAN.

Respectfully inscribed to Army, and the Board of Navy

I think that the Board are certainly at sea now! —

Navy Commissioners Pap Bowl

Three wise men of Gotham went to sea in a bowl

THE EXPLORING EXPEDITION AT THE SOUTH POLE, WAITING FOR STORES.

the Secretaries of the Navy and Commissioners, by

their humble servant

Robinson Crusoe

Engineers—the arm of the federal government most responsible for the rapid exploration of the West. Then, when Poinsett became secretary of war in 1837, he assigned Frémont to accompany the immigrant French scientist Joseph N. Nicollet on an extended survey of the Upper Missouri and Mississippi watersheds, meanwhile arranging his commission as a second lieutenant.

Nicollet became the second of three men to have a profound impact on Frémont's career. Together they formed an excellent team, and more important, Frémont obtained from Nicollet a solid scientific instruction in geology, botany, and zoology to complement his aptitude for mathematics and surveying. Much as he admired his scientific mentor, however, Frémont did not share his intense passion for scholarship. In fact, he was baffled by Nicollet's ability to become totally absorbed in his work and ignore the beauty of the scenery about them. "In all this stir of frontier life," Frémont marvelled, "Mr. Nicollet felt no interest

A lithograph printed in 1838, opposite, lampoons the U.S. Exploring Expedition, which was initially beset with delays, squabbles, and indecision. In the end, its achievements were heroic. Argillite carvings of sea captains, left, are attributed to the Haida people of Queen Charlotte Island. The one on the left was presented to the expedition by Hudson's Bay Company employees.

and took no share; horse and dog were nothing to him." All that mattered was the work at hand, which "engrossed his attention and excited his imagination." Indeed, "his mind dwelt continually upon the geography of the country, the Indian names of lakes and rivers and their signification, and upon whatever tradition might reveal of former travels by early French explorers."

Frémont spent two summers in the field with Nicollet and assisted him in drafting a map of the area they had studied. It was while working on the map that Frémont met his third patron, Thomas Hart Benton, one of the most ardent, fire-eating expansionists in the U.S. Senate. "Old Bullion," as Benton was known, had a grand vision for the West, a vision that had burned in his breast since Christmas Day 1824 when, visiting Thomas Jefferson at Monticello, he had come under the spell of the architect of American expansion. Always eager to acquire fresh information about western topography, Benton frequently visited Nicollet and Frémont in the Office of the Coast Survey as they labored on their map. Nicollet probably considered Benton a nuisance, but the Missouri senator's grand descriptions of America's western destiny excited Frémont, who was already developing a fascination for the West. As Frémont later recalled, these conversations were "pregnant of results and decisive of my life."

Decisive, indeed! Frémont became a constant fixture at the Benton residence, which included four lovely daughters as well as the eloquent senator and his wife. Frémont quickly became enamored of one of them, Jessie, then 16 years old and 11 years his junior. Her charms were such that two other suitors had already proposed marriage. As their friendship deepened, her alarmed parents attempted to nip the budding romance by having Frémont sent West on another surveying expedition. The ostensible purpose of the trip was to have Frémont gather the information along the Des Moines River that Nicollet needed to complete his map. The six-month absence did not have the desired effect, however. When Frémont returned, he and Jessie were secretly married.

Whatever his initial misgivings, Senator Benton finally welcomed Frémont into the family, for he could recognize in his son-in-law an agent of Manifest Destiny. If the Far Northwest was to come under American control, Benton realized, the government had to become more forceful in encouraging its people to settle there. Taking matters into his own hands, the persuasive and influential Missourian wasted no time in arranging with Colonel John James Abert, chief of the Corps of Topographical Engineers, to send his new son-in-law to survey the Platte and Kansas rivers to the Sweetwater River—orders which Frémont altered to include the Rocky Mountains as the goal of his reconnaissance. Accordingly, in the spring of 1842, Frémont left on the first of his legendary expeditions. So sure was Benton of Frémont's abilities that he sent along his own 12-year-old son, Randolph, whose role it was to show that even children could travel the trail safely.

Frémont's was hardly a select group. In addition to two dozen horsemen—mostly Creole and Canadian voyageurs and

A sampling of Wilkes expedition collections, opposite, includes coral, a stuffed caracara (upper right), a Patagonian armadillo, a Hawaiian human-hair necklace, and the voyage's chronometer observation book. Above, a taxidermist prepares bird specimens in an early Smithsonian laboratory. Preparation and cataloging of the thousands of Exploring Expedition specimens took decades to complete. In 1848, the Royal Geographical Society of London honored Wilkes with its Founder's Medal, which was restruck, left, for the "Magnificent Voyagers" exhibition.

unemployed trappers—and muleteers, who had charge of the carts, pack mules, and extra livestock, the little band of adventurers included two men whose names are forever linked with Frémont. One was Christopher—"Kit"—Carson, a young mountain man Frémont befriended on the boat from St. Louis. The other was Charles Preuss, a German cartographer who was to accompany Frémont on three of his five expeditions.

Preuss gave the expedition its scientific validity: he mapped the topography, collected plant and mineral specimens, and sketched the landscape. Theirs was a strange relationship, for the melancholy and obstinate cartographer harbored deep-seated feelings of contempt for Frémont, whom he considered "childish." Yet he served the explorer faithfully on two more expeditions before declining to join him on his fifth and last, signing on instead with Lieutenant Robert S. Williamson's Pacific Railroad Survey. He became very ill after his return to Washington, and killed himself on September 1, 1854.

What makes Preuss particularly fascinating is his diary, which he kept on all three journeys with Frémont. Written in German, it was inaccessible until recently when it was translated into English and published. The diary provides one man's remarkably blunt and candid appraisal of the Pathfinder, as well as important, on-the-scene accounts of early western exploration.

Although Preuss remains an obscure figure today, Kit Carson enjoys a reputation as a frontiersman second only to that of Daniel Boone. Indeed, his fame is due largely to the publicity he received through Frémont's writings. A complex person, Car-

son embodied much that gave the West its distinctive character. He could be brutal beyond belief in his treatment of Indians and Mexicans, yet he was highly regarded by his companions and devoted to Frémont.

The first expedition accomplished little of importance, for the explorers traversed well-known terrain to the South Pass of the Rocky Mountains. But the resourceful Frémont did attempt a few innovations to simplify the work of exploration. One was an inflatable rubber raft that could have been very handy had it been used properly. Frémont, however, tried to shoot rapids in it and nearly brought his passengers to an untimely end. They saved themselves and a few pieces of equipment, but they lost scientific instruments, notes, weapons, and the raft, which was damaged beyond repair. "It was certainly stupid of the young chief to be so foolhardy where the terrain was absolutely unknown," Preuss confided in his diary.

Thanks to Preuss, we also know that Frémont experimented with a daguerreotype camera on this expedition, which makes him the first explorer to photograph the West. Alas, this camera, too, was lost with the rubber raft. According to Preuss, it was a small loss, as Frémont had not mastered the art of photography anyway. "That's the way it often is with Americans," he wrote. "They know everything, they can do everything, and when they are put to a test, they fail miserably."

Despite his problems with rubber raft and camera, Frémont did have an undeniable flair for the dramatic. Spying a tall peak in the Wind River Range in what is now Wyoming, Frémont mistakenly declared it to be the tallest in the Rockies, and then proceeded to scale it and to plant an American flag at the summit. The gesture was typical of the exuberant explorer, and it was just such exploits that made him the darling of the expansionists.

Like so many of his actions, this one had its comic moments. Since the final ascent looked like an easy climb, Frémont carried no extra provisions or bedding. As a result, the fatigued and dizzy hikers had to spend a cold, windy, hungry night on the mountain. "The hike was disagreeable all around," Preuss grumbled. "No supper, no breakfast, little or no sleep—who can enjoy climbing a mountain under these circumstances?" In the end, a reorganized party of six men, including a black man who had to lug the barometer—"as a mulatto, [he] had no privilege to choose," Preuss remarked—reached the summit. The space was so small that only one man at a time could stand there. They fired their pistols, shouted "hurrah" a few times, drank their brandy, and unfurled a star-spangled banner carried by Frémont, who then took readings with the barometer that yielded an altitude of 13,570 feet. When Frémont returned to St. Louis, he found Jessie confined with their first child. In a grand gesture, he took the flag and spread it over her bed. "This flag was raised over the highest peak of the Rocky Mountains; I have brought it to you."

No matter that at least 30 peaks in the Rockies are in fact taller than the one Frémont scaled—his venture nonetheless marked a proud moment. Indeed, the image of Frémont waving a flag at the summit so captured the spirit of American expansionism that the U.S. Post Office, promoting the trans-Mississippi expedition in Omaha in 1898, chose to depict the scene on one of the first commemorative stamps it ever issued.

Back home in Washington with his wife and new baby daughter, Frémont began the task of writing his report, which he seemed to find more challenging than scaling peaks. "The horseback life, the sleep in the open air, had unfitted Mr. Frémont for the indoor work of writing—and second lieutenants cannot indulge in secretaries," Jessie learned. Consequently, she collaborated with her husband in drafting the troublesome report. Frémont got nosebleeds from the strain of writing, so he dictated and she scribbled, trying to maintain the furious pace of his storytelling. "It was hard," she later admitted, "but that was lost in the great joy of being useful to him, and so, swiftly, the report of the first expedition was written."

Well before the report of the first expedition was completed, though, Frémont and Jessie's father had plotted the second. In fact, it was Benton who actually worded the orders Frémont received from Colonel John James Abert, head of the Topographical Engineers, directing him to proceed beyond the range of the first expedition and "join on to your positions of 1842 on the Colorado of the Gulf of California. Thence continuing northwestwardly into the Flat-head country, and join on to Lieut. Wilkes' survey." That done, Frémont was to return east by the Oregon Trail and collect information for the construction of a chain of forts. As things turned out, Frémont's heroic

Known as the "Pathfinder" to a generation of westering Americans, John Charles Frémont, opposite left, lured settlers west with his vivid reports, maps, and descriptions of routes to Oregon and California. Flamboyant and ambitious, Frémont served in the U.S. Army's elite Corps of Topographical Engineers. Backed by his brilliant and equally ambitious wife, Jessie Benton Frémont, opposite right, and her father—Senator, orator, and voice of Manifest Destiny Thomas Hart Benton, right—Frémont made five well-publicized surveying expeditions to the West between 1842 and 1853.

sweep of the West, including what was technically an armed invasion of California, bore little resemblance to his instructions.

The second expedition was more ambitious than the first in every way. Leaving St. Louis in May 1843, the party numbered 40 men, among them the irascible Preuss, again Frémont's primary scientific adviser; Jacob Dodson, a free black member of Senator Benton's Washington household; two Delaware Indians; and Tom "Broken Hand" Fitzpatrick, another legendary mountain man. The indispensable Carson joined them later.

Ostensibly scientific, the expedition took on an ominously military aspect when Frémont added a 12-pounder mountain howitzer—supposedly as protection against Indians—to his other supplies and equipment. Indeed, except for Preuss, the little band of well-armed adventurers resembled anything but

surveyors. When Colonel Abert learned that Frémont had requisitioned the cannon, he ordered his enterprising lieutenant back to Washington for an explanation. His letter, however, reached St. Louis after Frémont had departed for the West.

Frémont kept his cannon, but it was hardly worth the trouble it caused. Never fired in anger or defense, it was used for occasional target practice, to celebrate Christmas, and to shoot buffaloes—"a cruel but amusing sport," reported Preuss—before being abandoned in the Sierra Nevada Mountains.

One of Frémont's contributions during this expedition was to name the series of intermontane depressions that contain the Great Salt Lake the "Great Basin." "I am doubtful if the followers of Balboa felt more enthusiasm, when, from the heights of the Andes, they saw for the first time the great

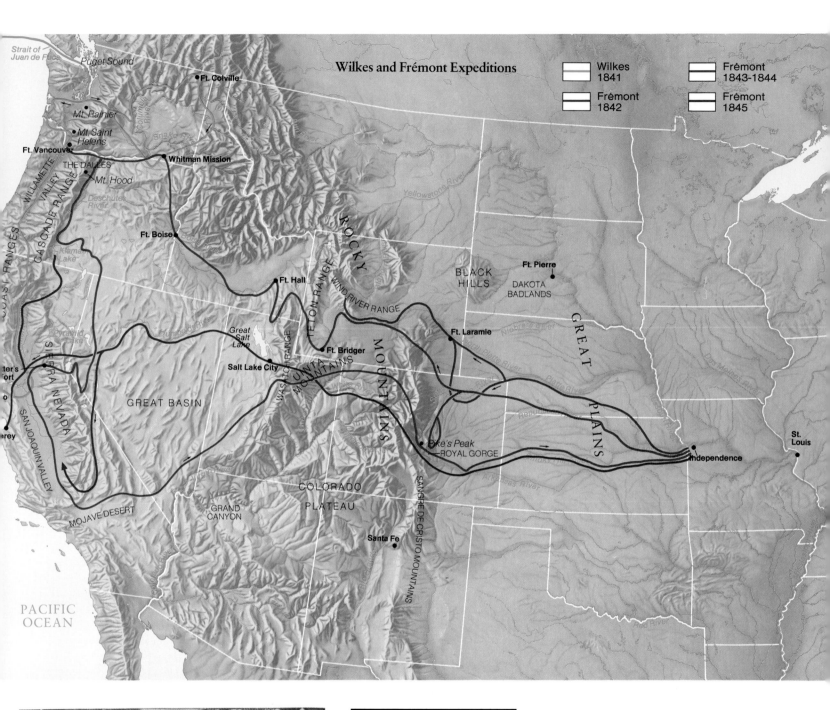

Wilkes and Frémont Expeditions

	Wilkes 1841		Frémont 1843-1844
	Frémont 1842		Frémont 1845

Strait of Juan de Fuca
Puget Sound
• Ft. Colville
Mt. Rainier
Mt. Saint Helens
Ft. Vancouver
THE DALLES
Whitman Mission
Mt. Hood
CASCADE RANGE
Deschutes River
WILLAMETTE VALLEY
COAST RANGES
Ft. Boise
ROCKY
WIND RIVER RANGE
TETON RANGE
BLACK HILLS
• Ft. Pierre
DAKOTA BADLANDS
Yellowstone River
Klamath Lake
Ft. Hall
Pyramid Lake
Humboldt River
Great Salt Lake
WASATCH RANGE
Ft. Bridger
UINTA MOUNTAINS
Salt Lake City
Ft. Laramie
MOUNTAINS
GREAT PLAINS
Niobrara River
North Platte River
SIERRA NEVADA
GREAT BASIN
Platte River
ter's Fort
SAN JOAQUIN VALLEY
Republican River
Kansas River
Independence
St. Louis
rey
Pike's Peak
ROYAL GORGE
MOJAVE DESERT
GRAND CANYON
COLORADO PLATEAU
SANGRE DE CRISTO MOUNTAINS
Arkansas River
Santa Fe
Red River
Des Moines River
PACIFIC OCEAN

Moving Camp, *opposite, from* Frémont's Memoirs of My Life, *depicts a scene in the Platte River Valley on his first trip to the West. In the Wind River Range of today's Wyoming, Frémont and his party spent a cold, hungry night in the open before he triumphantly planted* his flag on a peak he mistakenly thought was the highest in the Rockies. The 1842 feat made him famous and was widely depicted, as in this commemorative stamp, left.

Western ocean," he wrote. Since many trappers believed a whirlpool in the middle of the Great Salt Lake provided a subterranean outlet to the sea, Frémont was especially anxious to explore the lake. But the inflatable boat was leaky, and to keep afloat one of the men had to work the bellows constantly. Nevertheless, Frémont surveyed part of the lake and went out as far as a rocky island, where he and the boatmen spent the night. Convinced that no whirlpool existed and trusting their boat no farther, Frémont returned to shore, erroneously believing they had been the first men to break "the long solitude of the place." Frémont described the region in such glowing terms that Mormon leader Brigham Young was later to choose the site as the final home for his persecuted followers.

From the Great Salt Lake, Frémont proceeded to the Columbia River to fulfill the primary purpose of the expedition, which was to link his 1842 survey with the Wilkes survey. On this leg, he and Preuss busied themselves recording descriptive details of the terrain and collecting botanical specimens, spring waters, soils, and stones for later analysis. They determined the locations and heights of such notable peaks as Mount Hood, Mount Rainier, and Mount St. Helens, which, from a distance of 50 miles, they saw in eruption. And they added to their collections a sample of the ash with which the volcano had coated the whole region at the height of its activity the previous year.

Proceeding along the Snake River, they next visited the religious mission run by Marcus Whitman at Walla Walla. Preuss, as usual, was unimpressed. "I was so disappointed after all that to-do about the . . . settlement. I actually believed we would find a sort of paradise. But it is not much better than the miserable country which we have crossed. . . . The residence is a poor hut built of sod, a mill likewise built of sod. No garden; the corn is planted here and there among the shrubs."

From there they went by canoe to Fort Vancouver, a trip Preuss would have gladly missed. "Never have I experienced such a disagreeable journey on water." Frémont thought otherwise. "We were a motley group, but all happy; three unknown Indians; Jacob, a colored man; Mr. Preuss, a German; Bernier, creole French; and myself."

Now, his survey completed, Frémont could have simply retraced his steps and returned to St. Louis, but this he chose not to do. Evidently, his plan from the first had been to make a sweeping southbound arc that would carry him through parts of Nevada, California, Utah, and New Mexico. His men, Frémont later claimed, welcomed the challenge—"nor did any extremity of peril and privation, to which we were afterwards exposed, ever belie, or derogate from, the fine spirit of this brave and generous commencement."

What choice did they have? After resting several days, Frémont turned south towards Nevada, discovering Pyramid Lake. By late January 1844, the Pathfinder was deep in the Sierra Nevadas, which he decided to cross despite strong warnings from Indians that it would be foolhardy to do so. Forty-five days later the "brave and generous commencement" staggered down from the foothills and on to John Sutter's

Wild and remote, the rugged peaks of Wyoming's Wind River Range, right, have changed little since Frémont climbed one in 1842. Left, springtime waters fill the Platte River, often described by settlers following its banks to the West as "a mile wide and an inch deep." The route along the river was one of those traced by Frémont in 1843–44.

Fort Laramie or Sublette's Fort ~ near the Nebraska or Platte River

Gathered for trade, Oglala Sioux camp outside Fort Laramie in this 1837 painting by Alfred Jacob Miller. Frémont's party visited this fort, which was originally an American Fur Company post, in 1842 and 1843. Overleaf: After his remarkable expedition of 1843–44 to the Northwest and California, Frémont and his gifted German cartographer, Charles Preuss, prepared a set of seven annotated topographical maps of Frémont's route from the mouth of the Kansas River on the Missouri (the site of what is now Kansas City, Kansas) to the conjunction of the Walla Walla and Columbia rivers in southeastern Washington. Prepared to aid the growing tide of westward-bound settlers, the maps contained extensive notes on terrain, weather, availability of animal feed and water, and hazards—including hostile Indian tribes. Part of map Section 6 is shown here, representing a portion of the route as it paralleled a stretch of the river now known as the Snake, southeast of today's Boise, Idaho. Frémont regarded this arid, rocky stretch as "the most trying section for the traveller on the whole route."

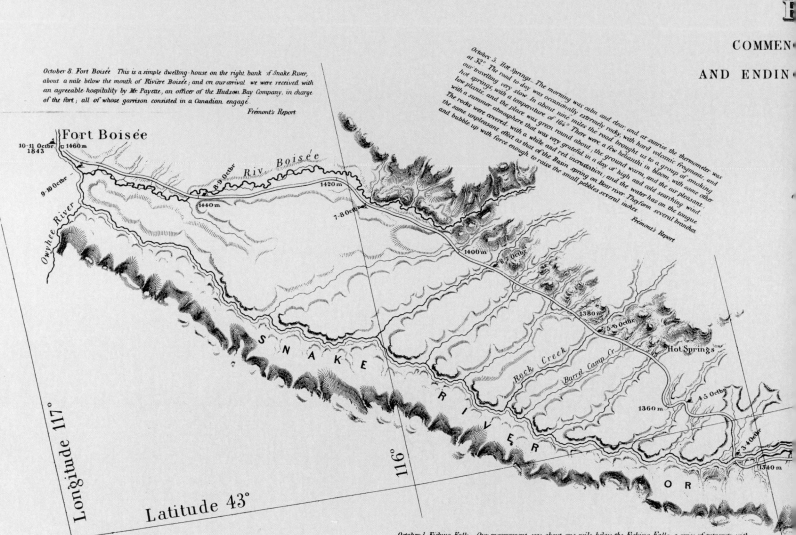

October 8. Fort Boisée. This is a simple dwelling-house on the right bank of Snake River, about a mile below the mouth of Rivière Boisée; and on our arrival we were received with an agreeable hospitality by Mr. Payette, an officer of the Hudson Bay Company, in charge of the fort; all of whose garrison consisted in a Canadian engagé.

Frémont's Report

October 5. Hot Springs. The morning was calm and clear, and at sunrise the thermometer was at 32°. The road to-day was occasionally extremely rocky, and our travelling very slow. In about nine miles the road brought us to a group of smoking hot springs, with a temperature above of 164°. There were a few helianthi in bloom, with some other low plants, and the place was green round about; the ground warm, and the air pleasant, with a summer atmosphere that was very grateful in a day of high wind and cold searching wind. The rocks were covered with a white and red incrustation; and the water has on the tongue the same unpleasant effect as that of the Basin spring on Bear river. They form several branches, and bubble up with force enough to raise the small pebbles several inches.

Frémont's Report

Fort Boisée

Riv. Boisée

Owyhee River

SNAKE RIVER

Rock Creek

Barrel Camp Cr.

Hot Springs

OR

Longitude 117°

Latitude 43°

Longitude 115°

Longitude 116°

October 1. Fishing Falls. Our encampment was about one mile below the Fishing Falls, a series of cataracts with very inclined planes, which are probably so named because they form a barrier to the ascent of the salmon; and the great fisheries from which the inhabitants of this barren region almost entirely derive a subsistence commence at this place. These appeared to be unusually gay savages, fond of loud laughter, and, in their apparent good nature and merry character, struck me as being entirely different from the Indians we had been accustomed to see. From several who visited our camp in the evening, we purchased, in exchange for goods, dried salmon. At this season they are not very fat, but we were easily pleased. The Indians made us comprehend, that when the salmon came up the river in the spring, they are so abundant that they merely throw in their spears at random, certain of bringing out a fish.

Frémont's Report.

October 6. Change in the face of the country. The morning warm, the thermometer 46° at sunrise, the sky entirely clouded. After travelling about three miles over an extremely rocky road, the volcanic fragments began to disappear; and, entering among the hills at the point of the mountain, we found ourselves suddenly in a granite country. Here the character of the vegetation was very much changed; the artemisia disappeared almost entirely, showing only at intervals towards the close of the day, and was replaced by Purshia tridentata, with flowering shrubs, and small fields of dieteria divaricata, which gave bloom and gayety to the hills. These were every where covered with a fresh and green short grass, like that of the early spring. This is the fall or second growth, the dried grass having been burnt off by the the Indians; and wherever the fire has passed, the bright green color is universal. The soil among the hills is altogether different from that of the river plain, being in many places black, in others sandy and gravelly, but of a firm and good character, appearing to result from the decomposition of the granite rocks, which is proceeding rapidly.

Frémont's Report.

METEOROLOGICAL OBSERVATIONS

Date	Time	Thermometer	Altitude	Remarks
1843 Septbr 22	sunrise	41° Fahr.	4779 Feet	Wind S. begins to run
	sunset	42°		do. sky partly clear; partly rainy clouds
23	sunrise	32°		calm snow falling thick
	sunset	45°		nearly calm, clear over head
24	sunrise	35°		calm, overcast
	sunset	55°		breeze from S. clear
25	sunrise	46°		gale from S. clear
	sunset	55°		almost overcast
26	sunrise	40°		Wind S.W. rain last night
	sunset	44°	4252 Feet	sharp wind S.W. clouds and clear
27	sunrise	40°		slight breeze fr. S. rainy clouds
	sunset	45°		gale fr S.W. thunder in N. clear and clouds
28	sunrise	40°		slight breeze fr. S. rainy clouds
	sunset	45°		cold wnd. fr. S.E.
29	sunrise	36°		wind S.W.
	sunset	50°		do.
30	sunrise	28°		air fr. S.E. light clouds
	sunset	65°		wind squally fr. W. clear
Octbr 1	sunrise	55°	3173 Feet	wind W. clear
	sunset	74°		calm and clear
2	sunrise	48°		calm and clear
	sunset	70°		do. do.
3	sunrise	42°		air from S.E. clear and light clouds
	sunset	60°		do. do. do.
4	sunrise	47°		calm and clear
	sunset	57°		gale fr N.W. cloudy
5	sunrise	32°		calm and clear
	sunset	47°		wind N.W. overcast
6	sunrise	46°		do. do. do. rainy appearance
	sunset	51°	3226 Feet	do. do. clear
7	sunrise	45°		do. do. do.
	sunset	51°		do. do. do.
8	sunrise	38°		calm and clear
	sunset	62°		do. cloudy horizon
9	sunrise	36°		calm and clear
	sunset	68°		do. scattered clouds
10	sunrise	43°		calm and clear
	sunset	62°	1398 Feet	do. do.

Elevation above the Gulf of Mexico

TOPOGRAPHICAL MAP

OF THE

D FROM MISSOURI TO OREGON

THE MOUTH OF THE KANSAS IN THE MISSOURI RIVER

HE MOUTH OF THE WALLAH WALLAH IN THE COLUMBIA

In VII Sections

SECTION VI

m the field notes and journal of Capt. J.C. Frémont,

etches and notes made on the ground by his assistant Charles Preuss

Compiled by Charles Preuss, 1846

By order of the Senate of the United States

SCALE _ 10 MILES TO THE INCH.

Lithogr by E. Weber & Co. Baltimore.

Three Buttes

FORT HALL

Latitude 43°

Longitude 113°

114°

1180 m
18 22 Septbr
1843

FORT NEUF

22-23 Sptbr

Pannack R.

American Falls

24-25 Sptbr
1200 m

25-26 Sptbr

1220 m

26-27 Sptbr

Rain River

COLUMBIA RIVER

Sept. 24. American Falls. The river here enters between low mural banks, which consists of a fine vesicular trap rock, the intermediate portions being compact and crystalline. Gradually becoming higher in its downward course, these banks of scoriated volcanic rock form, with occasional interruptions, its characteristic feature along the whole line to the Dalles of the Lower Columbia, resembling a chasm which had been rent through the country, and which the river had afterwards taken for its bed. The immediate valley of the river is a high plain, covered with black rocks and artemisias. In the south is a bordering range of mountains, which, although not very high, are broken and covered with snow; and at a great distance to the north is seen the high, snowy line of the Salmon river mountains, in front of which stand out prominently in the plain the three isolated rugged-looking little mountains commonly known as the Three Buttes. Between the river and the distant Salmon river range, the plain is represented by Mr. Fitzpatrick as so entirely broken up and rent into chasms as to be impracticable for a man even on foot. In the sketch an nexed, the point of view is low, but it conveys very well some idea of the open character of the country, with the buttes rising out above the general line. By measurement, the river above is 870 feet wide, immediately contracted at the fall in the form of a lock, by jutting piles of scoriaceous basalt, over which the foaming river must present a grand appearance at the time of high water.

Frémont's Report.

30 Subterranean River _ Immediately opposite to us, a subterranean river bursts out
y from the face of the escarpment, and falls in white foam to the river below. In the views
you will find, with a sketch of this remarkable fall, a representation of the mural precipices
close the main river, and which form its characteristic feature along a great portion of
A melancholy and strange looking country _ one of fracture and violence, and fire.
Frémont's Report.

WIS FORK OF THE COLUMBIA

1320 m
2 Octbr Fishing Falls
30 Sptbr 1 Octbr
1300 m
1280 m 29-30 Sptbr
Rock Creek
28-29 Sptbr
1200 m
27-28 Sptbr
1240 m
Goose Creek
Swamp Creek

1. The figures on the road indicate the distance in miles from Westport Landing.

2. This is the most trying section for the traveller on the whole route. Water, though good and plenty, is difficult to reach, as the river is hemmed in by high and vertical rocks and many of the by-streams are without water in the dry season. Grass is only to be found at the marked camping places, and barely sufficient to keep strong animals from starvation. Game there is none. The road is very rough by volcanic rocks, detrimental to wagons and carts. In sage bushes consists the only Fuel. Lucky, that by all these hardships the traveller is not harassed by the Indians, who are peasable & harmless.

3. West of the Fishing Falls, salmon, fresh and dried, can be obtained from the Indians.

Mount St Helen's with smoke from the crater hovering in a peculiar form over the top of the mountain

Canadian artist Paul Kane painted Mount St. Helens in 1847 from the mouth of the Kattlepoutal River in British Columbia. "There was not a cloud visible in the sky at the time I commenced my sketch . . . suddenly a stream of white smoke shot up from the crater of the mountain, and hovered a short time over its summit; it then settled down like a cap."

fortress on the American River, having survived treacherous passes, high drifting snow, and numbing cold. The party eventually made its way down the Sacramento and San Joaquin valleys, through Oak Creek Pass (which they believed to be Walker Pass), onto the Mojave Desert and eastward over the old Spanish Trail, and then along the Duchesne and what was then called the South White River back to Independence, which they reached in July.

Jessie Frémont, meanwhile, had been in St. Louis anxiously awaiting her husband's return. As before, they collaborated to publish the official report. The Senate, thanks in part to the efforts of Senator James Buchanan, ordered 10,000 extra copies printed together with Frémont's report of the 1842 expedition as *A Report of the Exploring Expedition to the Rocky Mountains in the Year 1842, and to Oregon and North California in the Years 1843-44.* An accompanying map by Preuss marked a substantial advance in western cartography. In 1846 Preuss prepared another map which, divided into seven sections, represented the Oregon Trail in detail from the mouth of the Kansas River to the confluence of the Walla Walla and Columbia rivers. The inclusion of pertinent comments from the *Report* all along the route made the map a valuable companion for emigrants, who were heading for Oregon in ever increasing numbers.

Frémont's third expedition, which began in June 1845, is still shrouded in controversy and mystery. It seems safe to surmise, however, that the expedition was concerned more with conquest than with exploration. Frémont's orders made no mention of California; he was to survey the Arkansas and Red rivers and determine the points at which the 100-degree longitudinal boundary line of the United States touched those rivers. Nevertheless, by December Frémont had again reached Sutter's Fort, and, shortly thereafter, he held a secret meeting with Thomas O. Larkin, the American consul in Monterey, California. This conversation, he insisted, was entirely innocent, but the Mexican authorities were understandably suspicious of the 60 well-armed "scientists," who had arrived without warning.

Although Frémont was allowed to spend the winter there, he was ordered to leave the following March. This he did, but only after a spate of saber rattling. He had not proceeded very far when he was overtaken by a messenger carrying letters from Senator Benton and Secretary of State James Buchanan which instructed him to "ascertain the disposition of the California people, to conciliate their feelings in favor of the United States. . . ."

This was all the encouragement Frémont needed. He rushed back to Sutter's Fort and quickly became embroiled in the activities that led to the independence of California. Although he was not present when the Bear Flag Republic was established with the raising of a homemade flag at Sonoma on June 14, he had certainly played a part in inciting the American settlers to move against the native Californians. By the end of the summer of 1846, much of California was under American control, and Frémont had been appointed military commandant.

Meanwhile, war with Mexico had broken out, and Frémont,

at the head of his California Battalion, emerged from the conflict a national hero and the governor of California. His triumph was to be short-lived, however, for he wound up in the middle of a quarrel between Commodore Robert F. Stockton and General Stephen Watts Kearny over who was the rightful commander-in-chief of California. Siding with Stockton, Frémont initially refused to obey Kearny's command, although eventually he agreed to do so. Things went from bad to worse, and at one point, no doubt smarting from recent humiliations, Frémont challenged Kearny's aide, Colonel Richard B. Mason—who was to replace Frémont as governor—to a duel. Fortunately, it never took place.

In June 1847, Frémont was compelled to follow Kearny on the long trek back east, where the general planned to place him under arrest for mutiny and insubordination. After his son-in-law's arrival, Senator Benton demanded a court-martial, so that Frémont could be "justified and exalted." Months later, however, Frémont was convicted of mutiny, disobedience, and conduct unbecoming to an officer, and ordered dismissed from the army. When President Polk remitted the penalties but let the conviction stand, Frémont resigned. The impetuous lieutenant had overstepped the bounds of military propriety and deserved censure, but his father-in-law saw things differently. "Columbus . . . was carried home in chains," and, similarly, Frémont, "the explorer of California and its preserver to the United States, was brought home a prisoner . . . to expiate the offense of having entered the Army without passing through the gate of the Military Academy."

Court-martial or not, Frémont's influence was enormous. His *Report* became the pattern for the long series of topographical survey reports in the years to follow. The fact that his expeditions had been only loosely predicated upon scientific research and his *Report* politically inspired and romantically written does not diminish their importance. Even the exalted Baron Alexander von Humboldt lavished praise on its scientific revelations and on the author's "talent, courage, industry and enterprise."

And well he should have, for Frémont initiated the topographical mapping of the Far West based on field reconnaissance. Using the map prepared by the Wilkes expedition, Frémont constructed and issued the first scientific map of the trans-Mississippi West. "It fills up the vast geographical chasm between the two remote points," he could rightfully boast, "and presents a connected and accurate view of our continent from the Mississippi River to the Pacific Ocean."

Despite the importance of his work, Frémont had to share the Washington limelight with Wilkes, who fancied himself the leading authority on Oregon and the California coast. Moreover, with his salary and federal appropriation to publish the scientific results of his expedition, the naval officer had achieved a most enviable position. This must have been particularly galling to Benton, who had worked so hard to build and enhance the reputation of his son-in-law. Had it not been for Wilkes, Frémont would have been the reigning expert in the nation's capital on the Oregon territory. Benton must have

Frémont's cantankerous cartographer, Charles Preuss, confided to his private diaries that he frequently disliked Frémont and nearly always hated the expeditions' primitive living conditions. Nonetheless, he accompanied the Pathfinder on three of his journeys. Preuss used modern mapmaking techniques to create the map of Utah's Great Salt Lake, below.

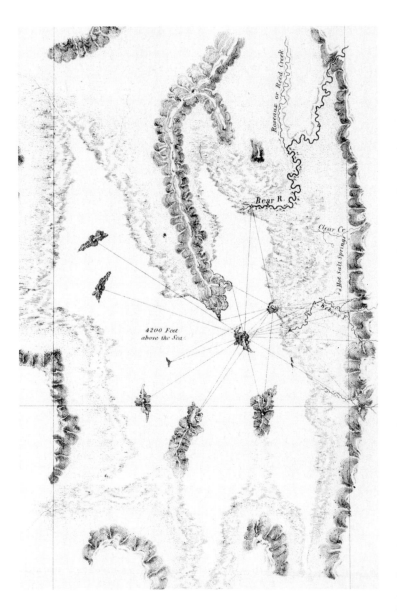

Preuss sketched Pyramid Lake in Nevada, left, in 1844. A modern view from almost the same vantage point, above, depicts the 500-foot-high pyramid and the other strange tufa mounds and rock formations that intrigue visitors to this day.

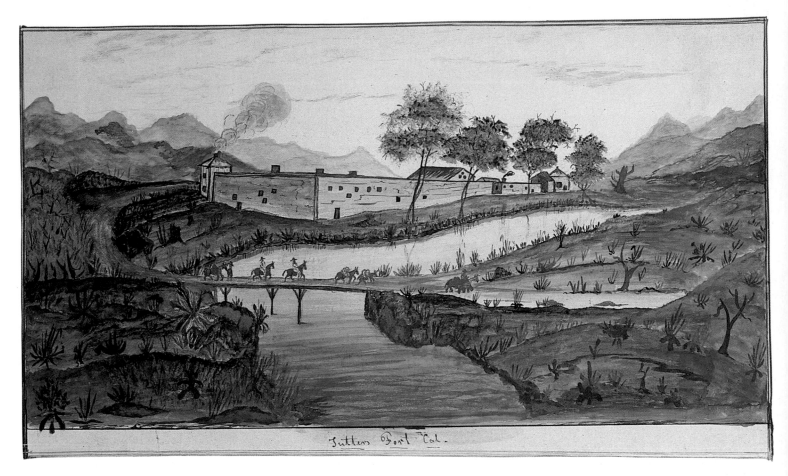

Sutters Fort Cal.

marvelled at the resilience of Wilkes, who had managed to survive his court-martial with career and scientific reputation intact. Frémont, on the other hand, enjoyed some distinction as a scientist, but was bereft of income and career, although he was to lead two more expeditions into the West. That is why Benton missed no opportunity to steal the thunder from Wilkes. In fact, Old Bullion challenged Wilkes twice, and both challenges resulted in lengthy disputes in the local press. If these confrontations served no other purpose, they demonstrated to Benton and the Washington community that the Stormy Petrel well deserved his nickname.

For both Frémont and Wilkes, their reports and scientific publications are the standards by which their contributions as explorers are measured. In this regard, Frémont suffers greatly when compared to Wilkes, for he managed to lose most of his scientific collections before getting out of the wilderness. Those plant specimens that did survive he gave to Professor John Torrey, the Princeton botanist, who catalogued them.

Indeed, whatever the political and military implications of Frémont's third expedition, it was not without scientific merit. Torrey combined the plants that survived from the second expedition with those from the third and published *Plantae Fremontianae, descriptions of Plants Collected by Col. J.C. Frémont in California*, which appeared as volume six in the *Smithsonian Contributions to Knowledge* (1854), and thus bestowed on the Pathfinder the distinction of being the first in a long line of government explorers whose work was honored

and supported by the Smithsonian Institution. Frémont's report also included 22 pages of meteorological data, which proved valuable in determining the extent of cultivable land in the Far West and helped begin the process of dispelling the myth of the Great American Desert. Frémont, of course, also gave considerable attention in his reports to the appearance, habits, and distribution of the many Indian tribes he encountered.

But it was in the area of cartography that Frémont made his most significant contribution. As historian William H. Goetzmann has pointed out, Frémont "went west for several reasons, but one of the most important of these was to . . . make a beginning toward the absolute measurement of its surface topography."

If Frémont was not the "scientist" one would have preferred, he succeeded beyond any reasonable expectations as a popularizer of the West. And try as they might, no one could ever replace the Pathfinder in the imagination of the American people. The public devoured his romantic adventures much as later generations devoured the dime novels of Ned Buntline and the stories of Zane Grey. In this work he was wonderfully served by his wife, Jessie, who wrote down his stories as he paced back and forth relating them. "I write more easily by dictation," he confessed when preparing his first report. "Writing myself I have too much time to think and dwell upon words as well as ideas." It was Jessie who gave his reports their incomparable style, making them as much contributions to American literature as to official government documents. Thanks to those reports,

During a grueling midwinter crossing of the Sierra Nevada in early 1844, Frémont and his men staggered through deep snow near Lake Tahoe, losing animals, equipment, and scientific specimens. In early March, they encountered a Mexican cowboy, or vaquero, who led them to Sutter's Fort, opposite, on the American River near what is now Sacramento. Sutter's Fort was later the site of the gold discovery that set off the great Gold Rush of 1849.

The vaquero below was painted around 1850 by James Walker, who had served in the American Army in the Mexican War and settled in California.

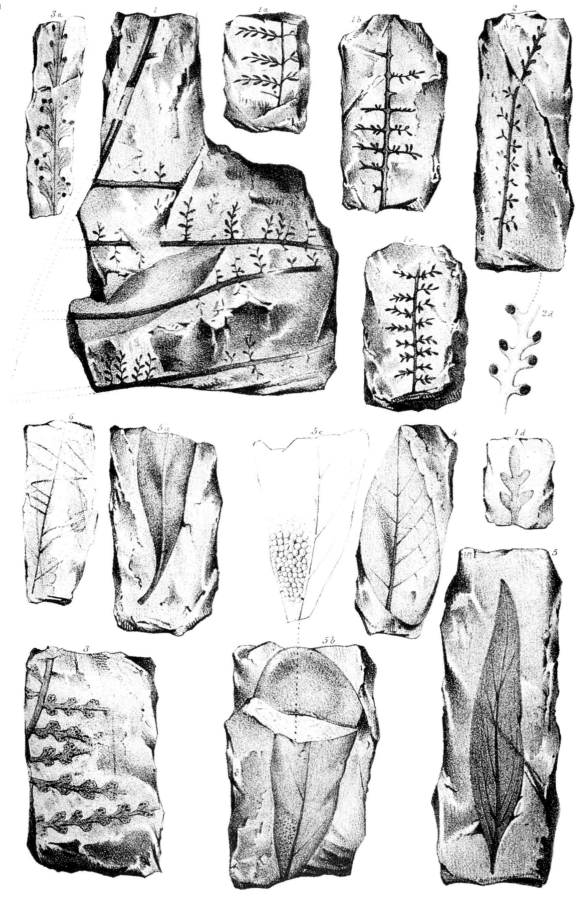

Named by botanist John Torrey for the leader of the expedition that collected it, Fremontia vermicularis, *left, flourished in the saline soil of Oregon and northern California. Fossil ferns, right, were among the many specimens, ancient and modern, that Frémont's parties returned to eastern scientists.*

the American people acquired other heroes as well, among them the flamboyant Kit Carson. "Mounted on a fine horse, without saddle, and scouring bareheaded over the prairies, Kit was one of the finest pictures of a horseman I have ever seen." Frémont's reports, printed by the thousands, were consumed by restless Americans eager to follow the paths into the Far West that he had blazed so dramatically and eloquently.

Wilkes, by contrast, lacked Frémont's charisma and flair. Nor did he have the benefit of a wife like Jessie to polish his prose and his image. Nonetheless, he did publish within a remarkably brief time after his return his official report, in five volumes plus an atlas of maps, entitled *Narrative of the U.S. Exploring Expedition During the Years 1838, 1839, 1840, 1841, 1842*. It is a candid account of the expedition in which Wilkes revealed the bitterness and acrimony that marred his relationship with his officers during the four-year voyage.

The scientific reports, although important, also had limited impact. These were prepared for the most part by the scientists who had accompanied Wilkes, though several were placed in the hands of specialists like Professor Torrey and Asa Gray, who prepared the botany volume, and Charles Girard of the Smithsonian, author of the volume on reptiles and amphibians. Unfortunately, the publishing process was so protracted and expensive that not all the intended volumes—the one on fishes, for example—could be published. All told, 19 volumes and accompanying atlases were published between 1845 and 1871.

The specimens that Frémont and Wilkes collected are also part of our story. Whereas Frémont returned from five expeditions with what was relatively speaking only a handful of specimens, Wilkes and his companions succeeded beyond anyone's wildest expectations. His men had assembled an astounding array of flora and fauna from all corners of the globe. Despite the wreck of the *Peacock*, which cost the expedition most of its entomology collection as well as some of the material obtained in Hawaii, their trove included more than 4,000 zoological specimens, representing nearly 2,000 new species. Of these, birds accounted for more than 2,000 specimens and included more than 500 species. The plant specimens numbered more than 50,000 and included some 10,000 different species. The live plants were used to establish the Washington Botanical Garden, which later became the U.S. Botanic Garden and still boasts one specimen that came back with Wilkes. The thousands of ethnographic artifacts made up one of the most important systematic collections in the United States from the Pacific Islands and the West Coast of North America. Add to this the remarkable gems, fossils, and corals the explorers obtained and the totals begin to boggle the imagination.

The United States was ill-equipped to receive these massive collections, and a good deal of material was lost before it came under systematic control. At first the collections were given to the National Institute for the Promotion of Science and were displayed in the newly constructed Patent Office Building in the nation's capital, but in 1857 they were turned over to the Smithsonian Institution, where they remain today. The speci-

mens were installed in the Castle in July 1858, and with that transfer the Smithsonian became the National Museum of the United States. The tragedy, of course, is that the United States, with only a little foresight, could have secured for posterity the specimens so carefully collected and returned by Meriwether Lewis and William Clark, the pathfinders who prepared the way for that generation of adventurers and explorers who preceded Wilkes and Frémont to the Pacific Coast.

Emanuel Leutze created this study for his monumental 20-by-30-foot mural, Westward the Course of Empire Takes Its Way. *A paean to Manifest Destiny, the great* mural was commissioned by Congress in 1860. It may still be seen in the Capitol.

Surveying equipment of the 19th century, below, includes a pendulum odometer (left), with its worn leather case, which was strapped to a wagon wheel to indicate the number of wheel revolutions and, through computation, the distance traveled; a brass compass with vernier resting against its mahogany box; a range finder in its half-cylinder metal box; a telescope that attaches to one of the vernier's sights; and a 33-foot iron surveyor's chain. Below right, a five-pound, .44-caliber 1850 Colt's Dragoon revolver, often carried by mounted troops accompanying early surveyors.

THE GREAT RECONNAISSANCE

Because of the success and popularity of the Wilkes and Frémont expeditions, the era before the Civil War witnessed a surge of government-sponsored exploration that historians often call "the great reconnaissance." By the end of the 1850s, virtually every region in the trans-Mississippi West had been probed and examined, albeit often hurriedly or even carelessly. The men entrusted with this monumental and strategically vital mission were the military mappers of the army's Corps of Topographical Engineers.

Founded in 1838, the year Wilkes set sail on his epic voyage around the world, the Corps came into its own in the 1840s. During this decade, the nation reached its full continental dimensions as a result of the Mexican War and the Oregon Boundary Settlement. Accurate surveys were thus essential to secure geopolitical control of these vast new areas—to defend them, to organize them into territories, and to identify and catalog their resources.

The Corps was an elite group whose officers, usually the most gifted graduates of West Point, never numbered more than 36 at any one time. It was also a somewhat short-lived group, ultimately destined to be merged into the Corps of Engineers during the Civil War. During its brief existence, however, the Corps of Topographical Engineers mapped the American West, conducting some two dozen major surveys during the 13 years between the Mexican and Civil wars. Yet the unparalleled accomplishments of the men of the Corps remain largely unsung. Few officers achieved either the fame or the notoriety of Frémont, but they were heroes all, and in their pursuit of knowledge they willingly, even enthusiastically, endured hardships and dangers to rival anything imagined by dime novelists.

Their mission was nothing less than the conversion of that great, wild domain of the West into a useful part of the United States, and they wholeheartedly espoused the philosophy of the

anonymous editorialist for the *New York Morning News* who wrote on December 27, 1845, that "... our manifest destiny [is] to overspread and to possess the whole of the continent which Providence has given us for the development of the great experiment of liberty and federated self-government entrusted to us."

John W. Gunnison was typical of the young men who joined the Corps. Born in rural New Hampshire in 1812, he entered West Point in 1833, graduated second in his class, and went on to a distinguished career as a topographical engineer and western explorer until his death in 1853 at the hands of Paiute Indians. He eloquently expressed his firm belief in the Corps in a letter to his family written soon after graduation. "When you think of an army *you must remember the corps to which I belong*," he boasted. "We took the place in 1838 of a corps of *civil engineers*, and though ready for the field of war, we are devoting time and labor during peace to the advancement of the interests of the whole people. We are building roads, surveying and clearing rivers, constructing harbors and facilitating business in every way, well knowing that whatever adds to the

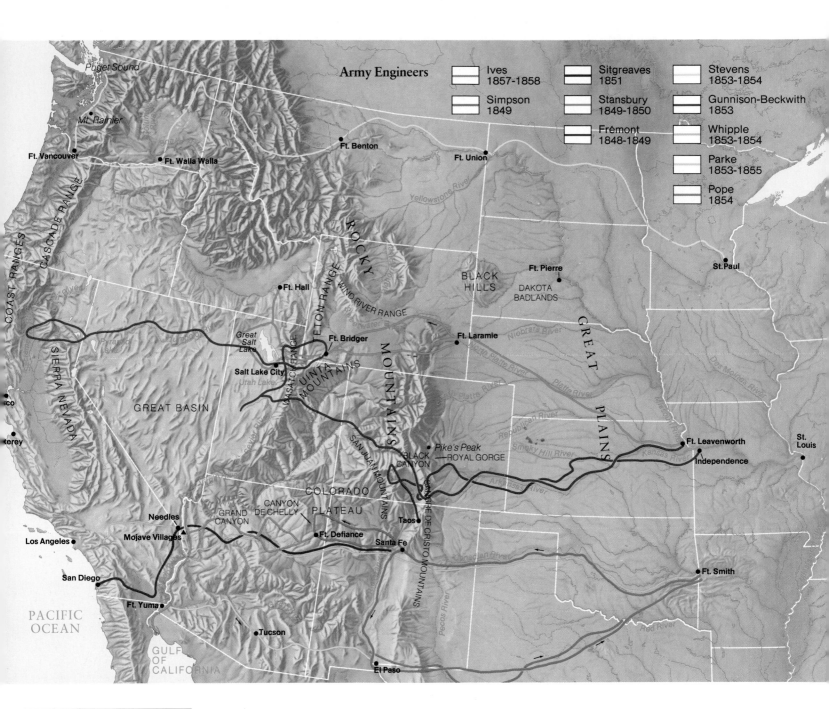

Army Engineers

Ives 1857-1858	Sitgreaves 1851	Stevens 1853-1854
Simpson 1849	Stansbury 1849-1850	Gunnison-Beckwith 1853
Frémont 1848-1849		Whipple 1853-1854
		Parke 1853-1855
		Pope 1854

On May 31, 1849, Captain Howard Stansbury of the Corps of Topographical Engineers and his party set out from Fort Leavenworth on an expedition to explore the valley of the Great Salt Lake. Arriving at the lake in the fall, Stansbury used a system of triangulation to survey both the Great Salt Lake and Utah Lake valleys. His crew erected 14 "principal triangulation stations," such as the one opposite, hauling the timber needed for construction from mountains as far as 20 miles away. A horn ladle and a woven basket and flask, opposite above, were collected in what is today southeastern Utah by Lieutenant John W. Gunnison of the Topographical Engineers, Stansbury's assistant on the 1849–50 Great Basin reconnaissance. The artifacts are attributed to the Ute Indians and now reside in the Smithsonian's collections.

After war broke out between Mexico and the United States in April 1846, red-whiskered Lieutenant William H. Emory, right, led a topographical detachment that accompanied General Stephen Watts Kearny's Army of the West to Santa Fe and on to California. Enduring great heat, rugged terrain, and hostile Indians and Mexicans, Emory and his men compiled more than 2,000 astronomical observations and took hundreds of barometric readings. Emory's official report of the expedition featured numerous illustrations, such as Lieutenant James W. Abert's sketch, Acoma No.3, above, portraying Indians with "their 'burros' laden with peaches" ascending "huge blocks of sandstone" to their village.

Perhaps the Topographical Engineers' most important assignment was delineating the new 1,800-mile boundary between the United States and Mexico after the war. Supervised by Emory, now a brevet major, the six-year Mexican boundary survey also accumulated a wealth of information on the region's geology, flora and fauna, archaeology, and Indians. The final Report was published in three volumes, the first of which included maps and such desert views as the one above. The volume on zoological specimens included the venomous beaded lizard, right, and a snake, Scotophis emoryi, opposite above, named for Emory.

wealth of individuals and opens communication strengthens all the sinews of war." Moreover, he added confidently, "there is no objection to our part of the army, for we pay for our bread."

As agents of Manifest Destiny, they accelerated western expansion by exploring new lands and writing up detailed reports on their findings, by surveying roads, by locating and improving navigable rivers and harbors, and even by attempting to find subsurface water in desert country. Most important, the Corps completed the first scientific mapping of the West and defined national boundaries. Their expeditions usually included civilian artists, naturalists, cartographers, and daguerreotypers. Indeed, some of the most important figures of the arts and sciences served as assistants to the Corps, such as talented artists Gustave Sohon, John Mix Stanley, and the Kern brothers, and geologist Ferdinand Vandeveer Hayden, destined one day to lead his own great survey of the West.

The most important work of the Topographical Engineers was delineating the boundary between the United States and Mexico, which alone took six years to accomplish. Much of the credit for the survey goes to Lieutenant William H. Emory, a

Arms, left, used by military escorts accompanying mid-19th-century surveying expeditions include an 1847 U.S. Cavalry musketoon (top), an 1842 U.S. musket (center), and an 1843 U.S. Cavalry carbine (bottom). Opposite, tiny gold castles on caps and collars identify the uniforms of Army engineers in 1851. The wool uniforms were ill-suited to certain western climes, but even an expedition in scorching heat up the Colorado River to Fort Yuma in 1850 couldn't dull the wit of Lieutenant George H. Derby. His humorous essays written under the pseudonym John Phoenix poked fun at Topographical Engineers and their surveys, and featured such characters as those at bottom.

Major.
Adj. General's Dept.

Captain.
Engineers.

1st Sergeant.

Musician.

Engineer Soldiers.

Published by Wm H. Horstmann & Sons, Military Furnishers, Philad.

"A low purple gateway and a splendid corridor, with massive red walls," wrote Lieutenant Joseph Christmas Ives in describing the entrance to Mojave Canyon, above, through which he passed on his expedition up the Colorado River from Fort Yuma in 1858. Ives and his party traveled upriver in the Explorer, opposite, a 54-foot paddle-wheeler that was dismantled in Philadelphia, shipped in pieces to the mouth of the Colorado, and then reassembled amid a gathering of curious Indians. Expedition naturalist John Strong Newberry gloried in the unprecedented opportunity for geological study that the river trip presented him, and produced the first geologic cross section of the canyon of the Colorado, opposite right, entitled Section of the Cañon of the Colorado on High Mesa West of the Little Colorado.

dedicated soldier and a keen scientific observer. Renowned among his classmates at West Point for his reckless courage, Emory was in charge of the topographical command attached to Colonel Stephen Watts Kearny's Army of the West during the Mexican War. In early December 1846, near an Indian village on the road to San Diego, Kearny's army ran headlong into a superior force of Mexican lancers. Although the Battle of San Pascual is considered an American victory, in fact the Mexicans could have destroyed Kearny's little army had they pressed their advantage. Emory fought well that day, living up to his reputation and indeed saving Kearny's life.

It is not for his bravery in battle that Emory is best remembered, though, but for his scientific analysis of the new territories acquired in the war. From 1849 until 1855, Emory was associated with the survey of the new 1,800-mile border between the United States and Mexico, initially as commander of the army topographers and eventually as boundary commissioner. His original *Notes of a Military Reconnoissance, from Fort Leavenworth, in Missouri, to San Diego, in California, Including Part of the Arkansas, Del Norte, and Gila Rivers,* submitted to Congress at the end of the war, contained the first reliable information in English about the Southwest.

Emory's final *Report on the United States and Mexican Boundary Survey* was a grand compendium in the tradition of the Wilkes expedition, with exhaustive scientific descriptions of the geography, geology, plant, animal, and human life of the region generated by a large team of military surveyors and civilian scientists and artists. Published between 1856 and 1859, its three volumes were well received; the botanical report, for example, compiled primarily by John Torrey, was hailed by no less an authority than Harvard botanist Asa Gray as "the most important publication of the kind that has ever appeared."

Emory was a quiet professional who shunned publicity, which could not be said of Lieutenant George Horatio Derby, a young topographical engineer who was also a wickedly talented satirist. After graduating from West Point and serving in the Mexican War, Derby was assigned to the army's Pacific Department and stationed in California, where, under the pseudonym John Phoenix, he kept local newspapers supplied with cartoons, burlesques, and parodies.

But Derby was also a highly competent soldier-scientist. Aboard the schooner *Invincible* in 1850 he sailed up the Gulf of California and then, with the use of a long boat, demonstrated the navigability of the Lower Colorado River. His reconnaissance also established for the first time the true relationship of the Colorado and Gila rivers, and led to the upriver explorations of the Colorado River canyons by Lieutenant Joseph Christmas Ives seven years later.

Only 29 at the time, Ives directed a thoroughly up-to-date expedition, complete with camera, that included such knowledgeable and capable veterans as geologist John Strong New-

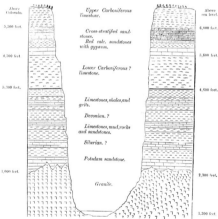

Overleaf: Redwall Cavern in the Colorado's Grand Canyon engulfs modern-day visitors. In 1858, Ives and a small party became the first white men to set foot on the canyon's floor.

berry, topographer F. W. von Egloffstein, and naturalist and artist Heinrich Baldwin Möllhausen. Ives commissioned a special shallow-draft steamer in Philadelphia, which was dismantled and shipped around Cape Horn to the mouth of the Colorado, then reassembled and christened the *Explorer*. A jaunty red paddle-wheeler with a deck-mounted four-pounder howitzer, the *Explorer* set out on its voyage on New Year's Eve 1857. For nine months the little steamer fought the mighty currents of the Colorado until, on March 8, it struck a submerged rock in Black Canyon and sustained minor damage. A few more miles of reconnaissance upriver in a skiff convinced Ives that he had reached the limits of the Colorado's navigable waters. Sending half of his party back with the *Explorer*, Ives headed eastward from the river with the other half through country "whose strange sublimity is perhaps unparalleled in any part of the world."

Ives was to make one more significant contact with the Colorado River. Guided by Hualpais Indians down "gaping chasms" that "resembled the portals of the infernal regions" to the mouth of Diamond Creek, Ives and his party, on an April morning in 1858, became the first white men to descend to the floor of the Grand Canyon. It would be another 11 years before John Wesley Powell, approaching from the other direction, entered the wilds of the Grand Canyon of the Colorado.

Although no photographs from his expedition survive, Ives's report is richly illustrated with woodcuts, engravings, and colored lithographs. It also includes von Egloffstein's maps of the

Lieutenant Simpson and his party were the first white men to view White House Ruin, opposite, and other canyon fortresses of Canyon de Chelly, the Navajos' tribal stronghold.

Attached to a military command with orders to quell the Navajos, Lieutenant James Harvey Simpson led a small topographical unit deep into the Navajo heartland in the summer of 1849, exploring such ancient Indian ruins as those of Pueblo Pintado, above, in Chaco Canyon and others in Canyon de Chelly, right. These sketches by Simpson's assistant Richard H. Kern still serve as important archaeological documentation of these pueblo cultures.

Surgeon, ornithologist, and naturalist S. W. Woodhouse, right, typified the eclectic background of many of the participants in the topographical reconnaissances of the 19th century. Opposite above, Woodhouse stands with his horse, "Davy," in July 1850 at the Bald Eagle Mound Camp during an ornithological survey in Oklahoma.

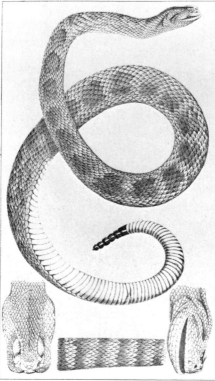

Beginning in September 1851, S. W. Woodhouse served as naturalist on Captain Lorenzo Sitgreaves's expedition across the Southwest from Zuni Pueblo in New Mexico. Losing the use of his left hand from the bite of a rattlesnake similar to the one at left, featured in Sitgreaves's report, Woodhouse was "dependent upon the exertions of the men" for much of his collecting. He also suffered from an Indian arrow wound, and had to tend to the wounds and illnesses of other expedition members. In the report, Woodhouse's zoological and botanical descriptions were complemented by the drawings of Richard Kern, such as that of the rough-barked cedar, opposite below.

Hostile Indians, scorching heat, and shortages of food and water plagued the Sitgreaves expedition, but the men finally reached Fort Yuma at the confluence of the Colorado and Gila rivers on November 30, 1851, and obtained rations "for the subsistence of the party to San Diego, California." Sitgreaves's report, right, contained useful information on and landscape drawings of this little-known region, such as Richard Kern's Ruined Pueblos, below. It also featured Kern's ethnological drawings of Indian tribes, including the first view ever of the Cosnino Indians, bottom, and Zuñi Indian Woman (Buffalo Dance), opposite.

33D CONGRESS, 1st Session. [SENATE.] EXECUTIVE.

REPORT OF AN EXPEDITION

DOWN THE

ZUNI AND COLORADO RIVERS,

BY

CAPTAIN L. SITGREAVES,

CORPS TOPOGRAPHICAL ENGINEERS.

ACCOMPANIED BY MAPS, SKETCHES, VIEWS, AND ILLUSTRATIONS.

WASHINGTON:
BEVERLEY TUCKER, SENATE PRINTER.
1854.

Colorado River area, which feature the new cartographic technique of fine parallel contour lines drawn directly on the plates to produce a three-dimensional effect, thereby representing in sharp relief the ruggedness of the canyon country.

Other reconnaissances in the Southwest by the Topographical Engineers continued to search for the best trails west, and to make important discoveries along the way. In the summer of 1849, Lieutenant James Harvey Simpson, accompanying Colonel John M. Washington's expedition out of Santa Fe, led the first American exploration of the Navajo stronghold in Canyon de Chelly and there encountered the spectacular cliff dwellings of the Anasazi, a people who had disappeared from the region centuries before.

Two years later, in September 1851, Captain Lorenzo Sitgreaves led an expedition from Zuni Pueblo in New Mexico westward across Arizona to the Colorado River, south to Fort Yuma and eventually on to San Diego. Scouting a wagon route that Simpson had described, Sitgreaves and his men suffered from rattlesnake bites and other illnesses, encountered difficult terrain and hostile Indians (who killed one luckless soldier and injured several others), and endured crucial shortages of food, water, and pack animals. In the end they could report no direct line to the Pacific.

In his report to Congress in 1853, Sitgreaves detailed some of the hardships and misadventures that his party had undergone. He also included descriptions of the land they had traversed, writing of the region around the Colorado, for example, as "the most perfect picture of desolation I have ever beheld, as if some sirocco had passed over the land, withering and scorching everything to crispness."

His physician and naturalist, Dr. S. W. Woodhouse, added more graphic detail to the Sitgreaves report. Bitten on the index finger of his left hand by a rattlesnake at the Zuni Pueblo as he was attempting to add the reptile to his collections, Woodhouse had to spend the remainder of the trek struggling to treat his own injury, as well as those of other members of the party, with only one hand. He tried every known remedy for snakebite—opium, iodine, silver nitrate. He even took the frontier advice of the expedition artist, Richard Kern—"that is to say, to get drunk." To do so, the physician reported, he drank a half-pint of whiskey followed by a "quart of fourth-proof brandy," and at the same time soaked the scarified wound in a cup of ammonia. Woodhouse also took ammonia internally, leading 20th-century physicians to wonder at his ability to survive his cures. (In fact, he never regained the full use of his hand.)

The step-by-step account of the doctor's efforts to overcome the effects of the snakebite filled much of his official report, which also included references to his ministrations to a mortally injured Mexican member of the party. Woodhouse reported apologetically that he was unable to perform an autopsy on the Mexican, given his own incapacity. He later described removing two stone-headed arrows from their critically wounded mountain-man guide, André Leroux, even though he himself had been shot in the leg.

As if such heroics were not enough, Woodhouse never lost

"The stillness of the grave seemed to pervade both air and water," wrote expedition leader Captain Howard Stansbury of the Great Salt Lake, which he first beheld in October 1849. Stansbury and his men were the first to travel the lake's circumference. The topographical party also reconnoitered possible railroad passes that were later used by the Union Pacific. Illustrations from Stansbury's report included Crossing of the Platte—Mouth of Deer Creek, right, and Valley Between Promontory Range and Rocky Butte—Camp No. 2. G. Salt Lake, above.

sight of his obligations to science, although he apologized in his report on the region's natural history for not being more productive as a naturalist. "I did not recover the use of my left hand for months afterwards, and this accounts for the small collection of birds, quadrupeds, and reptiles procured by me . . . being entirely dependent upon the exertions of the men." If no one was nearby to assist him when he saw a bird, reptile, or plant he wanted to collect, he "was forced to pass them by."

Perhaps this was just as well, for near the end of the expedition, as the explorers followed the Colorado south, they had to abandon their surplus baggage. The terrain proved so inhospitable that the mules began to die from exhaustion and lack of forage. Eventually, their own food gave out and they had to rely on mule meat for sustenance. The mule meat kept them alive, but it had the unexpected side effect of diarrhea, which the explorers had to endure for 10 straight days until they obtained a welcome change of diet upon reaching Fort Yuma.

At about the same time that Simpson, Sitgreaves, and other Topographical Engineers were surveying the Southwest, Captain Howard Stansbury and his assistant, Lieutenant John W. Gunnison, made a scientific reconnaissance of the Great Basin. Exploring the barren western reaches of the Salt Lake while Gunnison surveyed the region around Utah Lake to the south, Stansbury became the first person to recognize that the Great Basin had once been a prehistoric lake bed. "There must," he reasoned, "have been here at some former period a vast *inland* sea, extending for hundreds of miles; and the isolated moun-

Stansbury's expedition spent the winter of 1849–50 in Salt Lake City, where the captain and his assistant, Lieutenant John W. Gunnison, took the opportunity to learn more about the religious doctrines and social customs of the Mormons. Stansbury wrote in his report that "their dealings with the crowds of emigrants that passed through their city . . . were ever fair and upright," and characterized the sect as "a quiet, orderly, industrious, and well-organized society." Stansbury's report featured a view of the community, above, entitled Bowery, Mint, & President's House—Great Salt Lake City.

In 1848, John C. Frémont, shown at right in an 1850 lithograph, led a disastrous expedition to seek a railroad route to the Pacific. Against all odds, he attempted to cross the San Juan Mountains of the Southern Rockies in December. Frigid temperatures, icy winds, and heavy snows devastated first the mules, then the men. Frederic Remington's painting of a campfire scene, below, and a bleak Christmas menu, opposite below, illustrated Thomas E. Breckenridge's reminiscences of the expedition, published in The Cosmopolitan *of August 1896.*

tains which now tower from the flats, forming its western and southwestern shores, were doubtless huge islands, similar to those which now rise from the diminished waters of the lakes." On their return east in the fall of 1850, Stansbury and Gunnison, with the help of guide Jim Bridger, blazed a new trail across the Rocky Mountains through Cheyenne Pass in what is today southeastern Wyoming, saving travelers some 60 miles between Fort Laramie and the Mormon settlements at Salt Lake. The path was later followed to advantage by the Overland Stage, the Pony Express, and the Union Pacific Railroad.

Although the American people were the ultimate beneficiaries of these surveys, it was the lords of transportation who reaped their first benefits. Indeed, it was the desire to find a suitable railroad route to the Pacific that inspired most of the exploration carried out by the Corps of Topographical Engineers. Even as the first emigrant wagon trains were winding their way across the western landscape, visionaries back east were avidly promoting the idea of a transcontinental railroad.

The idea of a railroad to the Pacific had been voiced as early as the 1830s, but it was not until 1844 that Asa Whitney, a New York merchant grown rich trading with the Orient, presented to Congress a formal proposal for such a rail line. Under his plan, Congress would set aside a 60-mile-wide tract of land stretching from Lake Michigan to the mouth of the Columbia River, and profits derived from the sale and settlement of this tract would finance construction of the railroad.

A similar scheme was eventually approved after the Civil

War, but Whitney's idea was too revolutionary for its time. Moreover, it challenged the aspirations of the greatest Oregon booster of them all, Thomas Hart Benton. A railroad to the Pacific would be wonderful, Benton agreed, but it should not be approved without adequate thought and planning. "We must have surveys, examinations, and explorations made, and not go blindfolded haphazard into such a scheme," he warned his Senate colleagues.

And who better to conduct such a survey, of course, than his son-in-law, John Charles Frémont? Still bitter over his recent court-martial and eager to restore his tarnished image, the Pathfinder, financed by wealthy St. Louis interests, set out in October 1848 with 33 men to explore the 38th parallel, dubbed the "Buffalo Trail" by Benton, who saw it as a direct course between St. Louis and San Francisco. As for the formidable Rockies, they held no terror for the confident Frémont, now a seasoned veteran of mountain exploration.

Frémont had actually had some experience as a railroad surveyor, having helped plot the line between Charleston and Cincinnati before he left the Topographical Corps. It was natural, then, that he should claim that he was conducting the first expert survey of a railroad route to the Pacific. And despite the expedition's unofficial status, Frémont again entertained scientific aspirations: his party included the faithful Preuss as cartographer, the German botanist Frederick Creutzfeldt, and a gifted family of artists, the brothers Benjamin, Edward (Ned), and Richard Kern.

BILL OF FARE. CAMP DESOLATION
December 25, 1848.

— MENU —
MULE.

SOUP.
Mule Tail.

FISH.
Baked White Mule.
Boiled Gray Mule.

MEATS
Mule Steak, Fried Mule, Mule Chops,
Broiled Mule, Stewed Mule, Boiled Mule,
Scrambled Mule, Shirred Mule,
French-fried Mule, Minced Mule,

DAMNED MULE
Mule on Toast (without the Toast),
Short Ribs of Mule with Apple Sauce
(without the Apple Sauce),

RELISHES
Black Mule, Brown Mule, Yellow Mule,
Bay Mule, Roan Mule,
Tallow Candles.

BEVERAGES
Snow, Snow-Water, Water

Edward (Ned) Kern's artwork on his letter, above left, to his older sister Mary memorializes the death of Raphael Proue, the first of 10 men to perish on Frémont's fourth expedition. Either Ned or Richard Kern painted Natural Obelisks, *above, in the San Juan Range of the Rockies before severe weather and starvation forced a retreat.*

Experience and talent proved insufficient safeguards against a foolhardy idea, however. It defies reason that Frémont would attempt in the dead of winter to find a new pass over the Continental Divide in the Southern Rockies and then challenge the even more forbidding San Juan Mountains. Yet this was his plan, and so, after crossing the Sangre de Cristo Mountains at Mosca Pass in heavy snow, he and his men followed mountain-man guide Old Bill Williams up into the San Juan Mountains. There, with more than 10 feet of snow on the ground and the temperature falling to 20 below, Frémont's luck ran out. Williams lost his way, and on December 17 the explorers found themselves at an altitude of more than 11,000 feet in the midst of swirling blizzards. "Storm after storm continued and from hunger and the severity of the weather [the mules] . . . perished—nearly a hundred head of as fine animals as ever entered the mountains," Ned Kern recalled. The animals were the first to fall but the men were not far behind. "Hands and feet, ears, and noses of some people were frozen. . . . that old fool Bill lay down and wanted to die, just at the summit," Preuss marveled.

Ten men died from cold, starvation, or both on the grim, fragmented procession to Taos. "My food for 4 days consisted of the thigh of a [sage] hen that I cooked and recooked for breakfast and supper 8 times during those days rather meager soup that you would say," wrote Ned Kern when describing his ordeal to his sister. Kern also told of two companions who simply refused to walk any farther. "A few days after they were found dead—one lying by the side of a little fire the other sitting against the bank as if he had been looking at his friend—such were some of the scenes happening around us." Preuss wrote of a similar experience. "The last act of kindness the survivors could render to those who were too weak to go on was to light a fire for them. They would lie down, wrapped in a blanket, and shortly yield up the ghost."

Preuss himself was dour but durable. He survived, as did the Kerns, Creutzfeldt, and 19 others, yet even when they reached Taos in early February their troubles were not over. In their struggle to save themselves, the explorers had left behind almost all their equipment, notes, and scientific specimens. Old Bill Williams set out with Ben Kern and a few others in March to return to the San Juan Mountains and retrieve the property. They were never seen again and presumably fell victim to Ute Indians or renegade Mexicans.

Only the loss of the *Sea Gull* during the Wilkes expedition had taken more lives in the cause of American science, yet Frémont tried to put a positive light on the debacle. "The result was entirely satisfactory," he wrote. "It convinced me that neither the snow of winter nor the mountain ranges were obstacles in the way of a [rail]road."

Despite Frémont's bravado, the transcontinental railroad had not gotten off to an auspicious start. To make matters worse, the railroad quickly emerged as a bone of sectional contention, particularly among cities and towns in the Mississippi Valley vying with one another to become the line's eastern terminus. In the volatile 1850s, every issue and debate in Congress seemed to pit North against South, and the railroad was no

Gustave Sohon's Crossing the Hellgate River-May 5th 1854, *above, portrays a dramatic moment in Isaac I. Stevens's Pacific railroad expedition. One of four Pacific Railroad Surveys authorized by Congress in 1853, Stevens's survey followed the northernmost route and explored the vast region between St. Paul, Minnesota, and Puget Sound. The Pacific Railroad Surveys pooled the efforts of Topographical Engineers, artists, geologists, mineralogists, naturalists, and other scientists, and the resulting reports offered detailed descriptions of western landscapes and beautiful illustrations. Opposite, John Mix Stanley's* Puget Sound & Mt. Rainier From Whitby's Island *from Stevens's report.*

Captain John W. Gunnison led the Pacific Railroad Survey along the 38th parallel. Marching across Missouri and the "graceful grassy swells of the Kansas prairie," Gunnison's party toiled through the Sangre de Cristo Mountains and stopped to rest at Fort Massachusetts, below.

After surveying Cochetopa Pass and crossing the Continental Divide, the expedition continued on through the Wasatch Mountains down into the valley of the Sevier River. Here, on the morning of October 26, 1853, Gunnison, botanist Frederick Creutzfeldt, topographer

Richard Kern, and five others were massacred by Paiute Indians. Gunnison's assistant, Lieutenant E. G. Beckwith, took command of the expedition, and, after spending the winter in Salt Lake City, led his party out across the Great Basin and into California. The panoramic

view of the Sierra Nevada, bottom, near Noble's Pass in northern California, was engraved from an 1854 drawing by F. W. von Egloffstein and published in Beckwith's report.

exception. Finally, in 1853, amid intense factionalism and rivalry and skirmishes over route proposals, Congress passed the Pacific Railroad Survey bill, appropriating $150,000 for the determination within 10 months of the most "practicable and economical" trans-Mississippi railroad route to the Pacific. In making the appropriation, it called for as many surveys as there were "practicable" routes, which in fact were those with the greatest political support.

Three surveying parties took the field in the summer of 1853. Largest and best equipped was the one under Isaac I. Stevens, the enthusiastic and energetic young governor of Washington Territory, who blazed the northern route originally proposed by Whitney and now endorsed by the forceful Stephen A. Douglas of Illinois. John Gunnison, now a captain, was chosen to explore the path along the 38th parallel originally recommended by Frémont and Benton. The third party, commanded by Lieutenant Amiel Weeks Whipple, followed the 35th parallel, a route highly touted by Representative John Smith Phelps of Missouri. Exploration along the 32nd parallel, the southernmost route and the one favored by Secretary of War Jefferson Davis of Mississippi, did not begin until early 1854. It had been partially surveyed during the Mexican War, and Davis was confident it would be selected without further exploration. Enough skeptics challenged the route, however, that Davis finally agreed to include it in the survey, and so he sent out two parties, one from the West, led by Lieutenant John G. Parke, and the other from the East, under Captain John B. Pope. Lieutenants Parke, Henry L. Abbot, and Robert S. Williamson also explored the valleys and mountain passes of California for a route that could link the state's coastal cities with whatever transcontinental railroad was built.

In the strict sense of the word, the explorers conducted topographical reconnaissances rather than surveys. They were not expected to map out the exact routes the railroads would follow, but rather to collect information about the climate, soils, rocks, minerals, and natural history of each route, as well as estimate engineering difficulties, economic potential, and the availability of such necessities for railroads of the time as water and timber. Accomplishing these broad objectives required the talents of a variety of specialists. Thus, each survey team, led by a topographical engineer, included physicians, astronomers,

meteorologists, botanists, geologists, naturalists, cartographers, and artists, as well as military escorts, guides, interpreters, blacksmiths, hunters, and muleteers. As historian Henry Savage points out, "Never before had any significant area of the country been so thoroughly and systematically subjected to the inspection of so many trained observers."

With so many people tramping through so many remote areas of the West, trouble with Indians was inevitable. Indeed, the Corps had already lost one of its finest officers to Indians. In August of 1849, Captain William H. Warner was ambushed by a party of Pit River Indians as he was attempting to discover a railroad route from the Upper Sacramento River over the Sierra Nevadas to the Humboldt River. Both Warner and his guide, riding at the head of the column, were struck down by arrows.

The surveyors appreciated the risks and did their best both to protect themselves and to allay the fears of the Indians with whom they came in contact, but tensions ran high, and nerves were always on edge. On one occasion four men with Governor Stevens were so convinced an Indian was stalking them through the tall grass that they followed the old western maxim, "Shoot first and ask questions later." Approaching their supposedly well-riddled target they discovered only an irate skunk, which promptly made them unfit for polite society.

The most tragic incident occurred during the Gunnison survey. Captain Gunnison, now 41 years old and one of the Corps's most experienced topographical engineers, set out from Fort Leavenworth on the Santa Fe road on June 23, 1853. He was accompanied by Lieutenant E. G. Beckwith, his second-in-command, and a distinguished team of scientists and engineers, including the botanist Creutzfeldt and the artist Richard Kern, both survivors of the disastrous Frémont expedition of 1848. Gunnison's path roughly followed the one blazed by Zebulon Pike almost 50 years earlier—to the headwaters of the Arkansas, then across the towering Sangre de Cristo Mountains into the San Luis Valley at the headwaters of the Rio Grande. Gunnison had no easier time of it than Pike. After winding through rough terrain along the Upper Colorado and discovering the river that now bears his name, Gunnison struck the Spanish Trail where it crossed the Green River and continued on through the Wasatch Mountains and into the valley of the Sevier River, a desolate and arid region in west-central Utah.

Mojave Indians help Lieutenant Amiel Weeks Whipple's Pacific Railroad Survey forces cross the Colorado River, top. Setting out from Fort Smith, Arkansas, his party tracked the 35th parallel, crossing the towering San Francisco Mountains of central Arizona, above, the Colorado basin, and then the Mojave Desert and Coast Ranges into San Bernadino. Topographer and artist-naturalist Heinrich Baldwin Möllhausen drew The Petrified Forest in the Valley of the Rio Seco, New Mexico, right, and Spanish carvings found on Inscription Rock near Zuni, New Mexico, opposite.

Despite the hardships, Gunnison was quite pleased. "On reaching this plain a stage is attained which I have so long desired to accomplish: the great mountains have been passed and a new wagon road opened across the continent—a work which was almost unanimously pronounced impossible, by the men who know the mountains and this route over them." Much of the credit should go to the "energy, zeal, and ability" of his subordinates, he acknowledged in his official report. "That a road for nearly seven hundred miles should have been made over an untrodden track . . . through a wilderness all the way, and across five mountain ranges . . . and a dry desert of seventy miles between Grand [Colorado] and Green Rivers, without deserting one of our nineteen wagons, and leaving but one animal from sickness and one from straying, and this in two and a half months, must be my excuse for speaking highly of all the assistants of this survey."

Not everyone shared his enthusiasm. Like Frémont, Gunnison had his own German diarist along, and Creutzfeldt, like Preuss, had little good to say either about the expedition or its captain, whom he called "an old dog." At first the explorers were made miserable by heat and insects. "We proceed to get from the frying pan into a hell hole of ants and mosquitoes, which drive us to desperation," reads one entry. Creutzfeldt seemed particularly dissatisfied with their food and wrote in a typical entry dated August 21: "Our captain is mean as usual, we are eating bacon and bread, though vegetables, milk, eggs, butter and fresh meat can be had in the Fort."

A month later, nothing—at least in Creutzfeldt's estimation—had improved. "We go on to day senselessly in a desolate waste land without an idea where to get water or grass in all directions of the compass, and finally stop in this Arabia late in the dark night, on a Creek with some little water trickling in, but for its salty and bitter taste unpalatable. Men and beasts are suffering dreadfully. One wagon is left behind, the mules fatigued to death being unable to go on. All this because of great genius."

Only Indians ranked lower in Creutzfeldt's estimation. He thought Gunnison tolerated the Indians who continually besieged their camps begging food and gifts because he feared them. Whether Gunnison befriended the Indians out of fear or kindness will never be known. Whatever the motive, his policy was not effective. Ahead of schedule, with two months remaining before winter, he decided to explore the area around Sevier

113

Lake. "To explore the damned Sevier Lake and river, as it is called, we have to cross the river and . . . [go through] 2 passes and several valleys," Creutzfeldt grumbled to his diary. Nonetheless, he had no choice but to accompany Gunnison, who left his main party at a base camp and took the botanist, Kern, a guide, and eight troopers on the excursion to Sevier Lake. They never reached it.

For some time Gunnison had heard rumors of war between the Mormons and the Paiute Indians. "Parties of less than a dozen do not dare to travel," the captain wrote his wife on October 18 in his last letter home. He thought the worst of the troubles were over, however, when he set out for Sevier Lake. What he could not know was that a party of 20 Paiute hunters was also approaching Sevier Lake from another direction. They were led by a warrior named Moshoquop, whose father had been killed by white men only a few days earlier. The Paiutes were in a vengeful mood when they stumbled across the Gunnison party as it set up camp on the evening of October 25. While the explorers slept, Moshoquop and his followers surrounded their camp, planning to strike at first light.

They caught the surveyors completely by surprise. First awake had been the cook, who already had a kettle simmering above a small fire before the rest of the men had struggled out of their bedding. Gunnison was at the riverbank washing his

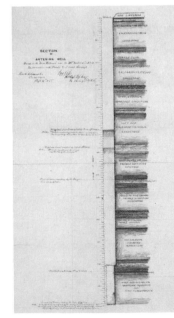

Heinrich Baldwin Möllhausen's A Conical Hill, 500 Feet High, *above, depicted the exposed strata of an isolated mound along the Whipple expedition's route, and accompanied that survey's geological report. The southernmost Pacific railroad route was surveyed by Captain John Pope and Lieutenant John G. Parke. Exploring the eastern section of the line in Texas from the Red River to the Rio Grande, Pope and his men had to contend with the treeless and desiccated* Llano Estacado, *or* Staked Plains, *of the Texas-New Mexico border. Pope believed that artesian wells, such as the one he sketched at left, could provide water for the growing of cotton.*

face, and Creutzfeldt, doubtlessly complaining about something, was warming his hands by the fire when the Indians
began shooting. The cook fell dead next to his campfire; the
botanist, a steel-tipped arrow in his spine, dropped beside him.
An Indian lying in ambush near Gunnison missed with his shot.
The captain pulled his cap-and-ball revolver, fired and missed,
and then rushed into the center of camp yelling, "We are
friends! We are friends!" He fell in a hail of arrows; 15 were in
his body when it was later found.

There was no resistance. As war whoops, gunshots, and the
screams of the dying rent the morning air, each man tried his
best to save himself. One trooper, bucked off his horse, hid in
brush for six or seven hours before sneaking away. Three
others also escaped, even though Indians chased two of them
for miles. The rest, including Gunnison, Creutzfeldt, and Kern,
were not so lucky. It was the most successful attack by Indians
yet against the U.S. Army in the West. Surprisingly, most of the
scientific material, including Kern's sketches, Gunnison's notes,
and Creutzfeldt's diary, was later recovered. Even Gunnison's
odometer was found, a few years later, some 70 miles away
from the scene of the massacre.

In the end, as far as determining the route for a transcontinental railroad was concerned, the Pacific Railroad Surveys
were a failure. Each expedition leader claimed his route was the

Colorado Desert and Signal
Mountain, *above, portrays the
"barren nature of the country"
as reported by Lieutenant
Robert S. Williamson, who led
one of two surveys of California
and the Pacific Coast. He and
Lieutenants Parke and Henry L.
Abbot explored mountain
passes and searched for possible
railroad connections between
cities in California, Oregon,
and Washington.*

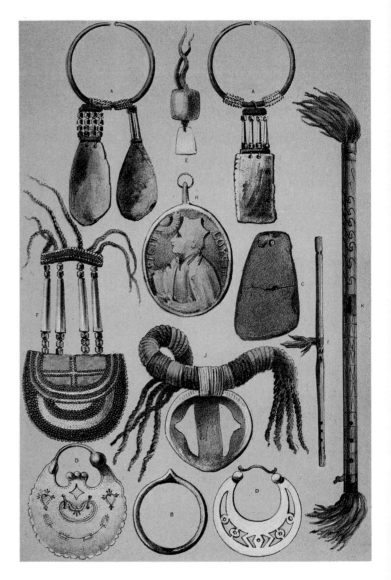

Published between 1855 and 1860, the 13 volumes of the Pacific Railroad Reports provided a comprehensive, illustrated record of the trans-Mississippi West's flora and fauna, Indian tribes, and geological and geographical features. A sampling of illustrations from the Reports includes a California hawk, left, a western grebe, below left, a prickly poppy, below, and a shoot of an evergreen oak, below right, as well as Indian artifacts, a spotted skunk, and a coast fox from California.

John Mix Stanley's Herd of Bison, Near Lake Jessie, *published with Isaac I. Stevens's* Pacific Railroad Report, *is one of the few remaining on-the-scene illustrations of the bison-filled* plains before the coming of the railroads and the increasing demand for buffalo hides in the East. By 1883 almost all the herds had vanished.

best, and the political boosters who had endorsed them to begin with were not about to change their minds. Jefferson Davis examined the reports and then, to no one's surprise, selected the southern route. The secretary of war did concede a disadvantage to the route in that part of it crossed Mexican territory, but he got around that difficulty by authorizing James Gadsden, U.S. Minister to Mexico, to purchase the area in question for 10 million dollars. Needless to say, this did not sit well with "Old Bullion" Benton. He informed his Senate colleagues that the southern route was "so utterly desolate, desert, and God-forsaken that Kit Carson says a wolf could not make his living on it." But what could you expect from graduates of the Military Academy, he blustered. "It takes a grand national school like West Point to put national roads outside of a country and leave the interior without one."

Although Congress approved the Gadsden Purchase, the route of the transcontinental railroad was not resolved until after the Civil War. And, ultimately, each route won, so that by the end of the century East and West were connected by a great network of railroads. The Central Pacific and Union Pacific (1869), the first to be completed, followed the route advocated by Benton and Frémont and marked by Gunnison and Beckwith; the Atchison, Topeka and Santa Fe (1881) followed Whipple's route; the Southern Pacific and Texas and Pacific (1882) followed the southern route; and the Northern Pacific (1883) followed Stevens's route.

Perhaps the most immediate beneficiary of the Pacific Railroad Surveys was the nation's scientific community, for the work of the Topographical Engineers and their civilian associates was memorialized in 13 often lavishly illustrated volumes issued between 1855 and 1860. A veritable encyclopedia of the West, these volumes offered narrative accounts of the individual expeditions as well as detailed reports on geology, botany, animals, and fishes, and ethnographic reports on Indian tribes. In scientific terms, the *Pacific Railroad Reports* marked the advent of specialization and teamwork in the study of the natural sciences. They also represented a cartographic milestone, as each expedition produced a detailed map of the country it surveyed. Lieutenant G. K. Warren, a brilliant young Topographical Engineer, then took this data and combined it with that available from other army expeditions to prepare the first scientifically accurate and comprehensive map of the trans-Mississippi West [see page 140].

Yet despite the enormous consumption of manpower and money the *Pacific Railroad Reports* represented, they still were largely superficial and disorganized. Jefferson Davis had the 10-month deadline to meet, and railroad promoters were anxious to get on with selecting the route and constructing the line. Nevertheless, while the country headed inexorably towards a tragic civil war, the enormous amount of knowledge assembled by the surveys was safely stored in the massive *Reports*. And the equally enormous quantity of scientific specimens, illustrations, and raw data upon which the *Reports* were based was safely stored in the Smithsonian, awaiting examination by a later generation of scientists and naturalists.

At their sorting tables in the
Smithsonian's Castle, curators
examine cultural artifacts and
natural history specimens. Even
before the Civil War, items from
the West arrived by the thousand.

"ARSENIC AND DIRECTIONS"

I t was more by accident than by design that the Smithsonian Institution came to be a patron of western exploration. In fact, it was more by accident than design that the Smithsonian Institution ever came to be at all. James Smithson, the English gentleman scientist who bequeathed half a million dollars to the United States for the institution that now bears his name, never specified the form it should take—only that it should exist "for the increase and diffusion of knowledge among men." A national university, an observatory, an agricultural institute, and a great national library were among the proposals for this marvelous bequest.

And they were all accommodated when in 1846, 17 years after Smithson's death, the bill establishing the Smithsonian Institution was passed. A museum, a gallery of art, a library, laboratories, and lecture halls were all to be housed in a specially constructed building. The precise direction the Institution would take was left to the Board of Regents, which had the good sense to select Joseph Henry as the Smithsonian's first executive officer, or Secretary.

The regents wanted someone of "eminent scientific and general requirements," and Henry certainly fit those particulars. Of a practical as well as a scholarly mind—he was an inventor of the electromagnet and of a rudimentary form of the telegraph— he launched as Secretary an international system for the exchange of scientific information and literature which is still intact today, as well as the renowned publication program, *Smithsonian Contributions to Knowledge*, which enabled the rapid

The plaited straw ornament at left was collected by U.S. Army officer Gouverneur K. Warren from Sioux Indians in the Upper Missouri River country.

Smithsonian Institute

dissemination of the latest scientific discoveries.

Henry recognized the importance of research collections and supported their acquisition, but "to amuse the citizens and visitors of Washington" with a museum was not part of his vision for the Smithsonian Institution. He adamantly refused to accept the collections of the Wilkes expedition, then housed at the Patent Office while the scientific reports were being prepared. The government should maintain the museum "as a memento of the science and energy of our navy," he wrote in 1848, but not as part of the Smithsonian. Its slender resources would be better spent in collecting specimens not yet studied, transmitting them to competent scientists and artists for scrutiny and illustration, and assisting them in their publications.

Fortunately for the future of the Smithsonian, Henry's resistance eroded during the next 10 years, in part because of the massive influx of specimens from the West in the 1850s, and in part because of his appointment of an assistant with original ideas about museums.

That assistant was Spencer Fullerton Baird, a dedicated naturalist and confirmed collector from Carlisle, Pennsylvania. As a teenager, Baird had often trekked 40 miles in a day in his relentless hunt for scientific specimens. In 1842 alone, he logged almost 2,000 miles and shot 650 birds. Artist John James Audubon became a grateful beneficiary of this voracious collector, and in return joined others in urging Henry to make Baird his assistant. Finally, in the fall of 1850, Baird came to the Smithsonian, an amazing young man of 27 who brought with

The spires of the Smithsonian's Castle rise above the trees in an 1852 watercolor by Richard Kern, opposite top. The distinguished American physicist Joseph Henry, opposite bottom, was selected in 1846 as founding Smithsonian Secretary, and presided over the building of the Institution's original edifice.

Joseph Henry's closest colleague, Spencer Fullerton Baird, above, arrived in Washington during 1850 to become assistant secretary of the Smithsonian. Highly recommended by fellow bird collector John James Audubon, left, the vigorous Pennsylvanian was to launch and assist dozens of expeditions to the American West.

Birdskins, opposite, were part of Spencer Baird's personal legacy to the Smithsonian—two railroad boxcars full of natural history specimens. The colorful Carolina parakeet (third from top) became extinct early in the 20th century. Below, a lithograph depicts a Smithsonian researcher at work amid the national ornithological collection. Feathered skins and fully mounted birds surround him.

him two boxcars of specimens and a hidden agenda.

Before Baird's arrival, Henry had already taken modest steps toward building natural history research collections, purchasing some material from collectors and acquiring some merely for the cost of its transportation to Washington. To Baird this was only a beginning. Envisioning a complete record of the nation's natural history, he launched a massive collecting program and became the key link between the federal government and the scientific community just as the government's systematic exploration of the trans-Mississippi West was surging.

Baird realized that these expeditions presented the Smithsonian with a unique opportunity to advance science, for much of the West's flora and fauna remained uncollected and undescribed. Seizing the opportunity, he saw to it that, whatever their primary mission, the government survey teams were accompanied by naturalists who collected for the Smithsonian. He also ensured that specimens were sent to the leading scientists and artists for examination, description, classification, and publication. Among those who benefitted from his largess were Joseph Leidy, paleontologist at the Academy of Natural Sciences in Philadelphia, and the botanists John Torrey and Asa Gray.

Baird's achievements were little short of miraculous. He was assistant secretary for 28 years and then, upon Henry's death in 1878, he became Secretary until his own death nine years later. As supervisor of publications at the Smithsonian, he was overseer for countless scientific reports, and he prepared many himself, especially on birds, mammals, and reptiles. He worked up the zoology for the Ives expedition, the fishes for Sitgreaves's Zuni River expedition, and three volumes of the *Pacific Railroad Reports*. In addition, he wrote a prodigious number of letters—3,050 in 1860 alone. He maintained a schedule that would have exhausted lesser men, working 15-hour days during the winter. Holidays were no festive interludes for him; he could get more work done then. Even on Christmas and New Year's Day, he could be found in his office writing letters, correcting printer's proofs, skinning birds, or cataloging specimens.

Encouraging and recruiting collectors, Baird continually expanded his network until eventually as many as 1,000 amateur and professional scientists were seeking, preparing, and shipping specimens from all over the globe to what in 1858 officially became the National Museum. A lucky few gained lasting fame when new species were named after them. For the most part, though, their only reward was seeing their names listed in the Smithsonian Annual Report and receiving another enthusiastic letter from Baird, full of thanks and further suggestions.

The Smithsonian records clearly document Baird's effectiveness as a manager of acquisitions. When he arrived in 1850, the Smithsonian had about 6,000 specimens; by 1858, that total had swelled to some 70,000. Perhaps a typical year was 1855, in which the Smithsonian received almost 500 packages—229 separate donations from 130 individuals. That year Henry claimed that the Smithsonian had the world's finest collection of American fauna. Over the next two years the number of recorded specimens doubled.

During Baird's first decade as assistant secretary, his major

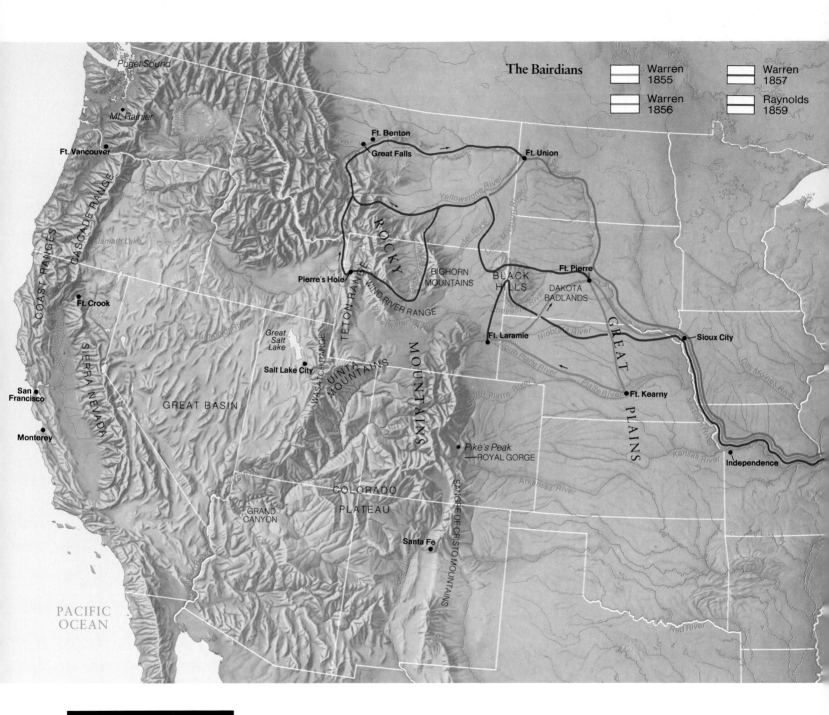

The Bairdians

| | Warren 1855 | | Warren 1857 |
| | Warren 1856 | | Raynolds 1859 |

In 1856 Baird recommended a young civilian geologist, Ferdinand V. Hayden, to the Army's Corps of Topographical Engineers. Though Hayden chafed somewhat under military leadership, he served with the Topographical Corps for several years. In the spring of 1859, he set out with Captain William F. Raynolds to survey what had hitherto been called Colter's Hell—Yellowstone country with its active geysers and other geothermal features. Snow falling in rough terrain like that in the Wind River Range of Wyoming, opposite, stopped the party short of its goal.

suppliers of natural history specimens were members of the military. As soon as an army officer was named to head an exploring expedition, Baird hastened to introduce himself and offer assistance. If the expedition had not been assigned a naturalist, Baird suggested likely candidates; if an officer wished to fill the role himself, Baird offered manuals and rudimentary training.

So effectively did Baird promote scientific collecting that many expedition leaders contacted the Smithsonian as they prepared to take the field. In his 1854 report, Baird described 26 government-sponsored expeditions since 1852, including the Pacific Railroad Surveys. "With scarcely an exception," he noted, "every expedition of any magnitude has received more or less aid from the Smithsonian Institution."

In addition to advice, training, and instructions for making scientific observations and collections in the various disciplines of natural history, the Smithsonian provided the explorers with all manner of supplies, such as shipping containers, alcohol, arsenic (a preservative), and scientific instruments. "Much of the apparatus," Baird claimed, "was invented or adapted by the Institution for this special purpose, and used for the first time,

with results surpassing the most sanguine expectations."

It was no simple matter ensuring that an expedition had all it needed, and it was the seemingly tireless Baird who handled the most minute details. As Baird's daughter later wrote, "No bride ever devoted more thought and attention to her trousseau than did my father to the fitting out of each of these explorers, and he watched the progress of each with anxious personal interest."

Baird's diary provides a fascinating insight into the way he and Henry served as the scientific hub of western exploration. On New Year's Day 1851, for example, after a meeting of the Smithsonian regents, Baird went to the White House to chat with President Millard Fillmore and Colonel James D. Graham, head of the scientific corps assigned to the Mexican Boundary Commission. "Had some conversation with [Graham] . . . respecting the appointment of a Naturalist to accompany him on his Boundary Survey," Baird recorded. "Promised to see the Secretary of the Interior on the subject tomorrow."

A week later, Baird talked again with Graham, who requested that Charles Girard accompany him. Baird, however, had other plans for Girard, his young French-born assistant. That very

afternoon he had discussed with Lieutenant Charles Wilkes a plan for Girard to identify and describe the reptiles that had been collected by the U.S. Exploring Expedition. Needless to say, Baird had his own candidate in mind for Graham—John H. Clark, a former student of his at Dickinson College. That evening he wrote Clark "to come on immediately."

The next day, January 9, found Baird "busy making preparations for [the] naturalist to Col. Graham's expedition." He ordered trunks and copper kettles for the preservation and shipment of specimens, and saw a second artisan about the lids. He then visited Wilkes's office and talked to Joseph Drayton, the artist and engraver, about the reptile report. "Thence to Smithsonian in hack and next to Capt. Stansbury's," where he examined the specimens just brought in by that officer from the Great Salt Lake. The reptiles had not yet been unpacked, but Baird saw "4 large bundles of plants. Many minerals. Mammalia, Badger, Foxes, Wolverines, Weasels. . . . Many birds . . . a new duck." From there he visited the Patent Office to see—"in 260 bottles"—Wilkes's reptiles. After dinner Baird attended to correspondence, then called again on Colonel Graham, who agreed to Clark's appointment and gave the assistant secretary a check for $60 "to procure [an] outfit." When the indefatigable Baird finally got home that night, Clark was there waiting for him.

During the next several days, Baird and Clark made further preparations. At the local market, the assistant secretary bought birds, fish, and rabbits in order to give Clark a refresher lesson in skinning such creatures. He returned to the trunkmaker and

Recumbent Indian, above, dominates the foreground of a detailed rendering of terrain in Nevada's Franklin Valley—one of the romantic touches F. W. von Egloffstein added to his artwork for the Beckwith 41st parallel expedition report of 1861. Several volumes of the encyclopedic Pacific Railroad Reports *contain natural history sections written by Spencer Baird in response to the flood of specimens sent back to Washington from the western wilderness. Baird's handiwork appears in the scientific descriptions of a salamander, opposite bottom, and the horned lizards or "toads," opposite top left. These creatures were encountered by the Stansbury expedition to the Great Basin in 1849. Baird himself found a new love in his investigation of the "slippery republic," the world of fishes. He took special delight in the sturdy, scoop-nosed specimen, opposite top right, collected by Dr. S. W. Woodhouse during Captain Lorenzo Sitgreaves's Zuni River expedition of 1851. James Hall, a leading paleontologist, described the fossil shell species, also at right, from the 1854 Pope railroad survey.*

Major William Emory's Mexican boundary survey of the early 1850s brought glimpses and souvenirs of an ill-defined southern frontier. In Arizona territory, right, Papago Indian women knock down cactus fruit with sticks. The herbarium specimen, opposite left, rests today in Smithsonian collections of the National Museum of Natural History in Washington, D.C. The frogs shown opposite right were depicted in Emory's expedition report of 1856. The quiet and scholarly nature of these items fails to reflect the expedition's political purpose— to establish secure borders with Mexico and push rail routes through to the Pacific. In 1853, at the time of the expedition, the United States negotiated the Gadsden Purchase of land from Mexico.

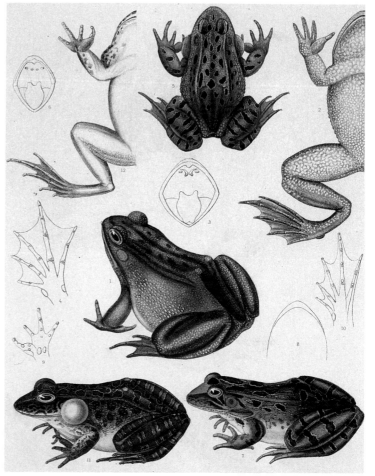

tinsmith to check on the copper kettles, and then inspected recently returned magnetic instruments to see if they were still serviceable. Finally, on January 16, he packed up a trunk with nets, traps, and other paraphernalia and forwarded it all to the southwestern border.

Baird's role now became that of exhorter. He maintained a supportive correspondence with Clark and his superior officers for the next several years. The young naturalist might complain of the barrenness of the country, "stretches of from 50 to 100 miles without living water, without grass, and without wood enough to boil a pot of coffee." The optimistic Baird would reply, "In the most unpromising localities there is always something."

Clark's first shipment of specimens arrived December 4, and by January 20, 1852, four cases of fish, reptiles, birds, and insects had come in. These, Baird boasted, were "the most extraordinary series ever gathered," and he informed Major William H. Emory, Graham's successor, "I don't believe there is his equal as a collector." To Clark, he wrote: Keep after birds and eggs. Look sharp for crabs and crawfish. Be alert to new small mammals, rats, and mice. "Get plenty skulls and skeletons."

Six weeks later another case arrived. "I am afraid Girard will go into a fever with the excitement," Baird wrote after opening the kettle in which the specimens had been shipped. "One of these days, when the results of the expedition are published, people will be astonished to find how much one man can do under difficulties. It all depends on training don't it?"

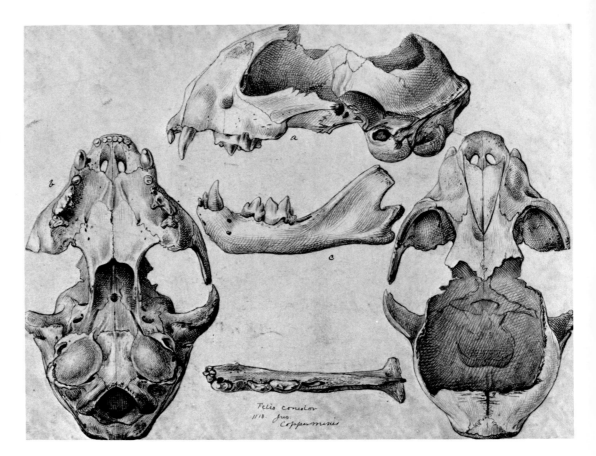

As naturalist for the Mexican boundary survey, Baird's pupil John C. Clark captured the American panther, Felis concolor, whose skull appears in several different views at right. Another of Clark's finds, the young wildcat illustrated below, may well belong to the same species.

Baird was encouraging to unknown, inexperienced naturalists as well as to those he handpicked. Visited by one neophyte-naturalist army officer about to leave for the frontier, the Smithsonian assistant secretary "gave him arsenic and directions" and hoped for the best. Indeed, Baird confided to his good friend, U.S. minister to Turkey George P. Marsh, half-jesting, half-boasting: "I fear I have much to answer for in the way of deluding unsuspecting young (and even old) men to possible destruction from bite of snake, scorpion or centipede, engulfing in caverns while in search of fossil bones, embrace of Krakens, when catching starfish on the seas; or some other undescribed species of calamity, the genus, even, of which is not yet known. The string of scientific expeditions which I have succeeded in starting is perfectly preposterous. Have you any idea of the activity of our navy and army at the present date? Expeditions by field and flood? Well, in nearly all I have a finger, and in several two hands."

As the enormous collections of natural history specimens and artifacts from the West and around the world continued to pour in, Joseph Henry came to see that there was no suitable depository other than the Smithsonian. In 1857 Congress appropriated funds for the curatorial care and display of government collections. Exhibit cases were built in the Great Hall of the Smithsonian Castle, and the National Museum of the United States came into being on the Mall. Spencer Baird, naturally, was its first director.

One of Baird's military collectors was John Feilner, a Bavarian mapmaker who had enlisted in the U.S. Army as a private in 1856. Stationed at Fort Crook, a little post in northern California, Feilner spent his spare time collecting natural history specimens, primarily bird skins and eggs. Acting on the advice of another immigrant naturalist in the army, Hungarian refugee John Xantus, who collected thousands of birds and other specimens for Baird, Feilner wrote to the assistant secretary in January 1859. "My collection of birdskins reaches now to the No. of over 300, not including mammals, and other sundry specimens. You may well imagine Sir the difficulty of their transportation, situated as I am should we be ordered from here to som[e] other Post." Would Baird be willing to store his collection in return for a complete set of specimens, including whatever Feilner collected in the future?

Thus began a long and unusual relationship between the immigrant soldier and the eastern scholar. "I hope," Baird responded, "that it will be in your power to make full collections in all departments of natural history, and especially in that of eggs." To assist his new recruit, Baird sent him two different kinds of shot, salt, three gallons of alcohol, five pounds of arsenic, 500 percussion caps, and a set of instructions.

A steady exchange of specimens and correspondence ensued. The following year Baird informed Feilner that he had sold some of his duplicate specimens for $40 and suggested he use the money to buy a double-barreled shotgun to facilitate his collecting. "I hope you are doing wonders among the birds," Baird urged, "and will do still more among the eggs. Don't

Geomys clarkii, Baird – Presidio del Norte. 6

Clark prepared the scientific description of the Pecos gopher, left, for Baird's Mammals of North America, *whereupon the diminutive rodent became known as* Geomys clarkii. *Another of Clark's namesakes, the species of snake at right, once bore the scientific name* Regina clarkii.

forget plenty of good skins of humming birds."

Baird was so pleased with Feilner's industry that he persuaded the young man's commanding officer to let him make a field trip to Klamath Lake, some 60 miles from the post. Undaunted by the fact that the lake lay in the heartland of the truculent Modoc Indians, the eager collector, accompanied by another trooper, left Fort Crook on May 13. While passing through the town of Yrkea a few days later, he wrote Baird, "I hope you upon my return to offer a favorable report of my labors." His only concern was the Modocs, rumored to be on the warpath. "If so—it won't be much favorable to me."

And indeed it wasn't. Five days later some 40 irate Modocs chased Feilner and his companion for six miles. Taking refuge in a settler's cabin, the two soldiers, assisted by several friendly Indians and white herders, were able to survive a siege of more than 48 hours. Only after killing the Modoc chief and several of his warriors were they finally able to drive the attackers away. Feilner sent the few specimens the Modocs had not destroyed to Baird.

With his enlistment soon to expire, Feilner sought Baird's assistance. "I need hardly tell you, that my ambition leads me to wish to be something better than an enlisted soldier." As an officer, he pointed out, he would have more leisure time for collecting. Unfortunately, his English was so weak that he had little hope of passing the required written examination. Nonetheless, he was willing to study hard if Baird thought it possible "that I, as a foreigner, without friends . . . could get a commission." Baird not only wrote a letter of recommendation to the secretary of war but also paid him a visit. "Sergeant Feilner is of very gentlemanly deportment, well educated, an accomplished topographical draftsman, and a thorough soldier. His gallantry in repelling with a single companion a much superior Indian force in May of 1860, in killing their chief, and capturing their property has been made the subject of special mention . . . in the last report of the Secretary of War. Sergeant Feilner has been a personal correspondent of mine for several years, and has furnished much information of interest relating to Natural History of Northern California."

Feilner received his commission just as the Civil War engulfed the country. He was transferred to the battlefields of Virginia, where he so distinguished himself that he rose rapidly to the rank of captain. Baird had no desire to see his competent collector meet an untimely though gallant death on the battlefield, however, so he succeeded in getting him sent west to join an expedition commanded by General Alfred Sully, who was heading to the Dakotas for reprisals against the Sioux after the Minnesota uprising. Feilner, assigned to the army engineers, received special instructions directing him to make a full report on the geology, botany, natural history, and physical character of the region covered by the Sully expedition.

Recently married and anticipating the birth of a child in a few months, Feilner relished the chance to leave the battlefields and work once again as a naturalist. Leaving New York City and his wife in April 1864, he went by train to Chicago and then to Sioux City, Iowa, where he joined Sully's army as it assembled for the anticipated strike against the Sioux. During this period Feilner corresponded frequently with Baird, who had furnished him with a fully equipped outfit for collecting in the field. "You will greatly oblige me, by sending me a work on geology—and giving me some instruction in that line." Feilner also needed a book on birds, having forgotten his own in the rush to get away, and a description of the "important species" in that part of the country. The pickings were slim in Iowa, however. During one brief outing he collected only 12 specimens. "Little is in this section of the country at present," he grumbled. "It is almost a wonder to see a bird on a tree."

Although Sully had yet to make his appearance, word had arrived that the Sioux were spoiling for a fight. Sixteen hundred lodges had already assembled, and 600 more were expected. "If so, much the better, all will be settled in one affair, and we won't have to go and look for them."

Feilner's last letter to Baird—accompanying a shipment of specimens—is dated June 3, the day before Sully's army left for the Sioux country. He apologized for the poor findings—"only one nest, one squirrel with skull, one skeleton of a mudhen and three bottles of insects"—but promised more when he reached the Dakotas. He had arranged his collecting gear in two boxes that could be carried by a mule, and had persuaded several enlisted men to be his assistants. One, hospital steward Sigmund Rothhammer, seemed so promising that Feilner had bought him a shotgun. "So far, I am prepared for every kind of march. All I want is luck."

Luck he did not get. As Sully's army moved north from Fort Pierre along the Missouri River, Feilner paused at a stream for a drink of water, unaware that three Sioux warriors were hiding in bushes just a few feet away. Shot twice, he died in "great agony" two hours later. Although his assailants were hunted down and killed, their deaths did little to temper the bitterness of Feilner's commanding officer. "It is hard that he should lose his life in this way," General Sully wrote. "It was all owing to his enthusiastic desire to collect as many specimens as possible for the Smithsonian Institute."

Yet Feilner's death did not end his work, for Rothhammer promptly took his place. "Nothing could give me more satisfaction than an opportunity to do my part in adding to the development of Natural History, that mother of all science, by devoting my energies and limited knowledge to a continuance of the same labors, which I was enabled to begin . . . through the kindness of my much lamented friend Capt. Feilner." And Baird did not forget his obligation to Feilner's widow, corresponding with her for more than 15 years and assisting her with problems she had with her pension.

The most important of Baird's military collectors was Gouverneur Kemble Warren, who was later to distinguish himself at Gettysburg and other battles of the Civil War. Handsome and intelligent, Warren graduated second in his class at West Point in 1850, and narrowly escaped being placed on the faculty. This he would not have relished. "I would rather rough it than be sent there before hard service had made me above reproach," he confided to his father.

Though his English was poor, German immigrant John Feilner soon won recognition both in the U.S. Army and among scientists for his collecting activities during his tours on the frontier. Like so many other naturalists, he corresponded with Spencer Baird at the Smithsonian and sent him hundreds of specimens, among them the sandhill crane and Lewis's woodpecker, above. The bow and arrows at left came into Feilner's possession after he survived an ambush by Modoc warriors.

Warren got his wish. Assigned to the elite Corps of Topographical Engineers, in 1854 he received the coveted assignment of compiling a comprehensive map of the trans-Mississippi West. It was at this time that he met Spencer Baird, and their friendship remained strong until Warren's death in 1882. During this period they maintained an extensive correspondence, exchanging scientific information, publications, and research papers. Baird also proffered Warren advice, encouragement, and assistance, and in return received a wealth of natural history specimens and a significant collection of western Sioux artifacts, as well, of course, as the officer's unflagging gratitude.

Warren's map, produced when he was only 26, was a cartographic triumph—"the first reasonably accurate map of the American West," in the words of one historian. In part to gather information for this monumental work, Warren conducted three surveys of what is today the northern Great Plains—in 1855, 1856, and 1857—covering extensive areas of the Nebraska and Dakota territories. During these expeditions he also collected numerous zoological specimens, which he then sent back to the Smithsonian for analysis and safekeeping.

All of Warren's specimens eventually came into Smithsonian hands, but it is his collection of Plains Indian artifacts that has always aroused a special interest. Like so many collections of Indian artifacts, this one was obtained after a battle.

In April 1855, Warren was ordered to accompany Colonel William S. Harney on an expedition into the Dakotas to punish Indians responsible for an unfortunate and needless incident that occurred the previous year near Fort Laramie. After a group of Sioux Indians had butchered a cow belonging to an emigrant wagon train, a hot-headed lieutenant named John L. Grattan and a group of soldiers were dispatched to a nearby Sioux village. Instead of gaining satisfaction for the incident, the impetuous Grattan got himself and 31 of his men massacred, marking the beginning of more than three decades of hostilities with the Indians of the northern plains. The Harney expedition contributed more than its share of bitterness to that legacy.

Commanding a force of 600 men, Harney easily found the Brulé Sioux village of Chief Little Thunder camped alongside the Oregon Trail on Blue Water Creek, a short distance from what is now Lewellyn, Nebraska. Terrified at the sight of Harney's troops, the Indians started to flee. Harney, however, to his everlasting shame, deceived Little Thunder with a white flag of truce in order to give his men time enough to surround the village. He then forced the Indians to fight.

The "battle" of Blue Water Creek was over before it began. Of the 400 Indians in the village, 87 were killed and 70, most of them wounded, were captured. Only five soldiers died. "The sight," Warren later reported, "... was heart-rending—wounded women and children crying and moaning, horribly mangled by the bullets." In one group were two dead women clutching their dead babies. Warren abandoned his attempt to sketch the battlefield in order to attend to the wounded Indians.

Warren later visited the devastated village and was struck by the vast quantity of clothing, weapons, and camp gear strewn about. Wishing to preserve a representative sampling of arti-

facts, he sifted through piles of material and systematically selected one or two fine examples of each type of object—decorated buffalo robes, beaded dresses, leggings, headdresses, blankets, quivers and shields—until he had collected some 100 items in all. Today some of these beautifully crafted artifacts are displayed in the Smithsonian's National Museum of Natural History, serving as reminders of the harsh course of America's Manifest Destiny on the plains.

Warren's 1856 expedition to the Yellowstone and Powder rivers country included in its scientific contingent the young geologist Ferdinand Vandeveer Hayden, yet another of Baird's collectors. Destined to become one of the nation's foremost paleontologists, Hayden had graduated from Albany Medical School with a burning desire to be a naturalist and, during February 1853, appealed to Baird for assistance in achieving his dream. "I feel as though I could endure cheerfully any amount of toil, hardship, and self denial provided I could gratify my strong desire to labor in the field as a naturalist," he wrote. "But I am poor, dependent entirely on my own exertions for my sup-

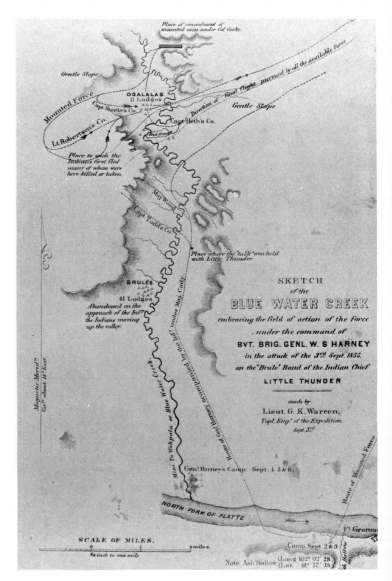

Gouverneur K. Warren, right, began his military career with action at the battle of Blue Water Creek in Dakota territory in September 1855. A skilled cartographer, Warren sketched the setting, opposite. The Sioux warriors were splendid horsemen, as shown above by artist Alfred Jacob Miller. At Blue Water Creek, however, they were greatly outnumbered, and the Americans inflicted many unnecessary casualties.

After tending to the wounds of surviving Indian women and children, Lieutenant Warren systematically collected the finest specimens of Sioux handicrafts, many still preserved at the Smithsonian. The bridle at right consists of red strips of blanket material sewn with small beads in floral patterns. The war club with massive blade below also came to light after the battle. The decorative leggings, opposite, belonged to a Sioux chief.

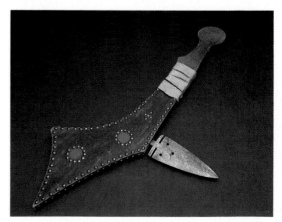

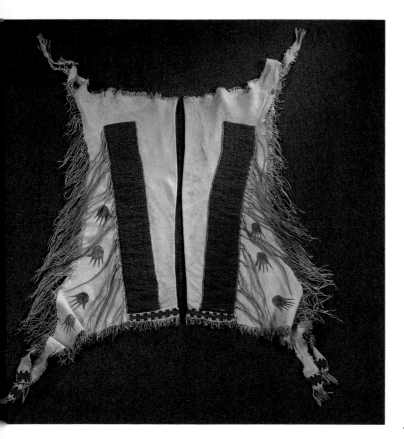

port, and every longing desire to engage in that most delightful of pursuits to me must be smothered by poverty." Could he do anything for the Smithsonian? Hayden asked. "I am willing to go anywhere, for any length of time and labor with the utmost diligence, . . . I have taken considerable pains to prepare myself for a collector."

At the time, Baird could offer Hayden only encouragement and the suggestion that he enlist in the army to take advantage of both a steady income and an opportunity to join the legion of army surgeons then dominating the field of natural history collecting. Instead, Hayden accepted an offer made by A. J. Vaughn, the Upper Missouri Indian agent, to work for him on speculation.

According to the agreement Hayden and Vaughn worked out, the Indian agent would pay the naturalist's expenses for a year's collecting in the Dakotas. The partners would share the profits from selling complete sets of specimens to wealthy collectors and universities. Vaughn, also one of Baird's acquaintances, agreed that all specimens would first be sent to the Smithsonian for identification and description.

Hayden worked industriously and in less than two months had collected about 500 different plant species "and many rare fossils." All the while he was trespassing in Sioux country, and they neither appreciated nor understood eccentric scientists no matter how ridiculous and harmless they appeared. Hayden must indeed have looked odd: "I . . . wander off alone for miles . . . with a Bag in one hand, Pick in the other, a Bottle of Alcohol in my vest pocket, and withal a gun to defend myself from Indians and Grizzly Bears." Once, in fact, Sioux warriors surrounded him, grabbed his bag, and dumped it on the ground. Amused to find that it contained nothing but rocks, they named the seemingly demented collector "man who picks up stones running" and let him go.

Hayden appreciated the danger. "The Indians are much opposed to anyone's getting specimens in their country and will yet make trouble with some one." Therefore, he explained to Baird, "it is not impossible that I may not live to return to the States. In case I should not, I wish you would take my collections and dispose of them as you may see fit. My Notes and Journals . . . I wish you to receive also."

He spent the winter at Fort Pierre, sorting and preparing his specimens for shipment to St. Louis and writing up his field notes. Those on geology alone filled 100 manuscript pages, and the specimens themselves, when shipped, weighed more than six tons. "Collected from a thousand localities and illustrating every phase of the Geology of the Upper Mo.," he boasted.

When he got to St. Louis the following spring, however, he discovered that many of the specimens he had shipped from the Upper Missouri were lost, stolen, or spoiled because no one had taken responsibility for them. "The labor of nine months lost," he lamented. Only the fossils remained in good condition. To make matters worse, Vaughn had sold some of their finer items to St. Louis fur trader Charles Chouteau, who planned to display them at his home. Thus, he wrote, "the collection has been placed in part out of my control. It was my

Warren's map, above, published in 1857, was the first consistently accurate picture of the trans-Mississippi West, much of it assembled firsthand in such areas as the Dakota Badlands, opposite.

wish to bring the whole on to Washington and as it is undoubtedly the finest ever obtained west of the Mississippi, it might have made a beneficial impression."

Hayden's arrangement with Vaughn had proved less than satisfactory, and he hoped something better could be arranged for the 1856 collecting season. Did Baird by any chance know of a government expedition heading for the Upper Missouri? Indeed he did. Impressed with the young man's diligence and dedication, Baird recommended Hayden to Lieutenant Warren, then in Washington preparing for his second survey of the Dakota country.

In February 1856, Warren made Hayden an offer he couldn't refuse—and one that changed his life. Hayden could join Warren's expedition for $200 plus traveling money or an annual salary of $1,000, for which he would be expected to supply valuable information on the Sioux country. He would also have the option of returning to the region with Warren the following year. *"Neither of these propositions, of course, contemplate any control over collections heretofore made by you."*

Hayden accepted, and Baird must have considered the arrangement a marriage made in heaven. By the end of May, after less than a month in the field, the soldier and the scholar—or "the Doctor," as Warren called him—were able to send Baird an impressive shipment of 291 birds, three squirrels, and five hares. "Every day almost we got some 3 to 5 species we had not got before," the delighted Warren reported.

Their bird collecting fell off somewhat during the course of the summer, but they more than made up for it in quadrupeds. If their harvest was typical of the naturalists roaming the West at that time, there is no wonder why the Indians came to resent them as much as they did other white trespassers. Of white-

tailed deer, Warren reported collecting two "fine" bucks, several skulls, and three fawn skins; of blacktails, two bucks and two does, as well as skeletons and several heads. Although their specimens of bighorn or mountain sheep consisted only of a large ram, the skin of a lamb, and the head of a ewe, they collected a splendid group of pronghorn antelopes—five pairs of skins, a dozen heads, and a buck skeleton. "We rather slayed them," Warren confessed, as "we did the *elk*." Of the latter, they obtained four pairs of skins, two pairs of skeletons, and many heads. "Oh, such splendid horns," Warren exclaimed. "They had such a charm for me that I hunted them a great deal, and we lived on the meat, which when fat and in season is first rate." Hayden had also obtained three wolf skeletons and the astounding total of 150 skulls. As for bears, they had been able to obtain only two skins and a few skulls. Rodents, too, were poorly represented.

They had tried to collect all they could find, Warren claimed, but more could have been obtained had there been time. Their biggest disappointment was sage hens; they had seen only one covey all summer. The Doctor managed to shoot one hen, but became so excited he lost his ramrod. "Altogether, rocks and all, we have a bulky and heavy collection and I don't see how we are to get it further than St. Louis, but we will see about that when it is there."

Hayden agreed with Warren. He felt that they had assembled a fine collection, but it had been hard work. "No Galley slave ever worked harder," he wrote Baird. "Indeed sometimes 12 or 15 hours per day. The results however will be the best proof if they all get home safely."

Hayden, personally, was proudest of his geological work. "The collection that I have made this summer is much finer and more extensive" than the one made last season. "Indeed taken all together it will make the finest collection of Fossil Plants in this Country."

All in all, he had enjoyed his season with Warren, in spite of the constraints of working with the military, and hoped to remain with him until something better presented itself. "In most respects I have had a fine time this season. Lt. Warren has afforded me every facility that was in his power and I have improved them all to the best of my ability and I hope to your satisfaction."

Hayden may have been satisfied with the outcome of their expedition but Warren was soon hurt and outraged to discover his young associate claiming the lion's share of the credit for their achievements. An article in the December 2, 1856, issue of the Washington *National Intelligencer* brought matters to a head. Making scant mention of either Warren or the War Department, it suggested that Hayden had conducted the exploration for the Smithsonian. Warren, who would have ignored the story had others like it not appeared elsewhere, confronted Hayden, then at his Rochester home.

"In a Rochester paper," Warren wrote, "it is stated you had received the appointment of Naturalist and Geologist (I think) to my party *from the Topographical Bureau*, from which it might be inferred that you were independent of me for your

Though the early sketch opposite shows Ferdinand V. Hayden dealing with insect specimens at a simple expedition table, fossils were his first love. At left he indulges in his personal pursuit of happiness, geological collecting. Indians called him "man who picks up stones running." Ft. Pierre, above, now Pierre, South Dakota, welcomed Hayden during the hard winter of 1854–55.

Bug Catching

situation." In the St. Louis *Missouri Republican*, "you are mentioned as if you were entirely distinct from my exploration." Still other stories reinforced the impression that Hayden alone had amassed all the collections. "You know that I labored nearly as hard in making the actual collections of natural history objects as you did; most of the large animals were killed or skinned and brought in by me; many of the birds I prepared entirely; my men did a great deal; many of the articles necessary to their preservation I purchased at my own expense, my accounts having been stopped." Then, to ensure the safe return of the specimens, "I gave up half of our boat and all our comfort to the collection, and all of us rowed like laborers to bring it a portion of the way down the Missouri River." Having performed all this labor, he continued, ". . . you may be sure it was no agreeable thing to me to see in a paper like the *National Intelligencer* that you had 'conducted' the exploration."

Warren could simply have dismissed Hayden and hired someone else in his place the following season, but he said he would not do this if the stories stopped and Hayden agreed not to publish anything about the results of their exploration without Warren's prior approval. "It is my wish to give you full justice for what you have done in my exploration," Warren assured him, "and I am sure you deserve all the credit in it that the exertions of any one man could win."

Although Hayden did accompany Warren the following season on an expedition up the Loup Fork of the Platte River to the Black Hills, their relationship was once again strained, ostensibly over the question of the disposition of their collections. "Warren is determined to keep the Smithsonian out of it," Hayden charged, and Warren, suspicious of Hayden's loyalty, felt that the naturalist placed himself and the Smithsonian ahead of the expedition and the War Department.

A dust-up was inevitable. It occurred one November morning when Warren called Hayden "a fool" and accused him of lying and dereliction of duty. Fearful of being fired on the spot,

Hayden held his tongue, but he vowed to have his revenge. "I intend now," he confided to Baird, "either to whip him or shoot him or else consider myself no man or gentleman."

Hayden never carried out his threats, but he harbored his resentment throughout the rest of the expedition. Never again, he vowed to Baird, would he work with the tyrannical and egotistical army officer, who "has treated me like a dog." He claimed to have suffered Warren's insults and indignities "patiently and submissively," confident that eventually justice would be done.

In addition to his ambitious and garrulous naturalist, Warren also had to contend with the Sioux, who refused to allow the expedition into the heart of the Black Hills. No doubt recalling the horrors he had witnessed at Blue Water Creek, Warren did not press the issue. As he explained in his official report, "I felt that, aside from its being an unnecessary risk to subject my party and interests of the expedition to, it was almost cruelty to the Indians to drive them to commit any desperate act, which would call for chastisement from the Government."

Nonetheless, despite the troubles that beset the expedition, Hayden and Warren added substantially to their collection of geological and other natural history specimens. Indeed, Hayden's catalog of their collections, included in Warren's *Preliminary Report of Explorations in Nebraska and Dakota, in the Years 1855–56–57*, offers an impressive testimonial to their energy: 47 species of mammals, 186 of birds, 28 reptiles, 65 mollusks, 1,500 plants, 423 mineral and geological specimens, 77 vertebrate fossils, 251 mollusk fossils, and 70 plant fossils. All the specimens, Hayden reported, had been deposited in the Smithsonian Institution.

Not yet prepared to rest on his laurels, Warren soon proposed yet another reconnaissance, this one to cross the Bighorn Mountains and explore the still mythical Yellowstone country. Acting on his recommendation, Congress appropriated $60,000 for the project. When the expedition left for the Yellowstone in the summer of 1859, though, it included as its commander Captain William F. Raynolds, who was heading up his first western reconnaissance. Warren's father had died earlier in the year, and the young officer had decided to relinquish command of the coveted expedition and accept the position of assistant professor of mathematics at West Point in order to be near his younger brothers and sisters, still living at the family home in Cold Spring, New York. Hayden must have been encouraged.

The Raynolds expedition was the last to be conducted by the Corps of Topographical Engineers. Marred by mutiny and by spring snows, it not only failed to find a satisfactory wagon road across the Dakotas, one of its primary objectives, but also to reach the Upper Yellowstone, the region that is today the national park.

One of Raynolds's minor irritants must have been Hayden, who persisted in his contentious ways. Hayden claimed that the army officer resented the naturalists and other civilians, and that he had charged that they behaved as if the expedition "had been fitted out simply to build up the Smithsonian Institution." This time, Hayden promised himself, he would not let such remarks bother him. "Such expeditions as these," he now realized, "are great things to bring out the weaknesses of human nature."

Certainly for Hayden, personality conflicts were a small price to pay for the opportunity to continue harvesting geological specimens from the fossil-rich Dakota-Wyoming region. It was the tireless "man who picks up stones running," in fact, who furnished eastern scientists with many of the raw materials needed to unlock the geological secrets of the Far West. Hayden's geological specimens were sent to his friend and colleague, Fielding Bradford Meek, who analyzed and classified them at his retreat in the Smithsonian Castle on the Mall. His fossils of extinct vertebrates went to another collaborator, the shy but brilliant Joseph Leidy of Philadelphia, who almost single-handedly established the science of vertebrate paleontology in the United States.

Raynolds may not have found a wagon-road route across the Dakotas during his two-year reconnaissance, but he did bring government scientists into the last major unexplored region of the Far West. His expedition, in fact, marked a transition between two eras of western exploration, the one dominated by soldier-explorers like Frémont, Gunnison, and Warren, the other by scientists and civilians. Hayden, as we shall see, remained an important force in western scientific exploration, but he had to share the limelight with a new generation of scientists that emerged after the Civil War and included scholars such as John Wesley Powell and Clarence King as well as their young and enthusiastic assistants. It mattered little to Baird and his colleagues at the Smithsonian, though, whether the laborers in the western vineyard were soldiers or civilians. The Smithsonian continued to provide the assistance, encouragement, and support needed to insure the scientific value of their work.

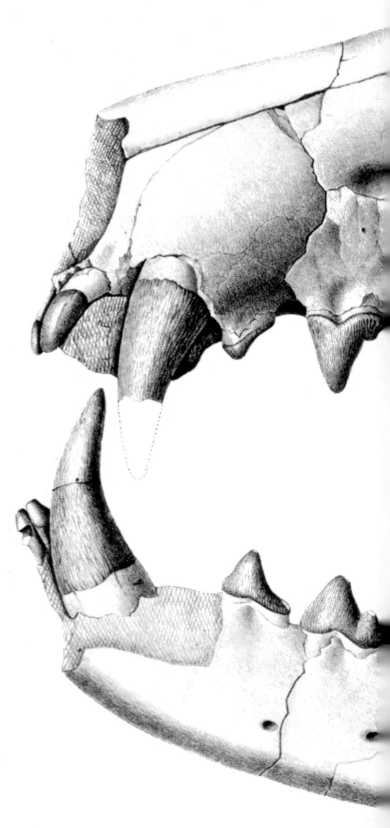

The skull of an extinct, hyenalike carnivore, shown in drawing at right, emerged from deposits of the White River country in South Dakota territory. Hayden, whose picture of the region appears above, and Smithsonian paleontologist Fielding B. Meek worked together in the field to retrieve the fossil.

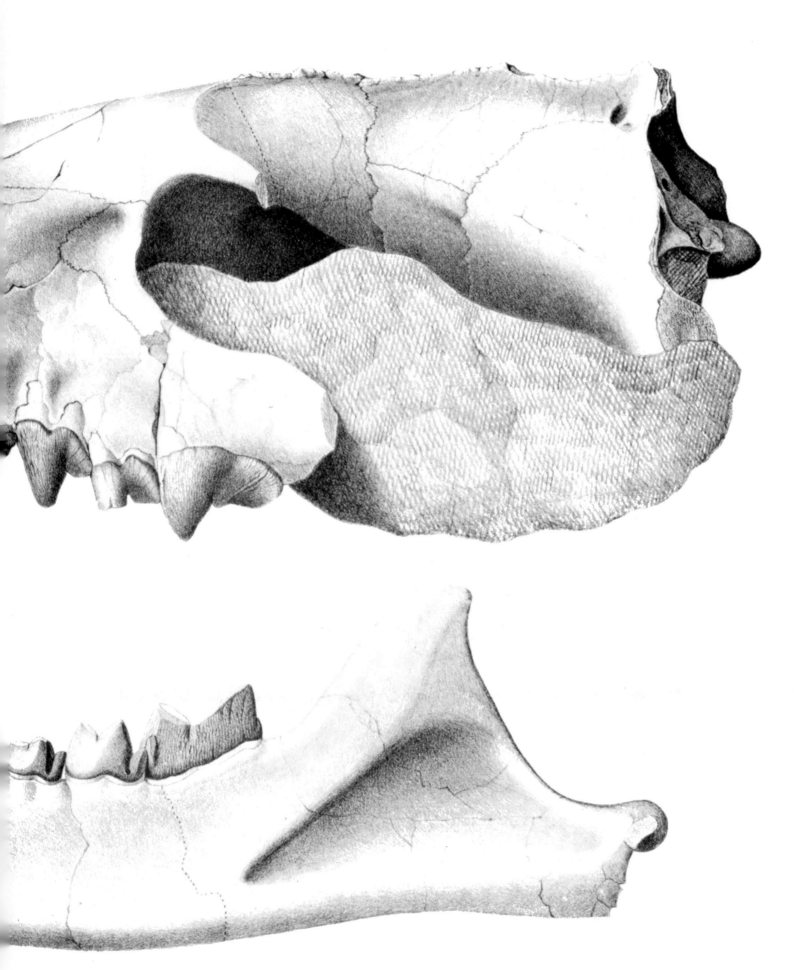

Epitome of the doughty frontier veterans who often accompanied government surveys, hunter Harry Yount poses in Berthoud Pass, Colorado, in an 1874 photograph by William H. Jackson. Yount, who procured game for the surveys led by Ferdinand V. Hayden from 1873 to 1878, later became the first ranger of Yellowstone National Park.

MEGATHERIA AT LARGE

"It is five o'clock, when the Megatherium takes its prey, that the most interesting characters of the animal are seen. Then it roars with delight and makes up for the hard work of the day by much fun and conduction." The year was 1863, and the writer was Robert Kennicott, a young naturalist destined to become one of the pioneer explorers of Alaska.

The beast he was describing for his father, however, was not some exotic animal from the West, but himself, for Kennicott was a charter member of a unique group of high-spirited young scientists. They called themselves "Megatheria"—or "great beasts," after an extinct genus of giant ground sloths—although they roamed not the wilderness, but the Smithsonian's Castle on the Mall. "We den in various rat holes about the building," Kennicott explained, "in the high towers and other queer places, where air is plentiful and fresh." Their keeper was Spencer Fullerton Baird, "just about the best and most wonderful man I ever did see." Their motto? "Never let your evening's amusement be the subject of your morning's reflections."

Admission to the Megatheria, an unorganized club of scientists, naturalists, and other individuals short on cash but committed to fellowship and scholarship, was easy to obtain. One simply had to apply to Baird, who opened the doors of the Smithsonian—literally—to those who, like himself, were devoted to advancing the cause of science. Membership in the club fluctuated greatly during the 20 or so years it flourished—young scientists were continually coming and going to the field, to the classroom, or to war—but it included some of the most eminent naturalists of the day: Ferdinand V. Hayden, John Torrey, William Stimpson, Edward D. Cope, James G. Cooper, John Strong Newberry, William H. Dall.

Longest in residence as a Megatherium was Fielding Bradford Meek, "a very excellent and Honorable gentleman with fine feelings and extremely modest, though he is now one of our best paleontologists," wrote Kennicott. "He is perhaps the best in certain specialties in America." Meek lived and worked in the Castle from at least as early as 1861 until his death from tuberculosis in 1876, studying the fossils shipped to the Smithsonian from the various western expeditions. He methodically described the specimens in paper after paper, many of which carried Hayden's name as coauthor, though "the Doctor"—as Baird called him—did little of the actual writing.

After a youth of poverty and poor health, Meek suffered increasingly from deafness, which made him even more diffident. He seemed content with his spartan, solitary life. "I do not like hotels, boarding houses or private families," he wrote to Newberry before a visit to his fellow Megatherium at Columbia University in 1869. "I also prefer to spend my evenings with the books and specimens. I can hear and understand what they say, and they require neither small talk nor formalities." Described by Kennicott as "wholly devoted to science," Meek is well represented in the collections of the Smithsonian, but the single item that says the most about this scholarly recluse is his drawing of his pet cat, under which he wrote, "the only family I have."

For the most part, the Megatheria followed a routine. At about eight A.M. they began making their appearance—from behind exhibit cases, through hidden doors, "and out of all sorts of comical places." The halls of the Castle would then echo with the "How! How!" of salutation, supposedly in imitation of the call of the Megatherium in the wild. Down the scientists would go to their dining room in the basement and fall upon their breakfast "with a wild roar." The next stop was Baird's office to examine the mail and chat for half an hour or so, and then off—each to his own lair—to study bones, fossils, plants, or whatever "treasure" might have arrived from the West or some other distant place. Kennicott's den was the "snake room," which he could reach only "through some hundreds of feet of dark cellar passage." There he was safe from interruption. After hours he was free to use Baird's office, which offered a fireplace and gas lights.

In the evening the Megatheria reassembled in their basement dining room and supped on bread, beef, and coffee "made of peas." On rare occasions, when one of their number had some extra money, they feasted on oysters and ale and scuppernong wine.

The "conduction"—conversation—more than compensated for the humble fare. They talked of faraway places and adventures they had had or hoped to have. Anyone was welcome to share their meals, but visitors were forewarned that the Megatheria respected only honor and science. Rank or status protected no one from barbs or witticisms, but "laughing and animated conversation" provided the antidote for Megatherium bite, and humor made their dining room "brighter than sunlight." As a result, few turned down an invitation to dinner. "So excellent is the source of conduction, that . . . vulgar outsiders, who think that the Megatheria must be rather dry sticks from their pursuits, are caused to open their eyes very wide when they are allowed to see the Megatherium eating its prey or on a frolic."

And frolic they did. When Bruno Kennicott, Robert Kennicott's brother, visited the Castle one rainy day, he ended up joining the young naturalists in a hop-and-jump race about the Great Hall. "Darned if I ever did see such men," Bruno Kennicott marveled. "I suppose Stimpson and some of 'em are big naturalists but they act mighty like small boys." Later, out west, Indians would similarly wonder at the curious behavior of grown men who spent every waking moment peering at plants, animals, and rocks.

Smithsonian Secretary Joseph Henry was not always amused by the antics of the Megatheria and once tried to evict the frisky boarders. Meek could stay, he told Baird, but the young naturalists had to find other lodging. "I have concluded that the making of the Smithsonian building into a caravanserai has been carried a little too far." He was especially concerned about their excessive use of the gas lights. "I wish to impress some of the

gentlemen with the fact that sun light is cheaper than gas light and answers all purposes equally well."

Henry's strictures had little permanent effect, however, and the Castle remained a haven to an assortment of dedicated, earnest professionals throughout Baird's tenure. The assistant secretary knew just how essential their help was in sorting, describing, and assimilating the vast collections that arrived at the Smithsonian each year.

Busy as he was, Baird still had time to entertain and visit with the young scholars. "Prof Baird is at all times as conducive as his work will allow him to be and when he will allow himself a few minutes out," Kennicott informed his father. The Megatheria especially appreciated invitations to his home for supper and

conversation. "When Mrs. Baird's health is not a subject of anxiety to him and his work doesn't crowd too much, he is always ready to keep us laughing—making up for any loss of time by setting us at work on some odd job before we leave."

When out in the field, members of the group sometimes felt deprived of the Castle's social and intellectual stimulation. "I should be very happy to be one of your pleasant circle at the Smithsonian this winter," Newberry wrote from the Mojave Indian villages of the present-day California-Arizona border area in February 1858. Serving as geologist on the Ives expedition up the Colorado River, Newberry griped good-naturedly to Hayden about the monotonous scenery and the equally monotonous diet, both characterized by an excess of sand. He sorely

When they weren't in the field collecting and observing, the Megatheria, a high-spirited band of young scientists under the benevolent guidance of Smithsonian Assistant Secretary Spencer F. Baird, inhabited the Institution's Castle, descending at evening from garret laboratories for food, games, and "conduction," as they termed good conversation. Perhaps taking their fanciful name from the fossil Megatherium, right, a representative of an extinct genus of giant ground sloths, the Megatheria included the four pictured opposite, left to right: William Stimpson, Robert Kennicott, Henry Ulke, and Henry Bryant. Some Megatheria actually lived in the Castle, although none in quarters as grand as those of Secretary Joseph Henry, opposite top.

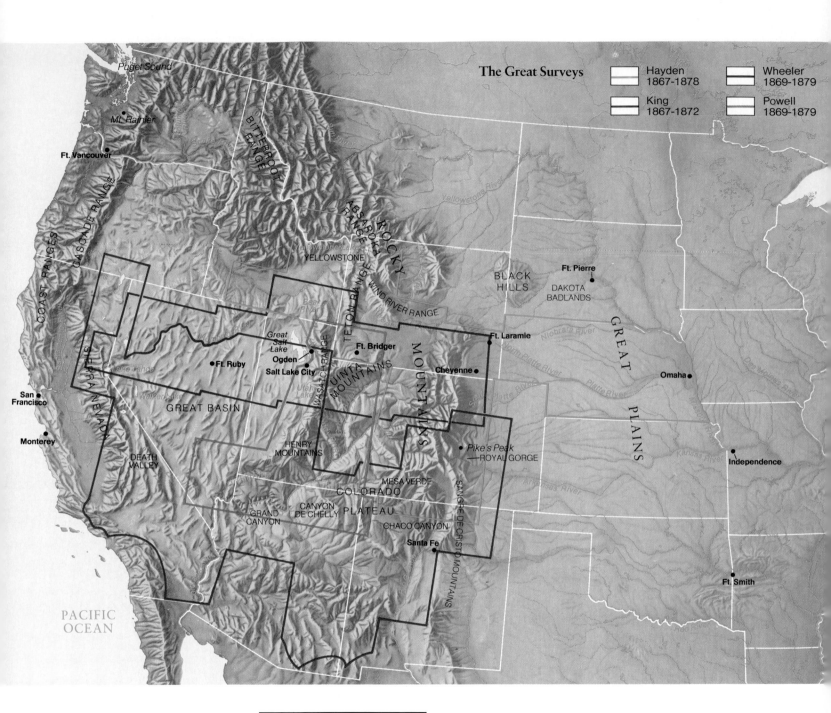

The Great Surveys

Hayden 1867-1878   Wheeler 1869-1879

King 1867-1872   Powell 1869-1879

During the 1870 Hayden survey, Ferdinand V. Hayden and his party stopped for a meal by the North Platte River near Red Buttes, Wyoming. Fifteen of the 20 men on the expedition appear in the photograph, opposite top, by William H.

Jackson. Left to right, they are: sitting, Charles S. Turnbull, John H. Beaman, Ferdinand V. Hayden, Cyrus Thomas, a hunter named Raphael, and Arthur L. Ford; standing, left to right, two cooks, Sanford Robinson Gifford, Henry Wood Elliott, James Stevenson, Henry D. Schmidt or Schmitt,

E. Campbell Carrington, Lester A. Bartlett, and William H. Jackson. Opposite bottom, Smithsonian mineralogist F. M. Endlich carried this surveyor's compass on the Hayden surveys from 1873 to 1879.

missed "studying abundant material, eating comforting food, sleeping on good beds, washing clean and dressing neatly every day, and having a good time generally."

Not even the Civil War could completely dampen the spirits or suspend the work of the lively Megatheria. Jittery Union patriots were alarmed on occasion at what appeared to be signals from the Smithsonian Castle's towers to Secessionists lurking across the Potomac. Invariably, the lights proved to be lanterns carried by late-toiling and sometimes reveling Megatheria climbing the stairs to their beds.

Ferdinand V. Hayden was one member who answered the Civil War's call to arms, exchanging his geologist's pick for a surgeon's scalpel. It was the only time during his career that he practiced medicine. His action was so out of character that his fellow naturalists could not believe he was serious. "Here . . . we want you," Stimpson wrote a few months after Hayden had enlisted. "Plenty of sawbones can take your present place . . . but no one here. The Megatheria is revived. Kennicott, God bless him, has come back. Barrel of ale in the cellar. Digestion howls in the Den at Dinner. Jolly Conduction. Advancement of Science. Freedom from carking care. Friendly sodality. This is *Home*. The Smithsonian is pleasanter than ever."

But Hayden was serious, and he remained at his post until

General Robert E. Lee's surrender at Appomattox, attaining the rank of brevet lieutenant colonel. Even then he did not return. Instead, he joined the faculty of the medical department of the University of Pennsylvania, where he taught mineralogy and geology.

Hayden may have taken a position in academia, but his heart yearned for the West. In 1866 he traveled to the Badlands of the Dakotas, as he had before the war, and returned with his usual wagon load of fossils, which he handed over to Meek. What he desperately wanted, however, was his own expedition, one that would be free of meddling army officers, one that he could organize and command himself.

It was Spencer Baird who turned his dream into reality. In 1867, the new state of Nebraska was planning to use surplus federal funds to commission a survey of the state's geology and natural resources. Always alert to scientific opportunities for his volunteers, Baird informed Hayden immediately. "If you want the place you had better come at once and see about it. If you had not carried off my copy of your geology of the Upper Missouri I might perhaps have clenched the matter . . . on the spot!"

Hayden saw his opportunity. "I feel so earnest about that matter—I can accomplish so much if I can get that place," the excited geologist replied. Leaving nothing to chance, he appealed to politicians, fellow scientists, and army officers—including Major General G. K. Warren—for support and was soon in charge of the Geological Survey of Nebraska under the direction of the Commissioner of the General Land Office. He was to conduct a general natural history survey of Nebraska and also to point out potential economic resources. This combination of objectives was to become Hayden's hallmark as his modest survey developed over the following decade into the biggest and best known of the great surveys of the West that were launched and supported by the federal government after the Civil War.

Then, spurred by the Homestead Act and the enormous influx of European immigrants, and by fresh discoveries of gold and silver, a human tide swept across the Mississippi River. The government needed specialized information about the trans-Mississippi West—its agricultural, ranching, mining, and timber potential. American science blossomed like western wildflowers in the spring. Baird's Megatheria were ready, standing foremost in the ranks of the new generation of explorers. Like graduate students at a university, they had served their apprenticeships and were now prepared to repay with scientific achievements their alma mater and their major professor.

At the head of the class—at least as geologist—stood Hayden. He was by no means the only one in the field, but he quickly became the most dominant and popular. Although the $5,000 appropriated for his first Nebraska survey was not much with which to launch a comprehensive exploration, it posed no handicap, for his days as a struggling explorer living hand-to-mouth in the trans-Missouri country had taught him how to make a little money go a long way. Typically, in his expedition preparations, he begged and borrowed as much as possible.

From the army he obtained supplies and equipment—surplus wagons, condemned horses and mules—and from Baird the usual collecting kits and assistance. "I hope you will get together all the little things you can for me to save Expenses," he wrote to the assistant secretary shortly after receiving the appointment. "I must do a great deal of work with small means. Some good will result from it." A month later he sent Baird another appeal. "Can't you put up a box of apparatus. Two of those screw cap cans, apparatus for catching insects, &c. I would like to work up the zoology of Nebraska. Also the botany. If you have any boards for binding plants or anything in that way let me know. Let me know what you can furnish me."

In return for assistance, Hayden promised to send Baird all his natural history collections, which had not been mentioned in his instructions. It was a promise Hayden would keep throughout the years of his survey. The archives of the Smithsonian hold a score of letters from Hayden to Baird describing collections about to be dispatched or already on their way. And each year's collections, it seems, were better than ever. "I shall send you a vast amount of collections, perhaps . . . the best things I have ever had," Hayden wrote in November 1868. He made almost the identical claim the following year: "Never in my life, have I had so successful a trip." Nor did his enthusiasm wane in succeeding years. "Our work this summer will be the best work," he boasted in July 1873, during his Survey of Colorado. "We will show what can be done with a careful organization and a plan." Already, his collection of insects was "the best" he had ever seen, while the photographer, W. H. Jackson, had taken almost 200 pictures "of the choicest scenery," most of them "panoramic views." By the end of the survey, "all the important mountain ranges will thus be brought out."

Always, Hayden kept an eye out for the rare and unusual. Once he found a black-footed ferret for Baird, and his letter suggests that the creature, nearly extinct today, was virtually unknown even a century ago. "It has a light color, back sort of yellowish gray, white nose, black feet and legs, about the size of a mink and the most vicious little scamp I ever saw," Hayden wrote from Russell, Wyoming, in 1868. "Jim thinks it is your long sought animal and it is a novelty to every one here."

In camp near Salt Lake City, survey leader Ferdinand V. Hayden, above, enjoys a fresh-air meal with assistant chief James Stevenson, topographer Frank Bradley, and wife Emma Woodruff Hayden. Years later, Stevenson married anthropologist Matilda Coxe. Their artifact-bedecked Washington, D.C., home, right, reflects their many collecting trips to the Southwest. The 1873 Hayden survey split into six teams to cover much of Colorado, southern Wyoming, and eastern Utah. Led by William H. Jackson, a photographic party roamed over the region independently, taking pictures for science—and for the folks back East. One of the latter, a camp on Clear Creek, near Denver, appears opposite.

"Jim" was James Stevenson, a young man who first went West with Hayden as a member of the Warren expedition of 1856. Stevenson served as Hayden's executive officer during his post-Civil War surveys and was the first to hold that position in the United States Geological Survey. In time he became interested in American Indian ethnology and married Matilda Coxe, one of the nation's first female anthropologists. Together they studied the Pueblo people of the Southwest, obtaining major collections of pottery for the Smithsonian in the process. In 1887 Stevenson contracted Rocky Mountain spotted fever and died the following year, one of the few members of the great surveys to die as a result of his activities in the field.

A major impetus behind the Nebraska survey was the hope that the lush prairies concealed great veins of coal that could be used as fuel in the absence of timber. Try as he might, however, Hayden found only lignite, or low-grade "brown coal." "I would be glad to find a workable bed of coal for the good people, but it cannot be." The news disappointed a great many, including one J. Sterling Morton, who had dug a 100-foot shaft on his farm in anticipation of striking coal. Quipped the editor of the Omaha Daily Herald: "I doubt whether Mr. Morton lived quite long enough to forgive Hayden for telling him the truth." Hayden did report finding impressive quantities of iron ore, however. Typically optimistic, he assured the unhappy Nebraskans that since the lignite could be used to smelt the iron, their state could "exert the same kind of influence over the progress of the great west that Pennsylvania exerts over all the contiguous states."

Indeed, Hayden's optimism became a key feature of his reports. He usually managed to find something positive to say about each region he surveyed, assuring him popularity among westerners, who willingly supported his annual requests for additional survey funds. It did not matter that his enthusiastic predictions were not always well founded.

Inevitably, though, such blatant boosterism got him into

In 1867 to 1869, Ferdinand V. Hayden, James Stevenson, and another old Hayden comrade, Fielding B. Meek, undertook a survey of the geology and resources of Nebraska. Left, the Niobrara River flows through what is today Agate Fossil Beds National Monument in north-western Nebraska. Hills and outcrops along the river often contain rich beds of fossils. From one of the Hayden surveys, James Stevenson sent Smithsonian Assistant Secretary Spencer Baird a long-sought specimen of a black-footed ferret (Mustela nigripes), *right. Uncommon even then, the black-footed ferret nearly disappeared in this century when its principal prey, prairie dogs, were poisoned by the millions. Once believed to be extinct, it still exists precariously in captivity and perhaps in some tiny undiscovered colonies in the wild.*

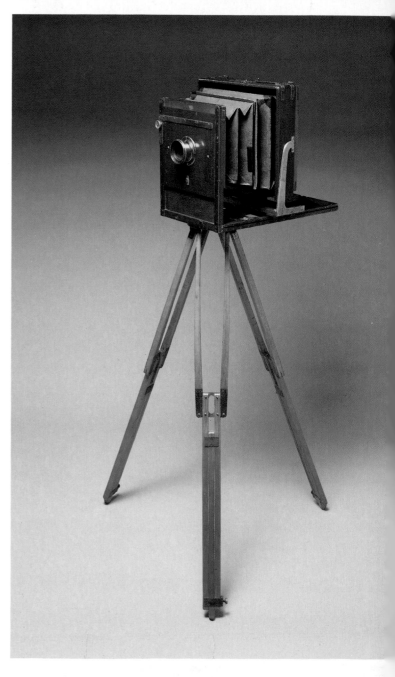

trouble. In 1869, one of his appointees, the Reverend Cyrus Thomas, noted more water and a more abundant harvest than normal during a survey of Colorado and New Mexico, prompting him to develop his "rain-follows-the-plow" theory. The explanation for the unusually plentiful moisture, Thomas wrote in his monograph, "Agriculture in Colorado," was "in some way connected with the settlement of the country; and that, as the population increases, the amount of moisture will increase. . . . This is the plan which nature herself has pointed out." Hayden, who should have known better, allowed this untenable theory to be published with his report, thereby exposing his survey to well-warranted scientific criticism.

In truth, Hayden worked at such a feverish pitch and published his reports on his explorations so rapidly that errors mar much of his writing, particularly his later surveys. A friend critiquing one of his articles scheduled for publication by the American Philosophical Society wrote, "I must say your style of narration is slovenly in the extreme and when it gets into print . . . I shall blush for the belles letters reputation of the society." Not only was the article obviously written at "railroad speed," but it had been punctuated into an "unintelligible mass" in places. "I wish to heaven," he pleaded, "you would give me a very little liberty to correct the proof." The secretary of the society, he warned, "is a man of delicate taste and is offended by slovenly writing."

The same sort of criticism was made of the many "discoveries" credited to Hayden's surveys, which covered so much ground so rapidly and superficially that some historians have described him as America's greatest tourist. "He worked with a telescope instead of a microscope," quipped one. This was no secret to his contemporaries. "The doctor goes too far in some of the claims he puts forward to the honor of original discovery," charged an editorialist in an 1872 edition of the *Engineering and Mining Journal*. Hayden, he continued, "should not exaggerate the novelty of his work. Every body knows how valuable is the work of his survey; he need not be 'monarch of all he surveys.' " With due respect for all "his real conquests and achievements," the editorial writer commented, the overly enthusiastic surveyor should be reminded that "the whole boundless continent ain't his'n."

Hayden ignored his critics, however, and each year saw him

William H. Jackson photographed one of his assistants, opposite upper left, leading Hypo, Jackson's favorite pack mule, during the 1871 Yellowstone expedition led by Ferdinand V. Hayden. A reject from the Army mule corps, sure-footed Hypo carried Jackson's bulky photographic equipment over terrain too rough for wagons. Mules not only carried packs but pulled wagons and even odometers, opposite upper right, which measured distance for mapmakers. Jackson used a heavy, wet-plate camera similar to one, opposite, carried on the 1872 Powell trip down the Grand Canyon. Survey photographers often lugged their 50-to-70-pound cameras into nearly inaccessible spots to get their pictures. Right, a survey cameraman, perhaps William H. Jackson, focuses on Yosemite Valley from the vantage point of 3,200-foot-high Glacier Point.

During the 1871 Hayden Yellowstone expedition, William Henry Jackson photographed his friend, painter Thomas Moran, left, at Mammoth Hot Springs. Perhaps more than anyone else, Jackson and Moran brought home the West's magnificent scenery to easterners. Lower right, Jackson made this image of the Hayden party as it entered Yellowstone in July 1871. Variously attributed to Jackson and to another fine survey photographer, John K. Hillers, the photo at upper right of the Beehive group of geysers in Yellowstone was taken in 1878 or 1880.

Overleaf: Grand Canyon of the Yellowstone *by Thomas Moran. Exhibited today in the Smithsonian's National Museum of American Art, this 7-by-12-foot painting captured the imagination and admiration of Americans when Moran produced it following the Hayden survey of Yellowstone in 1871.*

On Ferdinand Hayden's 1873 survey, William H. Jackson took his most famous photograph— the Mountain of the Holy Cross, *opposite, a legendary peak in the Sawatch Range of the Colorado Rockies. The image inspired a poem by Henry Wadsworth Longfellow and a watercolor by Jackson's old friend, Thomas Moran, reproduced in the chromolithograph above.*

more popular in Washington and the West, and his survey more handsomely supported by Congress. In 1869, not only did he receive $10,000—twice as much as in the preceding two years—but his survey was removed from the supervision of the General Land Office and transferred to the Department of the Interior with the lofty title, the United States Geological Survey of the Territories. The following year this princely sum was increased to $25,000 for a survey of Wyoming and adjacent territories. Hayden had arrived.

It was already July by the time he received his appropriation for the 1870 survey, and Wyoming (old-timers liked to joke) had only two seasons: the Fourth of July and winter. Despite his need for haste, Hayden stopped in Omaha to visit Jackson Brothers, Photographers. The year before, Hayden had met one of the brothers, William Henry Jackson, who was taking pictures along the Union Pacific Railroad. Always alert to ways to publicize his work, the explorer recognized instantly the impact photography could have in promoting surveys. Now, browsing in Jackson's cluttered studio and studying his photographs of landscapes and Indians, Hayden was all the more convinced.

Hayden got his photographer, but the American people were the true beneficiaries, for Jackson had an artist's eye and a scholar's dedication. Only 27 when he signed on, Jackson was to spend nine seasons as a member of Hayden's team. During that time he took hundreds of photographs, many of which today are priceless works of art as well as invaluable resources for scholars interested in measuring geological, ecological, and botanical changes that have occurred in the western landscape over the past century.

Jackson was only one of several memorable people who signed on for the 1870 survey. "Potato John" Raymond was the cook, a six-foot, four-inch giant who earned his nickname by vainly trying to boil potatoes at an altitude of 12,000 feet. Edward Drinker Cope, one of the great 19th-century paleontologists, was a fellow Megatherium and, like Jackson, surveyed with Hayden for the better part of a decade.

In the field from early August until January, the surveyors of the 1870 expedition followed a route that took them north along the North Platte River to the Sweetwater River, through South Pass and on southwest to Fort Bridger, near what is today Wyoming's border with Utah. From there they explored south into the Uinta Mountains and up to the sources of the Muddy and Bear rivers, eventually working their way to the Green River and up to Green River Station in Wyoming Territory. They then headed east along Bitter Creek and through Bridger's Pass and the Medicine Bow Mountains to Cheyenne. "For every mile on the map," Jackson later wrote, "we covered between two and three on the ground—up mountainsides, down stream beds, across country—to gather rock specimens, to survey and map, and to paint and photograph."

And photograph he did! Certainly no one worked harder. Jackson lugged around 300 pounds of heavy and unwieldy equipment, including a portable darkroom of his own design, a variety of chemicals, and hundreds of fragile glass plates. Little wonder he needed his own wagon.

Panorama from Point Sublime by William H. Holmes depicts the Kaibab division of the Grand Canyon of the Colorado. The illustration is one of a number executed by Holmes for an atlas in Clarence Dutton's Tertiary History of the Grand Cañon District, published in 1882 to present the geological findings of Dutton's 1879 U.S.G.S. survey of the Grand Canyon, an expedition accompanied by Holmes. No one has ever surpassed Holmes's combination of magnificent scenery and scientific accuracy to reveal the vast topographical and geological complexity of the Grand Canyon.

Glass plates, of course, represented advanced technology. Photographers of the day exposed their images on sensitized glass plates that had to be kept moist until developed. During his first season with the Hayden survey, Jackson used a camera with 6½-by-8½-inch plates. Discovering that these were too limited for the majestic landscapes of the West, however, the following year Jackson switched to a camera that could handle 11-by-14-inch plates. By the end of the Hayden surveys, he was toting an enormous device that took 20-by-24-inch pictures. He even developed a camera that could photograph 360-degree panoramas.

When working in mountainous terrain, Jackson used pack mules to transport his equipment. His favorite was Hypo, a

stubby creature with cropped ears who could carry his cameras, tripod, dark box, chemicals, water keg, and a day's supply of plates. "Hypo," he recalled, "was good for as many miles as my horse was, and together we covered an enormous amount of ground off the road from the wagon party."

Not all his mules left Jackson with fond memories, however. One cantankerous beast named "Gimlet" slipped his pack, leaving a trail of broken glass. "The Doctor himself was the first to notice," Jackson recalled. "By that time Gimlet had scattered most of his load. All my 11-by-14's were irreparably shattered. I have never been so distressed in my life."

The actual picture-taking was another challenge. After unpacking and setting up his equipment at each site, Jackson needed at least 45 minutes to prepare a plate, make the exposure, and develop it. Often the shot took much longer. When photographing the 132-foot Tower Falls of the Yellowstone River, Jackson first had to clamber down the steep gorge to the bottom, lugging his camera all the way. Then he had to climb back up, prepare a plate, go back down, expose it, wrap it in a wet towel to keep it moist, and then climb back to the top to develop it. Because he had to repeat the entire process for each view, he had only five photographs to show for an entire day's work. But then, what photographs they were!

Jackson's most famous photograph is probably that of the Mount of the Holy Cross, which he took in 1873 during the Hayden Survey of Colorado. One day, as the expedition wound through the Central Rockies, the fabled cross suddenly appeared in the distance. The first to see it was Jackson. "Near the top of the ridge . . . , as I clambered over a vast mass of jagged rocks, I discovered the great shining cross dead before me, tilted against the mountainside."

The photographer immediately started to set up his apparatus, but, by the time he had assembled everything, clouds had obscured the cross. Jackson returned below timberline to camp, but as soon as dawn broke he climbed back up the mountain, determined to get his picture. The cross now was visible, but this time he was foiled by the temperature: it was so cold that water froze. When the day warmed up enough for him to use melted ice water to prepare his plates, shadows were beginning to move across the face of the mountain. Working as rapidly as possible, Jackson made eight hurried exposures, which resulted in some of the finest pictures of his long career.

Hayden completed his 511-page report on the 1870 survey in time to impress Congress before it adjourned the following spring. "Never," he wrote in its preface, "has my faith in the grand future that awaits the entire West been so strong as it is at the present time, and it is my earnest desire to devote the remainder of the working days of my life to the development of its scientific and material interests, until I shall see every Territory, which is now organized, a State in the Union." No wonder westerners loved him. And Congress, with encouragement from both Speaker of the House James G. Blaine and Hayden himself, awarded him $40,000 for the first official government exploration of the legendary Yellowstone country.

Even Hayden did not have the audacity to claim "discovery" of the fabulous country that is today Yellowstone National Park. Indeed, at least two other expeditions preceded him in this region—the Folsom-Cook group in 1869 and the Washburn-Langford-Doane party in 1870. It was actually Nathaniel P. Langford, a Montana businessman and member of the latter expedition, who spearheaded the movement to establish a national park. Langford, accompanied by several leading citizens of Montana and a military escort consisting of Lieutenant Gustavus C. Doane and five soldiers, spent some 30 days exploring the Upper Yellowstone and coined the names of some of the park's natural wonders—Old Faithful, the Mud Geysers, the Devil's Den, Crystal Falls. And when Langford and his companions discovered some enterprising Montanans erecting fences around one of the region's spectacular geophysical features, they hit upon the idea of trying to persuade the federal government to preserve the area as a national park.

Langford wrote a number of articles to publicize the region's phenomena, including one for *Scribner's Monthly* entitled "The Wonders of the Yellowstone." Truman C. Everts, a member of Langford's party who had gotten lost during the Yellowstone expedition, wrote another piece for *Scribner's* entitled "Thirty-seven Days of Peril." The article, which included some crude sketches by one of Doane's soldiers, recounted many of his adventures in the wilderness. One reader concluded that the author "must be the champion liar of the Northwest." More credible, perhaps, was Lieutenant Doane's official report to the

One of the greatest of the West's surveyors, Clarence King, left, was an accomplished climber and mountaineer when in 1867 he undertook his Geological Exploration of the Fortieth Parallel in the hope of establishing a transcontinental railroad route. King's photographer for the first two years of the survey, Timothy O'Sullivan, photographed "Karnak Ridge," below, a jumble of fractured rhyolite columns in Nevada's Trinity Range named for its fancied resemblance to the Karnak temple in Egypt. Bottom, O'Sullivan made this image of his equipment wagon and mules in the barren Carson Desert of Nevada during the 1867 King survey.

War Department. Hayden, for one, was certainly impressed. "For graphic description and thrilling interest," he declared, it was not surpassed "by any official report since the times of Lewis and Clark."

Hayden, of course, was determined to see the wonders of the Yellowstone for himself, and so, hastily assembling a party of 21 men and seven wagons, he set out from Ogden, Utah, in June 1871. This time, the celebrated landscape painter Thomas Moran was a member of Hayden's illustrious team. Tall and extremely thin, the 34-year-old artist proved a fortunate addition, for his magnificent landscapes immortalized the expedition. Hayden had not planned on taking along an artist; it was Moran himself who begged to be included, though he had never even ridden a horse before. He had, however, been the artist assigned by *Scribner's* to work up the sketches for Langford's article. The drawings had been crude, but they had excited Moran, especially the one of the Grand Canyon of the Yellowstone. When Moran learned that Hayden was organizing an expedition to the region, he asked to join the party, promising to pay all of his own expenses.

The trip cost Moran more than money. His bony body was not meant for horseback riding, and he frequently had to place a pillow between his posterior and the saddle. But he considered his aches and pains a small price to pay for the opportunity to test his artistic skills against such visual challenges as Fire Hole Basin, Old Faithful, and Tower Falls.

The entire survey came to appreciate the plucky artist—among other things, he taught the veteran explorers how to bake trout by wrapping them in wet paper and then building the fire above the fish—but it was Jackson who came to know him best, for they usually worked together. Jackson taught Moran how to use the camera, and the painter, in turn, helped the photographer with composition. Toiling side-by-side, the two artists captured for posterity the magnificent scenery of the Yellowstone country. Each day presented a new artistic challenge, until they reached what they agreed was the "pictorial climax"—the Grand Canyon of the Yellowstone. "Moran's enthusiasm," Jackson reported, no doubt with considerable understatement, "was greater here than anywhere else."

Moran was indeed enchanted, and he studied the canyon and its two waterfalls from every angle and perspective. From a spot known today as Artist's Point, Moran had a clear view of the Lower Falls with its awesome chasm, where cascading and churning water had carved a gorge more than 1,000 feet deep and twice as wide. Even more impressive were the dazzling colors of the gorge's rock walls—a fantastic array of yellows, browns, and reds. ". . . I have wandered over a good part of the Territories and have seen much of the varied scenery of the Far West, but that of the Yellowstone retains its hold upon my imagination with a vividness as of yesterday," the artist later wrote. "The impression then made upon me by the stupendous and remarkable manifestations of nature's forces will remain with me as long as memory lasts."

Shortly after sketching the Yellowstone's canyon, Moran

returned to his eastern studio where over the following months he transformed his sketches into finished paintings. His masterpiece, the "Grand Canyon of the Yellowstone," is an enormous canvas that measures 7-by-12 feet and took two months to complete. "I knew . . . [Moran] was going to paint a big picture," marveled one of his friends, "but I didn't know how big it would be. When I think of his carrying that immense canvas across his brain so long, I wonder that he didn't go through the door sidewise, and call people to look out when they came near."

Before removing his painting from its easel, Moran not only asked Hayden to approve his treatment of geological detail, but also honored him and his assistant, James Stevenson, by including them in the foreground. "The picture," Moran informed Hayden, "is all that I ever expected to make of it, and the indications are that it will make a sensation whenever it is exhibited." Indeed it did—and still does. Appropriately, this stupendous work is today in the custody of the Smithsonian Institution, where it serves as a fitting monument to the artist and his patron.

Although not alone in the effort, Hayden does deserve much of the credit for establishing Yellowstone National Park. He wrote his own article for *Scribner's*, complete with illustrations by Moran, which corroborated all that Langford had claimed and more, and he also presented key members of Congress with bound volumes of Jackson's most striking photographs. Faced with such formidable evidence, even the most diehard skeptics were convinced, and on March 1, 1872, President Grant signed the bill establishing the first national park of the United States. "This noble deed," Hayden wrote in his *Fifth Annual Report*, "may be regarded as a tribute from our legislators to science."

Hayden returned to his beloved West each year until 1878, his surveys ranging from the Yellowstone country in the north to the cliff dwellings of the ancient Anasazi Indians in the south. He may not have been the best or most competent of the explorers, but he set the standard against which all the others are compared. No matter that he located potential tourist spas as readily as mineral deposits, or that his work was often hastily done and sloppily described; his positive contributions greatly outweighed the negative. Because he succeeded in "selling" scientific exploration to a parsimonious Congress, he enabled promising young men—not all of them of the Megatherium Club at the Smithsonian—to gain first-hand experience in the field. It was these men who were to become the country's next generation of scientific leaders.

One of the most versatile of Hayden's young protégés was William Henry Holmes. As an art student newly arrived in Washington, Holmes had shared an instructor with Joseph Henry's daughter. Following her suggestion to visit the Smithsonian for subjects suitable for sketching, Holmes quickly came

The giant sand dunes of Mesquite Flat ripple towards the Grapevine Mountains in what is today Death Valley National Monument. In 1871, Lieutenant George M. Wheeler led an expedition across the already legendary Death Valley, almost losing three men to the 120-degree heat.

to the attention of Spencer Baird and several Megatheria, including Fielding B. Meek, who hired him almost immediately to sketch for some of his natural history reports. Then Hayden, with his eye for talent, tapped him to serve as a geological illustrator for his 1872 expedition, and thus was launched one of the most distinguished careers ever produced by the western surveys. With an unparalleled artistic technique, Holmes could sketch complex panoramas that accurately depicted hundreds of miles of twisted and faulted terrain. His drawings were masterpieces of draftsmanship, better than maps and sharper than photographs, with details of stratigraphy that eluded the best cameras of the day.

Holmes was more than an artist, however. In his 87 years, he became a central figure in Washington's scientific community, first as a geologist and then as an anthropologist and chief of the Smithsonian's Bureau of American Ethnology. Yet he never lost his love for art, and closed his career as director of the National Gallery of Art, bringing full-circle his long and remarkable professional life.

Hayden also assembled a vast library of scientific publica-

tions, his survey alone contributing four different sets of works. He issued bulletins, published major definitive monographs, and, for 11 straight years, issued annual reports that numbered hundreds of pages. Perhaps he was, as historian William H. Goetzmann claims, "one part sham and much of a showman." Yet whatever his flaws—and he had many—Hayden remained a staunch friend of both Baird and the Smithsonian. "I have but two objects in life," he wrote in 1873, while at the peak of his popularity, "My *survey* and the *National Museum.*"

Hayden's was but one of four great surveys of the West in the years following the Civil War. The leaders of the rival surveys— and that is what he considered them—were also giants of western exploration. Clarence King was the most dazzling. Equally at ease in mountain camps and in the drawing rooms of Washington and London, he was simultaneously an author, poet, explorer, adventurer, geologist, politician, and friend to statesmen and scientists. As his great admirer, historian Henry Adams, testified in *The Education of Henry Adams*, "His wit and humor; his bubbling energy which swept every one into the current of his interests; his personal charm of youth and manners; his

faculty of giving and taking, profusely, lavishly, whether in thought or in money as though he were Nature herself, marked him almost alone among Americans."

Although King lived until age 59, he had done practically all that would bring him fame by the time he was 39. At 21, in the midst of the Civil War, he and his friend James T. Gardner rode across the continent on horseback and became volunteer geologists with the California Geological Survey led by Josiah Dwight Whitney. Most famous of the post-war state geological surveys, the work in California set the standards for the federal reconnaissances that were to follow. King spent four years exploring the towering High Sierras, and his exhilarating experiences, which included feats of mountaineering and hairbreadth escapes from grizzly bears, formed the basis for the first of his two major books, *Mountaineering in the Sierra Nevada*.

He trumped his California survey adventure when, at only 25, he persuaded supporters in government to appropriate funds for the United States Geological Exploration of the Fortieth Parallel, which was to survey a 100-mile-wide swath of land from the crest of the Sierra Nevadas across the Great Basin to the western slope of the Rockies. King served as geologist in charge of this 10-year project, producing a seven volume report that included his second major work, *Systematic Geology*. His team's most publicized achievement was exposing the great diamond hoax of 1872, an effort by two con men to bilk millions from unwary investors. Applying principles of geology and their considerable knowledge of the area in which the dia-

Last of the Army surveymen, Lieutenant George M. Wheeler, right, seated at center, and some of his men relax in camp near Belmont, Nevada, in an undated photograph probably taken in the early 1870s. Wheeler's United States Geographical Surveys West of the One Hundredth Meridian included much of the Southwest. His parties passed through Santa Fe, New Mexico, site of the Church of San Miguel, above, and Canyon de Chelly, opposite, photographed by Timothy O'Sullivan.

mond field purportedly lay, King and several of his men located the secret field that had been salted with diamonds, rubies, sapphires, and other gems, and revealed it as a fraud.

In 1879, he was named director of the newly formed U.S. Geological Survey, a post that Hayden had coveted and expected to receive. King held his post for only one year, then retired from government service to seek his fortune in the mining industry. In this quest he was monumentally unsuccessful, and he died broken in health and finances on Christmas Eve, 1901.

Another of Hayden's rivals, one with whom he frequently feuded, was Lieutenant George Montague Wheeler, who headed the United States Geographical Surveys West of the One Hundredth Meridian. A member of the West Point class of 1866, Wheeler had missed the Civil War but hoped to make his mark as an army explorer in the West. He spent the years 1867 to 1870 mapping the deserts of the Great Basin south of the

area covered by King's surveys, and, in 1871, blitzed the Far Southwest. His teams crisscrossed Nevada, traversed torrid Death Valley, where three of his men almost succumbed to the 120-degree heat, and traveled up the Colorado River by boat as far as Diamond Creek in the Grand Canyon. Since Ives had already traveled up the Colorado to this point in 1858, and Powell had explored down the river in 1869, Wheeler's purpose in making this final leg of the journey is unclear. Sadly, Wheeler's party sustained the loss of three members to the Apaches after the end of the expedition proper.

Wheeler returned to Washington in January 1872, and, convinced that "the day of the pathfinder has sensibly ended," proposed a long-range plan to complete a map in 15 years of all the western territories. The lieutenant expected both the map—95 rectangles drawn in a scale of four miles to the inch—and the scientific findings of his survey to serve military objectives, but

John K. Hillers photographed part of Zuni Pueblo, New Mexico, opposite, around 1879 for the Smithsonian's Bureau of Ethnology. Zuni was visited by many explorers and surveyors, including Bureau of Ethnology chief John Wesley Powell, who had captained the first trip through the Grand Canyon in 1869. During Powell's 1871 Colorado River expedition, geologist's assistant John F. Steward, left, posed for the camera in scenic Glen Canyon, now drowned by Lake Powell.

Named for his wife, Powell's flagship Emma Dean, below, was photographed by Hillers in the Colorado's Marble Canyon during the 1872 expedition. Powell reconnoitered the river ahead from the chair lashed amidships.

his operations in parts of the West that had already been covered by King, Hayden, and Powell brought him into direct conflict with the civilians, who were determined to destroy his career. Garrulous as ever, Hayden blustered to one of Wheeler's aides: "You can tell Wheeler that if he stirs a finger or attempts to interfere with me or my survey in any way, I will utterly crush him—as I have enough congressional influence to do so, and will bring it to bear." Such feuds and overlapping explorations hastened the end of the independent expeditions and the formation of the U.S. Geological Survey in 1878.

Fourth of the national survey leaders and probably the best known today was John Wesley Powell, a one-armed veteran of the Civil War. In May 1869, after two preliminary explorations in Colorado, he set out from Green River, Wyoming Territory, with nine companions in four boats "to descend the Green to the Colorado, and the Colorado down to the foot of the Grand Canyon." By the time he emerged from the Grand Canyon of the Colorado 99 days and 1,500 miles later, one of his boats had wrecked and four of his men had quit. Ironically, three of these had left for the mountains only two and a half days before the expedition ended, and were ambushed and killed by Indians.

With public interest in his explorations greatly heightened by early rumors of disaster and now the news of the death of three of his men, Powell became an instant hero. He capitalized on his popularity by wringing $10,000 from Congress for continued study of the river, and in the spring of 1871 he embarked on a "Geographical and Topographical Survey of the Colorado River." This time, however, Powell went in style, strapping an armchair to the deck of his boat, the *Emma Dean*, which was named after his wife. From this vantage point he studied the river, gave orders, and, along one of the river's placid stretches, read aloud to his men from Sir Walter Scott's *The Lady of the Lake*.

During his surveys of the Colorado River and later of the Colorado Plateau, Powell sought to understand large-scale processes of nature. He eventually hypothesized that the Colorado Plateau was uplifted while the river carved out its intricate canyons. "The river," he explained, "was the saw which cut the mountain in two." His theories of uplift and erosion were a major step forward in understanding the geological forces that shaped the land not only in the trans-Mississippi West but throughout the world.

Powell also took a keen interest in the future of the arid lands of the West and put forth a number of ideas regarding their settlement and conservation in his most important work, the *Report Upon Lands of the Arid Regions of the United States*, published in 1878. In it he urged that all western lands be mapped and classified according to their potential use—agriculture, ranching, forestry, or mining, for example. He also wrote that the traditional eastern farm had no place in the arid West. Indeed, lack of water in these regions would severely limit settlement, and those who chose to defy nature and live here would have to cooperate in harnessing and using what meager water resources were available. Unfortunately, not everyone cared to heed this early proponent of conservation

and cooperation. Had they done so, our nation could perhaps have avoided such environmental catastrophes as the dust bowls of the 1930s that threatened to turn Jefferson's western garden into the Sahara described by Pike, Long, and other believers in the Great American Desert.

In 1878, the great surveys collapsed in a welter of bickering and controversy. Critics charged that they were wasteful and extravagant. Why spend money on four distinct surveys, each competing for favor with Congress and the public, when one would do just as well? Powell emerged as the leader of the movement to merge the surveys, and he was supported in this effort by a large segment of the scientific community as well as a majority of the Congress. The forces of efficiency and thrift prevailed, and the Hayden, King, and Wheeler surveys were discontinued, to be replaced by the United States Geological Survey. Clarence King was appointed its first director, but he was soon succeeded by Powell.

Although the demise of the surveys ended the era of the heroic explorer in the West, one wilderness still remained in North America to beckon daring, adventurous young scientists. This was Alaska, and it attracted a corps of scientific explorers as curious and hardy as those who earlier had challenged the trans-Mississippi plains and plateaus. Assisting them, as it had their predecessors, was the Smithsonian Institution, which continued to reap a scientific harvest from exploration. And in the forefront of those who hoped to unlock the secrets of the frozen north country were Baird's Megatheria, including the boldest and proudest Megatherium of them all, Robert Kennicott.

During his years as explorer and surveyor of the Colorado's plateaus and canyons, John Wesley Powell developed a keen interest in its Indian peoples, taking pains to gain their trust and learn their languages. In this John K. Hillers photograph, opposite, he speaks with

Tau-Gu, chief of the Paiutes. Powell compiled vocabularies, collected details of religion and lore, and championed the rights of Indians. Although he might not have approved of it, Lake Powell, above, largest artificial lake in the world, memorializes Powell's contributions to a host of scientific disciplines.

Both Kennicott Glacier, seen below blanketing Mount Blackburn in Alaska's Wrangell Mountains, and the freshwater cisco fish, Coregonus kennicotti, *below right, were named for naturalist Robert Kennicott, who in 1859 set off on a three-year expedition to the vast region that today encompasses Canada's Northwest Territories and Alaska.*

THE LAST FRONTIER

Almost every school child in America learns of "Seward's folly," which along with "Walrussia," "the Polar Bear Garden," and "Seward's ice-box" was one of the unflattering names that numerous wits of the 1860s gave to the territory of Alaska. It was Secretary of State William H. Seward, after all, who persuaded the United States to pay $7.2 million for this immense piece of real estate, which Russia, its financially troubled owner, then viewed as a frozen asset. What is not so widely known, however, is the Smithsonian's backstage role in Seward's efforts to enlighten not only the American public but also a reluctant Congress as to the benefits to be gained by this controversial transaction. His work was so successful that in less than two weeks—between midnight, March 30, 1867, when the treaty was signed, and April 9, l867, when the Senate ratified it by a vote of 37 to 2—Seward was able to convince an overwhelming majority of the Senate to confirm the purchase.

Seward had two invaluable allies in this campaign. One was Charles Sumner, chairman of the Senate Foreign Relations Committee, who delivered a three-hour speech on the Senate floor prior to the vote. The other was the Smithsonian's assistant secretary, Spencer Baird, who furnished Sumner with much of the information on the region's geography and natural history contained in the speech, which was described at the time as a "monument of comprehensive research." Baird not only met with Sumner five times between March 30 and April 9, but also spoke with Seward, several key senators, and the Senate Foreign Relations Committee. When Sumner later published his speech in the *Boston Journal,* he sent the proofs to Baird for correction.

The major source of Baird's information was the zealous and intrepid Robert Kennicott, who had recently spent three years in the Far North as a scientific explorer for the Smithsonian. His presence there had been the fortunate combination of Baird's foresight and his own willingness to challenge the far north-

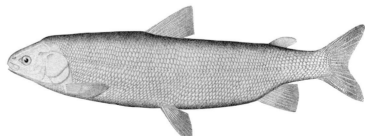

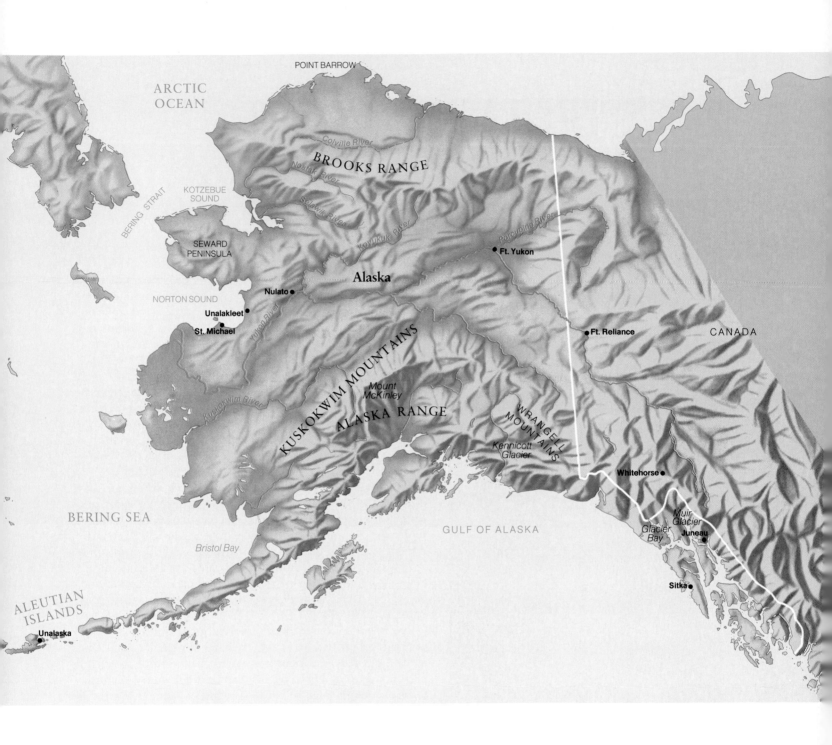

POINT BARROW

ARCTIC
OCEAN

BROOKS RANGE

Colville River

Noatak River

KOTZEBUE
SOUND

BERING STRAIT

Selawik River

Koyukuk River

Porcupine River

● Ft. Yukon

SEWARD
PENINSULA

Alaska

NORTON SOUND

Nulato ●

Yukon River

● Ft. Reliance

CANADA

Unalakleet ●

St. Michael ●

KUSKOKWIM MOUNTAINS

Kuskokwim River

Mount
McKinley

ALASKA RANGE

WRANGELL
MOUNTAINS

*Kennicott
Glacier*

Whitehorse ●

BERING SEA

Bristol Bay

GULF OF ALASKA

*Glacier
Bay*

*Muir
Glacier*

Juneau ●

ALEUTIAN
ISLANDS

Sitka ●

Unalaska ●

western wilderness of Canada, an area then administered for the British government by the Hudson's Bay Company, at a time when most American explorers and naturalists were still primarily interested in the trans-Mississippi West. Sadly, Baird's youngest and brightest Megatherium did not live long enough to learn of his importance to the acquisition of Alaska. He had died a year earlier, in 1866, at the age of 30.

Still, Kennicott had done much with the short time available to him. Raised a few miles northwest of Chicago on several hundred acres of land called "The Grove," he was so frail and sickly as a child that he received little classroom training, perhaps two years in all. Nevertheless, thanks to his father, a physician and botanist, Kennicott became fascinated by the study of natural history, making detailed observations of the behavior of various mammals and birds and collecting fishes and reptiles, including a number that were new to science. By the age of 18, the precocious youngster was sending Baird specimens for the Smithsonian's collections and sharing with him the results of his experiments on the effect of rattlesnake venom on animals. "I took two young kittens and two cedar birds and poured a drop or two of [the] virus down the throat of each," he wrote. "None of them appeared affected in the least." The assistant secretary responded with advice, encouragement, and books on natural history, much to the gratification of the elder Kennicott, who thanked Baird in a note written on the back of one of his son's letters: "As a *father,* and, once upon a

Emanuel Leutze's painting, right, commemorates the signing of the Alaska purchase document at four in the morning on March 30, 1867. Russian Ambassador Edouard de Stoeckl stands in the foreground by the globe, while Secretary of State William H. Seward is seated at left. A cartoon lampoons the purchase of Alaska, then known as Russian America, by the United States. Congress and the American public alike were generally ignorant as to the rich resources of Alaska, then still very much terra incognita. In the cartoon, an American stands ready to give the Russian iceman a big bag of money for a chunk of ice, while Seward awaits delivery in the cellar.

time, something of a Naturalist—or rather Botanist—I thank you, most sincerely, for your notice and encouragement of our son Robert—'Bob' is, in some respects, of the right stuff to make a Naturalist; and I should be greatly gratified should he be able to redeem the illusory promise of his father."

Bob did that and more. In 1856, when he was only 21, he helped found the Chicago Academy of Sciences; the following year, when the Academy became established, he began assembling collections for a natural history museum for Northwestern University. Deciding to extend the range of his collecting for the new museum beyond Illinois, in the summer of 1857 he embarked on a four-month expedition up the Red River of the North and across the plains to the west—"some distance north of the U.S. boundary line"—to "within a few miles of Lake Winnipeg." In mid-December, Kennicott went to the Smithsonian for the first time to classify and describe the material he had collected. There he came within the orbit of the assistant secretary, who quickly took a liking to the dynamic young man. "I know of no American naturalist who gives such promise," avowed Baird.

Kennicott spent the winter at the Smithsonian researching his specimens, went back to the Midwest to collect more the following summer, and then returned for another winter in Washington. It was during his second visit that he resolved to explore, under the auspices of the Smithsonian Institution, the vast area that is today Canada's Northwest Territories and, if possible, Russian America, as Alaska was then known. Although a few observant whaling captains—one might call them amateur

naturalists—and a few European scientists had already visited this part of North America, their work had been preliminary. No one had yet attempted a systematic survey, and the region remained, according to Baird, a "grievous blank."

Baird was indeed correct, for despite two centuries of Russian and British occupation, the Far Northwest remained little known, primarily because its visitors had for the most part been entrepreneurs rather than explorers. From the days of Vitus Bering, a Dane in the service of the Russian Navy who discovered Alaska, the region had endured one wave of exploiters after another—whalers, sealers, fur trappers, fishermen— each seeking to harvest economic wealth rather than scientific knowledge. Neither the Russians nor the British had cared to expend much in the way of funds for something as esoteric as the study of natural history, leaving wide the opportunity for the United States to undertake a comprehensive survey of Alaska's natural resources.

Robert Kennicott led the way. To finance his fieldwork, the young naturalist established a research fund underwritten by donors who were to receive sets of the specimens he collected. His contract with the University of Michigan, for example, dated April 25, 1859, states that in return for its donation of $250 to the "fund for Natural History explorations of Hudson Bay Territory under the direction of R. Kennicott," the university was to receive "a share pro rata of the specimens collected by the expedition." The university understood that all specimens Kennicott collected would first be turned over to the Smithsonian Institution, where they would be "divided among

Early explorer of the Far Northwest Robert Kennicott, opposite, traveled the region's waterways—including Great Slave Lake and the Mackenzie, Porcupine, and Yukon rivers— with Hudson's Bay Company voyageurs, seen at left portaging one of their canoes. Kennicott also stayed at remote Hudson's Bay Company trading posts, often enlisting the help of company employees in collecting birds and other natural history specimens.

the parties furnishing the means of making the exploration, each party receiving specimens in proper turn to the amount contributed."

The key person in this ambitious enterprise was of course Baird. He solicited the contributions, monitored the fund, purchased and shipped the supplies to Kennicott, received and sorted the specimens, and then doled them out to the investors, keeping one set for the Smithsonian and one for the Chicago Academy—Kennicott's condition for undertaking the survey. Somehow Baird managed to please all parties.

Kennicott's travels in the Far North would not have been feasible, however, without the support and protection of the Hudson's Bay Company. Indeed, were it not for the enthusias-

tic cooperation he received from this fur trade giant, which had been an economic force in the Canadian West for some 200 years before his arrival, Kennicott would have accomplished very little, and might even have been denied access to the area. Instead, because the company regularly serviced its outposts, Kennicott could usually travel in the company of experienced Hudson's Bay woodsmen.

To obtain enough scientific specimens to fulfill his contracts, Kennicott enlisted the aid of Hudson's Bay Company personnel, Indians, missionaries, and anyone else who came his way. At any one time, he might have a dozen collectors at work snatching eggs from nests, trapping and shooting birds and animals, and recording meteorological phenomena. Some were

satisfied to receive Kennicott's good will in return for their services as well as the opportunity to have their name forever linked to a previously unknown species. Others were paid. In fact, Kennicott offered his collectors just about anything within reason. One man was presented with an accordion destined, undoubtedly, to enliven long evenings.

Good whiskey was especially popular. "Of course for my own use I wouldn't spend a cent so," Kennicott was quick to assure the assistant secretary, "but . . . nothing from me would be more acceptable to the gentlemen on whose good offices my success entirely depends." They usually had to content themselves with "a villainous liquid" they called beer, made from locally grown barley. "You see what efforts are made to procure the element of conduction!!"

Getting the whiskey to Kennicott was not always easy, however. The Hudson's Bay Company voyageurs, the project's paddling and portaging baggage handlers, were so thirsty that they often found even the alcohol used in preserving specimens to their liking. To ensure delivery, therefore, Baird wrote "poison" on the alcohol containers and splashed them with creosote so they would "smell bad."

Baird also sent letters of appreciation to Kennicott's collectors. These letters, Kennicott insisted, would effect "more for science . . . than I shall in a year's work. Do you not know that you have a persuasive way with you that enables you to make every body do just as you like—as far as any external influence can have effect?"

"I have, of course, received a new name, by which I am called by the Indians," Kennicott wrote in his journal on July 3, 1861. "It is che-tsoh-kah-kieh—*(che-tsoh, a bird, and* kah-kieh, *chief, or master)," although, he went on, they usually "call me* Che-tsoh." *Kennicott sent the Smithsonian hundreds of bird skins and eggs, among them the skins, opposite, of (from upper right) a spruce grouse, a white-fronted goose, a ruffed grouse, a willow ptarmigan, and a sharp-shinned hawk. Kennicott also collected numerous mammal skins and skulls, such as those of wolverines, below, which he called carcajous (from the French word for the animal) and characterized as "rascally beasties."*

The "element of conduction," books, and flattering letters may have kept the Hudson's Bay Company factors and their assistants at work for the advancement of science, but such inducements did not work with the Indians. "I can get scarce any thing from them, and what few specimens I do get I must pay large prices for," Kennicott grumbled at one point. "So long as an Indian isn't hungry—or in fact *very* hungry—he is as independent as you please and quite scorns the idea of working for any thing less than very large pay, if he will work at all." To enlist their help, Kennicott needed sewing needles (he once ordered 5,000), calico shirts and cloth, ribbons, fake jewelry, brightly colored cotton handkerchiefs—"at least two feet square"—and guns, especially double-barreled percussion shotguns. Whatever their cost, the shotguns were worth twice that to Kennicott. "By offering such a grand and generally unattainable prize, I could induce an Indian to spend his whole year hunting specimens for me."

Kennicott launched his wilderness odyssey on May 19, 1859, departing Fort William on the northern shore of Lake Superior with the spring brigade of the Hudson's Bay Company, which

was setting out to collect the furs and replenish the stores at its outposts in Manitoba and Saskatchewan. The brigade consisted of three birchbark canoes, each 36 feet long and four feet wide. In addition to an eight-man crew, composed of Iroquois Indians and French Canadians, each canoe carried 3,000 pounds of scientific and trade cargo.

Kennicott at first admired the voyageurs, who were often of mixed Indian and French-Canadian ancestry, marveling at their stamina and endurance, their cheerfulness and politeness, and their ability to live off the land, eating just about "any thing in the shape of fish or bird. A crow and pair of pigeon hawks, which I shot a few days before, were eaten, and I think they would eat eggs so nearly hatched that the chick could almost *peep,*" he noted in his journal. Kennicott learned much from his hardy traveling companions, including how to swear in French, chew tobacco, and—perhaps his most valuable lesson—be less trusting. "The damned voyageurs [have] plundered me of my provisions," he reported in disbelief from Norway House, his first stop, a Hudson's Bay Company trading post located at the northeastern shore of Lake Winnipeg. "I had enough to have furnished a decent allowance after using what was required for the voyage—confounded thieves, liars and rascals, generally, these French Red River half breeds."

Fortunately, the staff at Norway House welcomed him so warmly that Kennicott soon forgot his rude introduction to this region of the Far Northwest. The Hudson's Bay people were so interested in his work, in fact, that he had no trouble recruiting

volunteers to collect specimens and undertake meteorological and other observations. His only regret was having too few copies of Baird's collecting instructions to pass out. "All of these men are bricks, all intelligent and *gentlemen,*" he assured the assistant secretary, ". . . [so] you see I'm not exactly a Martyr! to science when I go north. Frozen nozes, hard fare, etc only will give zest to the whole."

Kennicott was so pleased with his situation that he promptly promised to spend several years at his survey. "As a devotee to science I think it decidedly my *duty,*" he insisted, adding that he would be "a great fool did I neglect the opportunity to be the first naturalist in this unknown region." Baird, of course, was delighted at the offer. "Half a dozen years will not exhaust the country, certainly not three or four; and as long as you are satisfied to remain, and can do it without distressing your family, I will be very glad to have you [there]."

Despite initial optimism, however, the young naturalist quickly came to appreciate the difficulty of the task before him. "I am in wo!" he wrote some 39 or 40 miles below the Cumberland House trading post on the Saskatchewan River, his second stop. "The bird nesting is a dead failure. I have not gotten over five or so nests since leaving Norway House." Not only were eggs scarce but so were birds and animals. In the past two weeks he had seen but one Canada jay and two woodpeckers. "You may suppose I feel a little blue. . . . If it were not for the fine insects I'm getting I should be quite discouraged." After one storm, he had been able to pick up 50 species of beetles on

the shores of Lake Winnipeg, thrown there by the waves. Kennicott was confident he could also make handsome botanical collections, but no one had subscribed for plants. "Can't you get some Botanist to go $250?" he pleaded. "I have a plant press and enough good blotting paper for several hundred plants beside a little thin paper and may yet get more, and am going into plants."

Plants were not high on Baird's list of desirable specimens, but he did wish to build up the Smithsonian's egg collections. "Make eggs the specialty, particularly waders and geese. But get plenty of all, and more, too." Baird also wanted skulls. "Get plenty of single skulls of beaver, mountain foxes, wolverines, etc. Can't have too many."

"I judge from what you say," Kennicott responded, "that I'd better lose a rare bird or mammal than a rare egg and shall act accordingly. But I'll get both! Only the egg *first*."

Alaska's infamous mosquitoes quickly proved a bane to egg collecting. "[They] are so exceedingly numerous and horribly voracious as to prove a serious detriment to collecting. I think," Kennicott told Baird, "I've lost some pounds of blood during the last week by them. But I could endure their bites if they would keep out of my eyes. I've lost several fine birds and opportunities to kill parents of nests, by their flying into my eyes and destroying my aim when about to shoot." Kennicott was not exaggerating; another 19th-century Alaskan explorer concurred, "Cold is nothing compared to the mosquitoes; of the two give me fifty below zero."

Try as he might, Kennicott could seldom find enough eggs to satisfy either Baird or himself. "I do wish I could just see you a moment when you opened the little package I shall send you with this [letter]," he wrote in November 1859. "But alas I fear you'll expect more than I have yet obtained. The egging was a dead failure; but wait. Next Spring!"

It was not until the spring of 1861 that Kennicott was finally able to reap a bountiful harvest. Writing on June 23 from "Duck's eggs Paradise"—Fort Yukon in Russian America—he exclaimed: "Hurrah! for the Youkon every time! And hurrah for rare ducks eggs (But Damn and double damn all musquetoes in general and Youkon musquetoes in particular)." With the assistance of a Hudson's Bay employee and a half dozen Indians, Kennicott already had in hand more than a bushel of eggs. One Indian, "a *regular brick* of a savage," had brought him 76 eggs of the lesser scaup, *Aythya affinis*, all found along the edges of one lake.

The long winters also proved more difficult than Kennicott had anticipated. He endured three on this trip—at Fort Simpson on the Upper Mackenzie, near the foot of Great Slave Lake; at Fort Yukon, about 120 miles inside Russian America at the Arctic Circle; and at La Pierre's House, a mountain post about 200 miles from Fort Yukon. A handful of Hudson's Bay Company employees, most of them Red River *métis*, or half-breed French-Canadian Indians, usually kept him company at these isolated stations. Kennicott would collect what he could, usually small birds and animals, dream of home, and wait for

spring. One day was like any other—breakfast at eight, supper at four—with activities dictated by the availability of the limited natural light. Meals consisted of dried reindeer and moose meat, potatoes, fish, tea, sugar, bread, and butter, with an occasional dish of rice or raisin pudding for variety. At night the men would swap stories, drink, smoke, and play whist.

Kennicott had intended to keep a detailed account of his activities, but his field notes, journal, and letters went unwritten. In March 1860, during his first winter, he confessed, "I have been *hybernating* this winter. I've been in the most apathetic state you can imagine." Trying to write had been like "purgatory," and, he added, "It seems a little tough to exist in such a *less than vegetable state* for 8 or 9 months for the sake of the 3 or 4 months of shining summer and fall—a good part of which it takes to thaw ones brains out!" By the end of his third winter, he was ready to leave the North Country, and it was only his promise to Baird to explore more of Russian America that kept him there. "I will confess that I would on my own account, much rather go out as soon as possible—for I find this Damned apathy rendering me about half idiotic, and I'm getting alarmed lest it gets fixed upon me as a habit—or disease—not to be gotten rid of even when I leave this monotonous life."

Kennicott worried continually about his lethargy and failings as a collector, but Baird reassured him. "You have done yourself great injustice in writing as if your last spring's operations were a failure. It was so far from the case that you far exceeded my expectations." Kennicott had obtained many rare species of birds, including a tern known only from a single specimen in the British Museum. "A curious fact in the zoology of the Slave Lake and Fort Simpson district," Baird wrote, "is that it is almost exclusively eastern in its type, very few Pacific or Rocky Mountain species."

Although pleased overall with Kennicott's specimens, Baird was distressed at the condition of the eggs. "Many of the big eggs were much broken," he complained. To prevent this from happening, he told Kennicott, each one should be wrapped separately. He also found fault with the holes Kennicott had drilled in the eggs to drain the fluid. "A well prepared egg to the amateur is worth ten times as one with big holes, many persons refusing to have the latter, however rare, on any terms."

When Baird suggested that certain eggs would fetch a high price from private collectors, Kennicott rejected the idea of selling them for profit unless it was necessary to obtain funds to keep him in the field. "But if you mean any pecuniary benefit to

Englishman Frederick Whymper, artist on the Western Union Telegraph Expedition, sketched explorers making their way up the Yukon River during the springtime break-up of the ice, opposite. The youthful William H. Dall, above, assumed command of the expedition's Scientific Corps after Kennicott's death. Dall's sketch of the Russian post of Nulato, right, on January 1, 1867, documents the first telegraph poles along the Yukon River. The Stars and Stripes tops one pole, followed by the Masonic and Western Union flags and then the flag, also shown above the sketch, that Dall designed for the Scientific Corps. Dall was somewhat premature in flying the American flag over the post, for the United States was not to complete its purchase of Alaska for another three months.

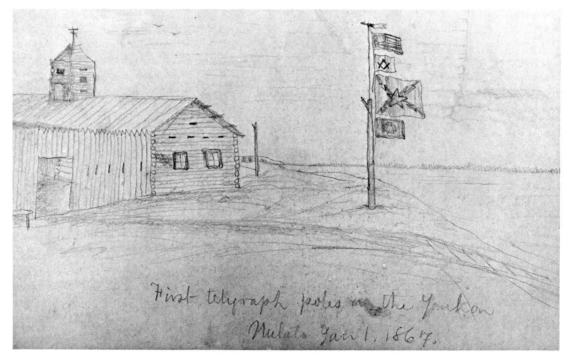

First telegraph poles in the Yukon
Nulato Jan 1, 1867.

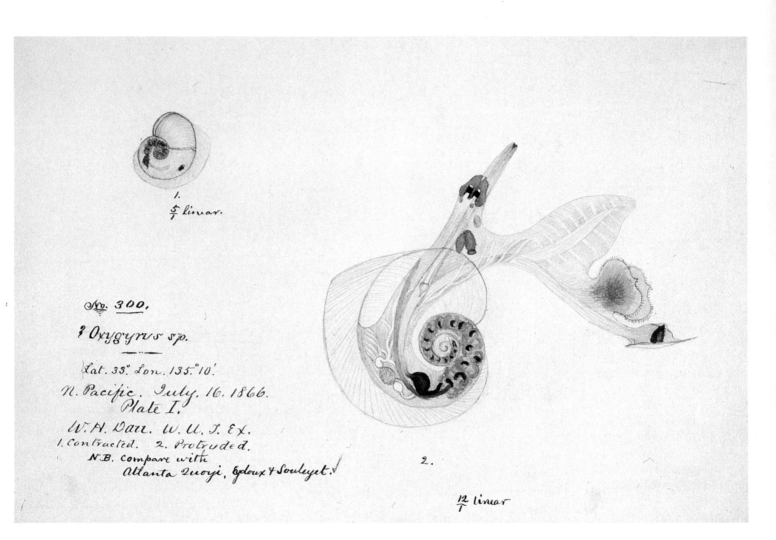

No. 300.
? Oxygyrus sp.
Lat. 35°. Lon. 135.°10'.
N. Pacific. July. 16. 1866.
Plate I.
W. H. Dall. W. U. T. Ex.
1. Contracted. 2. Protruded.
N.B. Compare with
Atlanta Quoyi, Eydoux & Souleyet.

1.
5/1 linear.

2.

12/1 linear

accrue to me from the sale of my specimens I object to it entirely. I never expected nor do I wish to receive any pay for my services. All I want is to have my expenses (clothes included) paid, and then if I arrive at home clear of debt I'll be quite content with my pecuniary affairs. You see 'tis very pleasant to think myself an honest devotee to Science. But I lose much of my own esteem if I work for money instead of Science."

During his three years in the northwestern wilderness, Kennicott ranged over an incredibly extensive area. The distance between Fort William on Lake Superior to Fort Yukon in Russian America was more than 2,500 miles as the crow flies, and much longer as the rivers wind. Yet this accounted for only part of his wanderings, for he logged additional mileage at each of the places he visited. At La Pierre's House in the fall of 1861, for example, he laid 150 traps along a 50-mile circuit and ran his trapline by dog sled at least three or four times a week from mid-October until Christmas.

Fortunately, the young man from Chicago did not have even the threat of an Indian attack to trouble his mind. Having been spared the bitter conflicts of their southern brethren, the Canadian Indians were at least tolerant if not friendly toward strange white men, a fact that greatly impressed Kennicott. "I

go to bed and to sleep with dozens of them in my room, and my things scattered about, and I do not think I ever had so much as a pin stolen," he marveled.

If Kennicott had any enemies, they were enemies of the mind. Isolation must undoubtedly have been a terrible cross to bear for the buoyant young man, of whom his fellow Megatheria could write, "Kennicott's voice was ever the most cheery, his tale the freshest, and his song the blithest." His journal entry for Christmas Day 1861, when he was mushing along the trail to La Pierre's House near the Arctic Circle, shows him trying to rally his spirits. "We had crossed the highest part of our track over the [Rocky] mountains just at the first appearance of the gray light in the southeast, which precedes the first real daylight by several hours at this season, and here, about nine o'clock on Christmas morning, I stopped and smoked the last of my cigars to the health and conduction of the family circle assembled at 'The Grove' and to the 'Megatheria,' and then sang, 'Do they miss me at home.' But the temperature was more than 40° below; too cold for cigars or sentiment, so I got on my sled, relieved my feelings by a yell . . . which started my dogs off on a gallop, and rode down the mountain singing *La Claire Fontaine* and other voyaging songs."

Kennicott often pondered the idea of an extensive collecting

No. 309.
Clio sp.
Pl. VIII. Lat 51.50' Lon. 161.26'.
N. Pacific Ocean
W.H. DALL. coll. fee. et pinx.
Aug 2. 1866.
W.U.T.E.E.

Clime elegantissima
Dall

1.
2.
3.

Oral aspect.

trip to the Russian settlements. "I dream bright dreams of the Anderson River Eskimo, musk oxen, a trip to the sea coast, and white geese & owl's eggs," he once wrote lyrically to Baird. Despite such dreams, however, Kennicott abruptly left for home in the spring of 1862. He gave conflicting reasons—his father's illness, his mother's wishes, his desire to fight in the Civil War. Most likely, however, it was the need to escape isolation and boredom. The fact that he had done little writing or collecting during his travels in the months before his departure suggests that all was not well. Historian Donald Zochert can only suspect "that what he sought during these last silent months in the North, he had not found. What he found, he had not sought."

After several weeks at home, Kennicott returned to the Smithsonian in order to assist Baird in sorting the collections from his Arctic expedition, which, despite his self-doubts, were extensive. But these were difficult days for him. Although the Megatherium Club was in full bloom and he was once again surrounded by fellowship and science, he found no peace of mind. Writing to Roderick MacFarlane, one of several Hudson's Bay Company employees he had recruited and who was to send more than 10,000 Arctic specimens to the Smithsonian, Kennicott cautioned: "Don't be in a hurry to leave the North,

MacFarlane. I assure you there is little comfort in the outside world. . . . It's all very well to talk of the delights of the civilized world, but give me the comfortable north where a man can have some fun, see good dogs and smoke his pipe unmolested. Damn Civilization."

One dream remained firm for Kennicott, however: "to establish a good museum of Natural History in Chicago"—a "*Young Smithsonian*," as he described it to MacFarlane. And in 1864 he accepted the curatorship of the Chicago Academy of Sciences. "I of course can't expect to make a Baird of myself, but having him for a close ally in all matters I hope to make our Chicago museum 'give track' to the progress of science."

Kennicott was working to make that dream a reality when events took him north again, this time as commander of an expedition to establish an intercontinental telegraph. For several years prior to the Civil War, a number of promoters had hoped to set up a communications link between Europe and America. Cyrus Field, for one, was attempting to do so by means of a trans-Atlantic cable. Others considered a route through British territory and Russian America and across the Bering Strait and through Siberia to be more feasible, and in 1865 they launched the Western Union Telegraph Expedition. Kennicott, at Baird's urging, agreed to head the team that ex-

plored the route through Russian America.

Although by temperament and personality Kennicott was unsuited to the task, he viewed it as a way of completing his unfinished survey and even persuaded Western Union to employ a "Scientific Corps" of six naturalists as his assistants. The most important of these was William Healey Dall, who went on to become the dean of Arctic explorers.

Kennicott had met Dall, who was only 19 at the time, at the Chicago Academy of Sciences. Now that he was seasoned in the field, Kennicott felt he could recognize "the right stuff to make a Naturalist": "I've got a prize here in Young Dall of Boston," he bragged to Baird in November 1864. "He is quite a conchologist and works like a brick." Three months later he offered Dall a position with his team. "If you are willing to work one or two years with no greater *pay* than $30 per month and expenses—But with a good opportunity to do a big thing in Natural History—and on a field where the *best* man stands first, then as your friend and well wisher I urge you to go with us!!"

Ironically, the Western Union Telegraph Expedition launched Dall's career, but it destroyed Kennicott. The high-strung scholar was not suited for an expedition run under businesslike, even quasi-military discipline and regulations, including the requirement that its members wear uniforms. Almost immediately Kennicott began feuding with his fellow officers, while at the same time suspecting the motives of his superiors. Dall, who accompanied him to San Francisco, the departure point for the trip to Alaska, wrote that Kennicott was in such "a great state of excitement" that he appeared drunk. Anyone seeing him, he confided to Baird, would have considered him "insane or incapable of doing the work set before him. . . . He is absurdly suspicious of everyone." Kennicott, doing nothing to dispel that notion, warned Baird that "should anything happen to me . . . so that I never return it might be that some evil disposed person should by misrepresentations make it appear that I have not done my duty by the Company."

The problems, which were certainly enough to daunt any leader, bear an amazing resemblance to those that had beset Charles Wilkes and the great U.S. Exploring Expedition nearly 30 years earlier. There were arguments over discipline as well as what route to follow—in this case, across Alaska—and conflicts between the naturalists and the company's officers, who were interested in advancing science only if it advanced their enterprise. Dall described the officers as "a set of the usual fast men of no particular forte . . . most of whom find it fashionable and easy to deride Natural History, always beginning and ending [comments] with '*bugs*.'"

Logistics were a nightmare. The vessel that was to carry the party up the Yukon River was at first delayed for repair near the river's delta, then foundered on rocks, leaving the explorers to exist on army rations. And there were never enough sled dogs for the amount of work to be done. "Things don't look at all pleasant and I wish I were quite alone with a small outfit of my own choosing," Kennicott confided to Baird only a few months into the enterprise. "I could then go in with a lighter heart than I now do when I have the safety and comfort of the others to

look after." Dall's summation of the trip was more succinct: "one, long, weary, fight."

Kennicott had planned to spend his first winter at Fort Yukon, but unforeseen difficulties forced him to stay at Nulato, an isolated Russian trading post on the Lower Yukon. Although two other members of the expedition were with him, the inactivity did not wear well on the restless leader, who became increasingly depressed. One morning in May 1866, unable to sleep, he left the post and failed to return. Searchers found his body a short distance away. His pocket compass lay near him. Although some thought he had committed suicide—he had, as his companion Lieutenant Charles Pease related, written out "directions for the carrying on of the explorations" sometime before dawn—the prevailing opinion was death by heart attack.

Dall, who had remained aboard Western Union's ship as acting surgeon, did not learn of Kennicott's death until four months later. Grief-stricken when he heard the news, he had no doubts as to the cause of death. "He was murdered," he wrote to his future wife Elizabeth Merriam, "not by the merciful knife but by slow torture of the mind. By ungrateful subordinates, by an egotistic and selfish commander, by anxiety to fulfil his commands, while those that gave them were lining their pockets in San Francisco." On the first anniversary of Kennicott's death, Dall went to Nulato and carved the following inscription on an oak board: "To the Memory of Robert Kennicott, Naturalist, Who Died Near This Place May 13, 1866, Aged Thirty."

Dall wrote to Baird expressing grief and rage, but not surprise, for " . . . no one but me knows the fiery furnace in which he worked through . . . a legion of hell devils baiting him all the time." A second letter contained an offer to complete Kennicott's natural history survey, "for such time, health being spared to me, as you may judge proper and expedient." His only condition was that in addition to the Smithsonian set, Baird continue to send a set of specimens to the Chicago Academy as Kennicott had wished. Please reply at once, Dall asked, "for God knows, I don't want to stay."

Dall not only stayed, but he replaced Kennicott as chief of the Scientific Corps. He realized it was "a funereal sort of honor," for the expedition was disorganized and in disarray. The final blow came just a few months later in mid-July when Western Union abruptly terminated the expedition on learning that Field had at last succeeded in laying a trans-Atlantic cable.

Disappointed at the sudden ending of the expedition, Dall refused to leave. As he informed his future wife, "I have pledged myself . . . to Professor Baird to fight it out alone, as long as he judges best." To his mother he wrote, "My mission is to carry out Kennicott's work, and as far as it depends on me it shall be done."

And carry it out he did, even though it was not always easy. Like his mentor, Dall knew moments of frustration. The Russians were particularly aggravating—worthy companions when sober, he judged, but intolerable when drunk. "The Russians are *dogs*," he complained to Baird in a moment of ire. "If you come up bring plenty of rum & you can buy their *souls.*" His opinion of the Eskimos and Indians he encountered was not much better. "[James Fenimore] Cooper could never have introduced a Mahlemut [Eskimo] into his novels," he recorded in his diary. "The fat greasy blubber eaters would turn the stomach of any lady of fashion. He would search Russian America for a Mohican in vain. Mingoes all, are the savages; with the strength of men and the brains of children." He did appreciate their knowledge of natural history, however, and when an Indian brought him a bullfinch, claiming it to be the only one he had ever seen, Dall wrote, "As they are pretty sharp sighted in such matters, it may be concluded it is not common."

When Dall completed his survey, he composed the following testimonial, dated August 8, 1868, in his notebook. "I have endeavored to the best of my ability to carry out the original plan of Major Robert Kennicott in the exploration of this part of Russian America, in regard to Geology and Natural History. I have spared neither money, time, nor strength to forward this enterprise not in expectation of any pecuniary reward, but in the hope of being able to conduct my friend's beloved object, to a successful consummation. I hope I may say with out exaggeration that I have done as much during the past year (1867–8), as any one man, in my position could do, but I know if I had had an assistant, the collections might have been more than trebled—as it is, I know they are not insignificant.

"But I cannot close my work here, without remarking how great is the field for research as yet left almost untouched, in the coast from the Youkon-mouth to the Aleutian Islands, and from

meteorologist. Using the American Commercial Trading Company post, right, as head-quarters, Nelson roamed throughout the Norton Sound and Lower Yukon River region, collecting thousands of natural history specimens and cultural artifacts for the Smithsonian. Nelson's photograph of Kuskokwim Eskimos, above, is one of the many anthropological treasures in his monograph, The Eskimo about Bering Strait, *published by the Smithsonian in 1899.*

Nelson presented over 2,000 bird skins and 1,500 egg specimens to the Smithsonian, and much of his 1887 report on the natural history of Alaska was devoted to ornithology. Included in the report's 21 plates were Smithsonian bird curator Robert Ridgway's drawings of a gray or "Canada" jay (also known as the "Whiskey Jack"), right, and a willow ptarmigan, below, as well as, opposite, the heads of a spectacled eider (upper left) and a common eider, a willow ptarmigan (center), and a black scoter (bottom left) and a surf scoter, all of which were "colored from nature" by Nelson.

Fig. 1.

Fig. 2.

Fig. 3.

Fig. 4.

Fig. 5.

Unalakleet around the Kaviiak peninsula to Kotzibue or even the mouth of the Mackenzie R. and the interior of the country every where, except the valley of the Youkon of which I believe, I have made a pretty thorough reconnaissance—Geological & other wise—still, even there, much may reward a patient investigator.

"Time will prove the accuracy and value of my collections and observations and if they prove to be a useful contribution to the knowledge of the continent, I shall feel that my sacrifices of time, labor, and I fear, health, were not in vain."

Certainly the work of Kennicott, Dall, and their fellow members of the Scientific Corps had not been in vain. The Western Union Telegraph Expedition, despite its problems and premature end, had provided the opportunity for the first systematic scientific exploration of this great region. In his speech before the Senate on Alaska, Senator Charles Sumner noted his indebtedness to the expedition for "authentic evidence with regard to the character of the region, and the great rivers which traverse it." He referred specifically to the contributions of Henry M. Bannister, a member of the Scientific Corps, and Robert Kennicott, and said of the latter, "His name will always remind us of courageous enterprise, before which distance and difficulty disappeared." Sumner's greatest compliment, however, was to Spencer Fullerton Baird. "Sometimes individuals are like libraries," he declared, "and this seems to be illustrated in the case of Professor Baird, of the Smithsonian Institution, who is thoroughly informed on all questions con-

nected with the Natural History of Russian America."

In the end, the scientific contributions of the telegraph expedition were significant. Its personnel prepared topographical and geological maps, collected meteorological data, described species of plants and animals, and identified minerals. The expedition also shipped a vast array of representative specimens to the Smithsonian which, in turn, provided the data for numerous scientific publications. Dall, who personally assembled a massive collection of 4,550 rock specimens (those collected along the Yukon River between Fort Yukon and the sea were sufficient, he claimed, "to determine the geological formations [of Alaska] for 1,300 miles"), later credited the Scientific Corps with having identified 732 botanical species, 77 mammalian species, 211 bird species, and 52 insect species. Nonetheless, the real credit for the expedition's scientific achievements must go to Kennicott and Dall. As historian Morgan Sherwood, the authority on Alaskan exploration, points out, "Kennicott drew the blueprint for science; Dall carried it into the field."

Although Dall did not participate in the debates over the purchase of Alaska, he was delighted to raise the Stars and Stripes on February 3, 1868, at Nulato, where he happened to be visiting when the news arrived of Alaska's entry into the Union. He also took great pleasure in sending to the Hudson's Bay factor at Fort Yukon a letter addressed to "Fort Yukon, *United States of America.*"

Dall left Alaska in the fall of 1868, but he returned three years

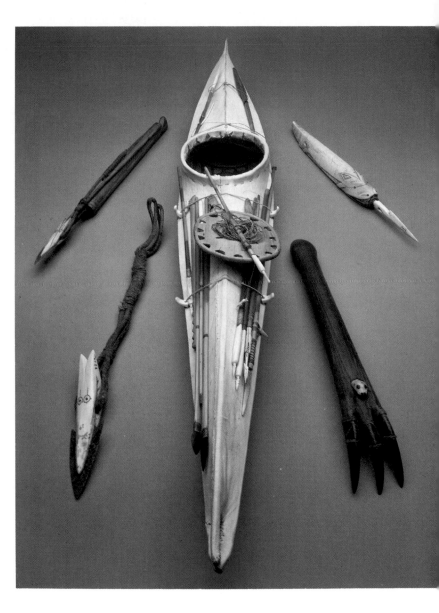

Edward Nelson's magnificent collection of Eskimo artifacts includes a mask, opposite top, showing a friendly tunghät, *or spirit, amid starry heavens (symbolized by the white feathers); a mask, right, of a fur seal rising for air (the disks representing the air bubbles the seal exhales as it rises); and a miniature of a fully rigged sea-going kayak, far right, surrounded by a hunter's tools, among them an ice scratcher (right foreground) used to imitate the sound of a seal's movement along the ice and thus lure other animals to the surface. Opposite bottom, a Nelson photograph documents Eskimos trap fishing on the Yukon River.*

Two other trained naturalists who served with the U.S. Army in Alaska and generated extensive collections for the Smithsonian were Lucien M. Turner and John Murdoch. Turner, the first U.S. Signal Service weather observer at St. Michael, collected numerous ethnological artifacts and natural history specimens. His Contributions to the Natural History of Alaska, *published in 1886, featured such animals as the Kittlitz's murrelet in winter plumage, opposite, and the Arctic eelpout, below left, then bearing the scientific name* Lycodes turnerii. *Murdoch served with the International Polar Expedition to Point Barrow of 1881–83, collecting such beautiful artifacts as the reindeer fur parka, left.*

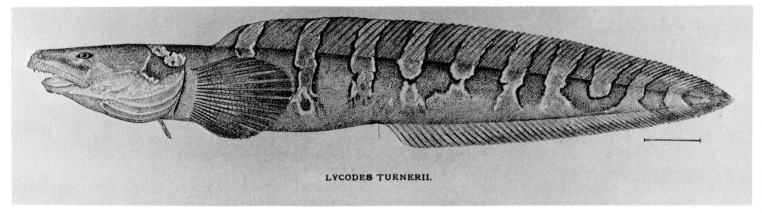

LYCODES TURNERII.

R. Ridgway

labor worthwhile: "the hope of solving the great problem of distribution of life, which seems possible and which would be a lasting satisfaction and comfort to me, as having been of some use to the scientific world in spite of my incomplete training."

Dall collected Indian and Eskimo artifacts throughout the dozen or so years he spent with the Coast Survey. These, he was amazed to discover, were increasingly in demand and therefore becoming increasingly scarce and expensive. "The collection which I presented to the S.I. in 1868," he declared four years later, "could not now be duplicated for $2000.00 in gold if it could at all." He knew one man who paid a dollar for one arrow, "which I could once have bought for a needle."

Despite his lack of anthropological training, Dall became a leading authority on the native peoples of Alaska. His first major work, *Alaska and Its Resources*, was published in 1870 and described the distribution and customs of that land's Indians and Eskimos. It was followed by *Tribes of the Extreme Northwest* and by numerous papers on Arctic ethnology and archaeology. In fact, scholars believe he was the first to recognize Alaska's importance in the archaeological record of North America.

Three other government collectors—Lucien M. Turner, Edward W. Nelson, and John Murdoch—also figure prominently in the exploration of Alaska. Like Dall, none of them was in Alaska on the payroll of the Smithsonian, but each worked closely with the Institution and generated extensive collections for Baird and the National Museum.

Lucien Turner was the first person assigned to the U.S. Army Signal Service's meteorological station at Saint Michael, once the most important Russian fort in Norton Sound. He arrived at this isolated post, the earliest federal scientific presence in Alaska, in May 1874. Nominated as a weather observer by Baird, Turner was later lauded by Joseph Henry for putting together one of the most impressive ethnological collections ever presented to the Smithsonian. And when Turner left St. Michael in 1877, he was replaced by the even more productive Edward Nelson.

Born in New Hampshire in 1855, Nelson had for years aspired to become a naturalist, and he applied to Baird for a job with the Smithsonian. Although Baird himself had no work for him, he recommended Nelson as Turner's replacement at St. Michael. Like Turner, Nelson was more interested in collecting than in recording weather conditions, and so, again like Turner, he used volunteers to collect meteorological data while he scoured the countryside for specimens. His accomplishments were remarkable. Over the next three years, he logged nearly 5,000 miles by canoe, dog sled, and foot, visiting remote Eskimo and Indian villages as he assembled one of the world's most extensive and valuable collections of Alaskan ethnography, especially that relating to the Eskimos of Bering Strait. Indeed, Nelson was such an avid collector, acquiring even broken and discarded objects, that the Eskimos dubbed him "the man who buys good-for-nothing things."

Although Nelson is remembered primarily for the 10,000 ethnographic specimens he sent to the Smithsonian, his training

later with the United States Coast and Geodetic Survey and under its auspices continued the work in Alaska he had begun with Kennicott. Scrupulous about his obligations to the Coast Survey, Dall devoted his off-duty hours to collecting for the Smithsonian, for Professor Louis Agassiz at Harvard, and for botanist Asa Gray. In order to avoid a conflict of interest and to be certain that his scientific equipment was under his own control, he had paid for it entirely from his own pocket—"to the tune of about $350." Then, on Sundays and when the weather was too inclement to perform his assigned duties, he collected sea creatures. "The results are by no means insignificant or uninteresting," he confided to Baird. "This is private & on no account to be published or made public," he warned, but in fact he had assembled the finest collection of sea animals that has ever been collected on the Northwest Coast. "Mollusca have been fully collected and some extremely remarkable new forms, as well as living examples of very rare old ones, are my reward in this respect." The work had been extremely taxing, both physically and mentally, he admitted. It was "not like land exploration when one seems to gain strength from the very contact with virgin soil." Only one goal, he wrote, made all this was in ornithology, and he made important contributions to the zoology of Alaska as well. He supplied Baird with considerable information and specimens of all the forms of flora and fauna that came his way, including butterflies "secured by means of my hat." But his work in Alaska was cut short by the onset of tuberculosis, then rampant among the native people. He arrived in Washington in the fall of 1881, but was soon forced by ill health to seek the drier climate of the Southwest. Not until 1895 did he return to Washington and complete his monumental monograph, *The Eskimos about Bering Strait*, which was published in 1899. He devoted the rest of his long life (he lived until 1934) to natural history, becoming an advocate of wildlife conservation. His efforts led to the Migratory Bird Treaty Act with Great Britain and Canada and to passage of the Alaska Game Law of 1925.

John Murdoch was the naturalist designated by Baird to be a U.S. Army observer with the International Polar Expedition to Point Barrow of 1881–83. Later librarian of the Smithsonian Institution, he was the author of another pioneering monograph of Alaskan studies, *Ethnological Results of the Point Barrow Expedition* (1892). Significantly, Murdoch assembled and analyzed collections at about the same time as Nelson, but from an area in which the Eskimos had had considerably more contact with white men, most of them whalers. His collections thus reflect the influence of European culture on the technology and traditions of the Point Barrow Eskimos, and point up dramatic differences in their society from Eskimos farther removed from white contact.

By the 1880s, the Smithsonian's role in the study of Alaskan natural history had largely ended, in part because of Baird's waning interest and in part because of political squabbling. Some members of Congress saw little benefit from weather stations in Alaska; others resented Baird's manipulation of government employees. As a result, the Smithsonian's Alaska programs were cut back and its collaboration with other agencies curtailed. The business of exploring Alaska was then taken over by other government agencies, such as the U.S. Army, the U.S. Navy, the Coast Survey, and the U.S. Geological Survey, whose missions were economically more practical.

The most important military expedition in the years that immediately followed the purchase of Alaska was conducted by U.S. Army Captain Charles Raymond, who brought the first steamboat up the Yukon River in 1868. Reminiscent of the smoking monster that frightened the Indians along the Missouri River during the Stephen H. Long expedition a half-century earlier, the little paddle-wheeler *Yukon* also alarmed Alaskan natives as it churned more than 1,000 miles upriver to Fort Yukon. The primary accomplishment of Raymond's excursion was to claim Fort Yukon for the United States and force its British garrison across the international boundary into Canada. Raymond's only difficulty, aside from the hordes of mosquitoes and black flies that infest Alaska in the summer, occurred on the return trip in a small native skiff in late August. Rations ran out and his party would have starved had it not been for the timely assistance of an Indian named "Brother of New Years," who

A full moon rises over Muir Inlet in Glacier Bay, now a national monument in south-eastern Alaska. In 1879, naturalist John Muir explored and mapped this spectacular, glacier-lined bay, probing its many inlets by canoe.

No one did more to promote the magnificence of Alaska's wilderness than John Muir, above, whose vivid travel writings focused popular and scientific attention on the Far Northwest. Among Alaska's natural wonders are frosted nagoonberry leaves, opposite, and a cow moose feeding in Denali National Park, left.

had served as a guide to the Western Union Telegraph Expedition three years earlier.

The most famous person associated with Alaska in this period, however, was neither an official explorer nor a Smithsonian naturalist. He was John Muir, the father of Yosemite National Park and the savior of the giant sequoias. "To the lover of pure wildness, Alaska is one of the most wonderful countries in the world," he exclaimed in 1879 after his first visit. For Muir it was love at first sight, and he made six trips to Alaska before his death in 1914 at the age of 76. "I have found southeastern Alaska a good, healthy country to live in," wrote the great naturalist, who backed up his statement by hiking and camping over much of Alaska's rugged landscape, especially the glaciers that were his special love. Fascinated by Indian tales of a "big ice-mountain bay"—today Glacier Bay National Park—he traveled there by canoe with missionary S. Hall Young and gave his name to Muir Glacier. Always seeking fresh challenges with nature, Muir once climbed an Alaskan mountain in a driving snowstorm, prompting his Indian companion to mutter, "Muir must be a witch to seek knowledge in such a place . . . and in such miserable weather."

Muir was no witch but he could certainly enchant the readers of his numerous books, magazine articles, and newspaper stories. His rhapsodies about Alaska's natural wonders beckoned other nature lovers to follow him to this primeval wilderness, which they did, each summer by the boatload, even as America's last frontier was undergoing still another entrepreneurial onslaught, this time by gold seekers who were despoiling the wilderness Muir was trying to save. Indeed, because he became a national spokesman on preservation issues and helped establish the Sierra Club, John Muir was the naturalist whom the public came to associate most closely not only with California but also with Alaska.

Although huge tracts of land in Alaska were eventually surveyed, these efforts never matched in scope or personnel the expeditions that had so quickly and completely unlocked the secrets of the "lower" American West. Even today, parts of that enormous and exciting northern land remain less than well known, lending substance to historian Daniel Boorstin's claim that Alaska "was settled before it was explored".

Nonetheless, the explorations of Kennicott, Dall, and the others marked the end of an era of discovery that had begun with the hardy Norse voyagers a millennium before. By the end of the 19th century, only the inhospitable polar regions of the Earth remained to be explored. As we shall see, wealthy tourists were already visiting regions which a few years before had been regarded as utterly hostile and wild. And the forces of development and conservation had already begun their conflict—still unsettled today—over the best use of those millions of square miles comprising the American West.

Indians and bison yielding before her, the spirit of Manifest Destiny leads the parade of progress, stringing telegraph wire across the Great Plains in this print after a painting by John Gast. The Smithsonian still preserves Samuel F. B. Morse's original telegraph key, below right, which sent the first U. S. telegraph message in 1844.

END OF AN ERA

Floating down the Green River in the little 16-foot *Emma Dean,* John Wesley Powell approached one of the few remaining geographical mysteries of the United States—the middle reaches of the Colorado River as it plunged into and through the Grand Canyon, or, as Powell wrote, "the Great Unknown." Only 63 years had passed since Meriwether Lewis and William Clark had traveled down the Missouri, homeward bound after their epochal crossing of the continent. Now, in the summer of 1869, Powell was on his way toward completing the final phase of the initial exploration of the American West, and the first phase of truly understanding it. In the end he would be credited with discovering the region's last unknown river, the Escalante, and last unknown mountain range, the Henry. And he would be among the first to ponder and appreciate the region's very special nature.

Powell's adventure on the Colorado marked a transition, for the era of the great surveys by competing civilians and soldiers would be over within 10 years. The work of examining and defining the West then passed from the hands of the explorers, Army engineers, and topographers into the hands of scientific specialists and government teams of biologists, mineralogists, and paleontologists.

Between 1806 and 1869, most of the directives President Jefferson had laid out in his letter of charge to Captain Lewis had been fulfilled. Not only had the Missouri River and its principal streams been explored and "the most direct and practicable water communication across the continent for purposes of commerce" been determined, but now a transcontinental telegraph bound East with West. Even more remarkable, Powell's odyssey took place the same year that the iron horses of the Union and Central Pacific railroads snorted at each other across the golden spike at Promontory in Utah Territory. In fact, steam locomotives of the Union Pacific and the Burlington had hauled Powell's four wooden boats from Chicago to their launching point at Green River Station in Wyoming Territory.

Not everything in the West had met Jefferson's expectations,

of course. His "Stony Mountains," depicted on early maps as a thin picket line of peaks on the western edge of the Great Plains, proved to be a much broader, more imposing barrier to transcontinental commerce and settlement than he had anticipated. Nevertheless, within a remarkably short time, the federal government had gathered accurate knowledge of the trans-Mississippi West and the latitude and longitude of major geographical features. Detailed topographic and geologic maps were produced later by cartographers of Powell's generation.

The failure to preserve the scientific collections of Jefferson's great captains of exploration had been redressed. The creation of the Smithsonian Institution, established in time for the burst of federal exploration at mid-century, provided a haven for America's naturalists and their collections. Thanks to the foresight of Joseph Henry and Spencer Baird, the Smithsonian's program of describing, illustrating, and publishing new contributions to science worldwide, as well as preserving and cataloging the collections of the many government expeditions, made it a leader in international science. The Smithsonian marked its own entry into the 20th century by constructing the National Museum of Natural History, a massive showcase across the Mall from the Castle where the scientific legacy of the nation's 19th-century expeditions continues to be preserved, studied, and exhibited.

Chief among Jefferson's instructions to Lewis and Clark had been that they observe the nature, habits, and customs of the Indian "nations or tribes" they encountered. Jefferson required this information for both economic and military expediency. Trading with Indians was a major mercantile activity in the early years of the republic, and the new nation, if it harbored continental aspirations, needed to know the character and military disposition of the tribesmen beyond its borders. As a result, every expedition after Lewis and Clark made the collecting of information about Native Americans a matter of some importance. Even after the Civil War, when Indians no longer posed a threat to national security and had lost much of their economic importance as well, expeditions continued to furnish reports on them.

Although each of the four great post-Civil War surveys except Clarence King's observed Indians to some degree, Powell, to quote historian Wallace Stegner, "studied them with a passion." Gaining the trust and confidence of the plateau tribes of the Southwest, the one-armed explorer moved easily among them, recording customs, myths, and languages in scholarly detail. He did not use military escorts, even though he traveled through territory patrolled by some of the region's most militant tribes.

Thanks to Powell's interest and encouragement, Congress created the Bureau of Ethnology in 1879, appropriating $20,000 to support its work. Placed under the auspices of the Smithsonian Institution, the bureau—whose name was eventually changed to the Bureau of American Ethnology—was to be the repository of the "archives, records, and material relating to the Indians of North America, collected by the geographical and geological survey of the Rocky Mountains." To no one's surprise, Major Powell was named the first director of the bureau, a post he held until his death in 1902. Although the Bureau of American Ethnology was recently merged into the Smithsonian's Department of Anthropology, its archives remain intact in the National Anthropological Archives, where they constitute one

Eighty years of exploration, observation, and cartographic technique separate these two 19th-century maps. Opposite, a map titled "Louisiana" from the 1804 A New and Elegant General Atlas, *drawn by Aaron Arrowsmith and Samuel Lewis, reflects the lack of knowledge of the West and particularly of the mighty barrier of the Rockies before the return of the expedition led by Meriwether Lewis and William Clark in 1806. Left, John Wesley Powell's 1879 map of the rainfall patterns of the continent includes accurate details of the West's topography, executed with cartographic methods familiar to us today.*

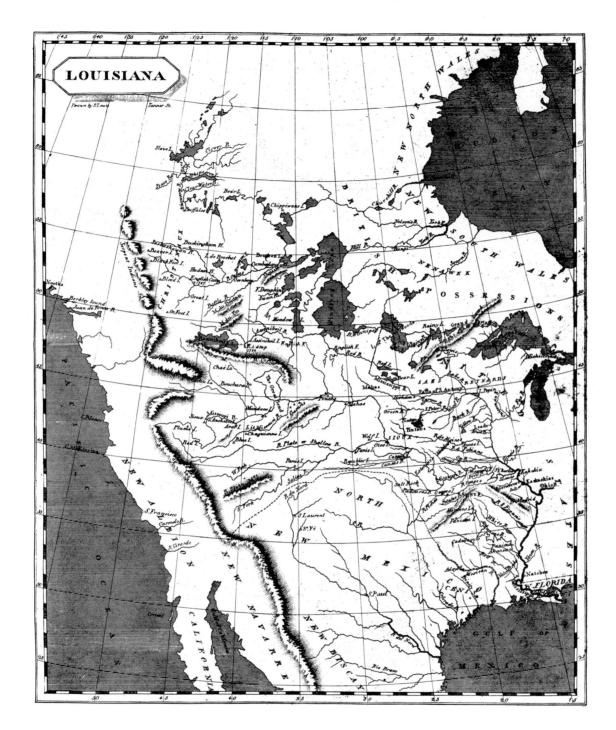

of the world's most important research collections on the Indian tribes of North America.

Powell's focus on the land and its uses was as Jeffersonian as his interest in Indian cultures. In fact, his studies of the Indians and their adaptations to the harsh environment of the Southwest led him to become deeply concerned about the conditions affecting agricultural development in arid regions, which include most of the western United States. Land-use policies developed a century earlier for the more humid East still governed the classification of lands for settlement and the allocation of water rights in the western mountains, dry plateaus, and deserts.

Powell recognized that such standards were unrealistic as well as unwise, his opinions running counter, quite naturally, to the rosy hopes of those who sought to control and exploit the West's water resources.

The Powell position on the administration of the arid lands of the West held sway in the expansionist post-Civil War United States only in the early years of his successful leadership of the new U.S. Geological Survey, and only while his Congressional backers could outvote those western politicians who found his views in opposition to their dreams. A fluke of legislative language had given Powell the unfettered right to spend the

appropriations for the U.S.G.S. without further Congressional oversight. Eventually, though, the powerful Major overstepped his bounds. Using money tagged for building reservoirs to make more topographic maps, and ignoring the growing strength of the western booster sentiment in the Congress, Powell had his funds and his clout removed. The ideas he had for the prudent development of the arid lands west of the 100th meridian came to some fruition in the mid-20th century, but not before the defeated veteran of the budgetary wars of Capitol Hill had long since departed the scene.

As the 19th century drew to a close, Jefferson's vision of the West as a land of yeoman farmers tending tidy homesteads remained largely unrealized. Instead, the West became a patch-work of conflicting interests that included homesteaders, ranchers, miners, railroaders, surveyors, and scientists. The tide of westward migration had reached new highs after the Civil War: more than four million settlers crossed the 100th meridian between 1875 and 1880 alone.

Few of these emigrants shared Powell's perspective. A far more typical outlook was that of the optimistic L. P. Brockett, author of the illustrated guidebook *Our Western Empire: or the New West Beyond Mississippi*. Listing the great pathfinder John C. Frémont (governor of Arizona Territory at the time) as one of his informants, Brockett provided his readers with 1,312 pages about the West's 11 states and territories and their ample attractions for the farmer, the rancher, and the speculator. "No pains nor expense," he claimed, "has been spared to gain from every source every fact which could illustrate their topography, geol-

Director of the Bureau of Ethnology and one of the most formidable figures of American science during the late 19th century, John Wesley Powell, left, works in his Smithsonian Institution office in 1894. Artist and archaeologist William Henry Holmes created the Bureau of Ethnology insignia, above, in 1879, using cliff dwelling and pictograph motifs from the Southwest.

ogy and mineralogy, climate, soil, productions, mineral wealth, pastoral facilities, population, accumulated wealth, education and religion, with notices of Indian tribes found in their borders."

Although Brockett admitted that there remained perhaps "a small modicum of truth" to the old idea of "a Great American Desert," he held that it was, nevertheless, largely a myth. Railroads were as important as rain to a region's development, in Brockett's view. He attributed the phenomenal 900 percent increase in the population of Dakota Territory, for example, to "the great enterprise and energy with which the railroads have opened the land to settlement and markets." In Frémont's Ari-

zona, growth had been at a more modest 400 percent, retarded by arid climate, hostile Apaches, and the lack of rail lines and wagon roads. "These difficulties are now in the course of removal," Brockett enthusiastically predicted, "the Southern Pacific having reached Tucson."

Indeed, the railroads more than anything else facilitated the rapid and dramatic transformation of the West. In 1871, for example, Albert Bierstadt made his third trip through the American West, crossing the heart of the continent to San Francisco in just six days. His first trip, 12 years earlier with the Lander expedition, had been a jolting, back-wrenching, five-month ordeal by wagon and horseback. In the decade between 1867 and 1877, John Wesley Powell traveled from the East to the Rockies and beyond some 30 times, and every trip after 1869 involved going at least part way by rail. Emigrants, explorers, scientists—all were riding the iron horse as the 19th century drew to a close. (In this new age of steam travel, did it seem possible that Frémont had once suggested that travelers *in extremis* could always eat a mule?)

Hastening the advance of the railroad had been the promise of rich mineral deposits hidden in the recesses of the mountainous West. This promise also magnified the role of the geologist and prompted Congress to create in the last quarter of the 19th century several agencies devoted to the earth sciences. Beginning in 1883, comprehensive surveys of general and economic geology were published annually in *Mineral Resources of the United States*. This report reflected the growing importance of statistical analysis in monitoring our nation's natural resources. A concerted effort was begun to locate mineral deposits and investigate on a systematic basis the geological history of the earth's crust.

The search for minerals also led to the discovery of incredibly rich deposits of fossil vertebrates. These discoveries, in turn, opened up an entirely different area of research and, regrettably, of competition as well. The dinosaur became a *cause célèbre*, as paleontologists fought like the creatures whose bones they exhumed in their frenzied effort to be first—first to find, first to identify, and then first to publish their fossils.

Union Pacific railroad men pose with their locomotive on a temporary wooden trestle over the Green River at Green River Station, Wyoming Territory, *1868. Workers raise a permanent stone bridge at left. As if to underscore the effect of railroads on western exploration, John Wesley Powell, his party, and their four boats traveled by rail* *from Chicago to Green River in the spring of 1869 to begin their epic transit of the Grand Canyon of the Colorado.*

Although Baird and his far-flung collectors participated in the competition for the scientific bounty lying within the sedimentary strata, they labored in the shadow of Professor Othniel C. Marsh of Yale University, the first professor of paleontology in America. Marsh was 37 before he first saw the West, courtesy of the Union Pacific. In 1868, after attending a professional meeting in Chicago, he took a railroad-sponsored scientific excursion to what was then the end of the line 60 miles beyond Benton, Wyoming Territory, just east of Rawlins. His conviction as he crossed the Green River that "entombed in the soft sandy clays . . . there must be the remains of many strange animals new to science" launched what was to be a 30-year career as one of the most prodigious paleontological collectors in United States history. "My first lesson in investigating the wonderful region," he later wrote, ". . . gave me the key to one chapter of its history, and from this other chapters opened one by one as year after year I returned West with ever-increasing zeal to continue the work."

Marsh combined scholarly genius with luck. He had started his life's work as a scientist while still a boy in upstate New York, accumulating fossils dug up by workmen building the Erie Canal. He was fortunate in both his mentors and his relatives: Colonel Ezekiel Jewett, Benjamin Silliman, Jr., and James Dwight Dana were his teachers, and George Peabody, founder of Yale's Peabody Museum, was his uncle. Independently wealthy, Marsh worked without salary in order to be free to explore and collect. And collect he did. With Yale students as laborers, the Union Pacific as his base of operations, and cavalry escorts for protection, Marsh quickly established himself as the nation's foremost paleontologist.

The cavalry was on hand because the best fossil beds were often found on lands that had been set aside for or were still claimed by Indians, many of whom bitterly resented continuing encroachments on their territory by whites. Their animosity, however, did not deter Marsh, who had the temerity to seek fossils in the Black Hills and the Badlands during the height of the Sioux wars. Invited by military friends to inspect fossil finds in the Badlands region south of the Black Hills, Marsh arrived at the Red Cloud Indian Agency near the promising fossil field on November 4, 1874, and began to plan his expedition. Recent discoveries of gold in the Black Hills, however, had stirred things up considerably, and the Sioux chiefs were in no mood to give their consent to Marsh's expedition. Wearying of delays and reluctant Indians, Marsh slipped out of camp just after midnight, located the fossil beds, loaded several wagons with bones, and then left the region just in time to elude a Sioux war party intent on finding the "Big Bone Chief."

Marsh later made amends to the Sioux by helping Chief Red Cloud expose flagrant abuses by officials of the Bureau of Indian Affairs. Thanks in part to his efforts, Congress forced the resignation of the Secretary of the Interior and other key officials of the Grant administration involved in the scandal. According to the *Nation,* which gave Marsh more credit than he probably deserved, ". . . there was only on the side of the Indians and the people of the United States a college professor doing work to

No sooner had the explorers and surveyors moved on than the farmers, miners, loggers, ranchers, oilmen, and others moved in. By the beginning of the 20th century, many of the West's resources were exploited, some already abused. From top to bottom: lumbermen use a "yarding donkey," or winch, to skid felled logs of Douglas fir in Washington, 1908; land-rush lawyers set up open-air offices, Guthrie, Oklahoma Territory, 1889; a Texas herd on the trail to a Kansas railhead.

From top to bottom: in Nebraska, homesteading former slaves pose before their "soddy," or sod house; gold-seekers pan for the precious metal in Rockerville, Dakota, 1889; would-be miners file over the Chilkoot Pass in 1898 during Alaska's Gold Rush.

which he had never been trained, and incited only by the desire to do his duty."

As Marsh's fame grew, so did efforts to enlist his paleontological services on behalf of the government. Such a connection did not interest him, however. As he explained to Baird and others, his collections had been made at his own expense and were his personal property. If he worked for the government, he would no longer be able to retain or control what he found. Eventually, though, as he later wrote, "the proposal made to me to aid the Government was more favorably presented by both the Director of the Geological Survey and Professor Baird," and on July 1, 1882, he agreed to serve as "Paleontologist in the U.S. Geological Survey." Five years later, he accepted an appointment as honorary curator in the Department of Vertebrate Paleontology of the United States National Museum, a position he held until his death in 1899.

Even though the special arrangement allowed Marsh to keep a set of type specimens for himself, Baird did not complain. Seeing only a small portion of these on a visit to Yale in 1871, the Smithsonian's ever-effusive assistant secretary claimed Marsh had collected more fossils of scientific value than all the other expeditions to the West had been able to obtain for the Institution. The extent of Marsh's cooperation, however, was not fully realized until after his death. According to an inventory of the material at Yale destined for deposit in the National Museum, the Smithsonian received 1,200 trays of specimens, 200 boxes from the field that had never been opened, and 90 prepared specimens. Five freight cars were required to ship this material, which weighed some 80 tons. In addition, Marsh himself had sent the Smithsonian two car loads in the years preceding his death. According to Charles D. Walcott, who had succeeded Powell as director of the U.S. Geological Survey, the actual number of specimens in the Marsh collection, which ranged from "minute teeth of fossil mammals to individual specimens weighing from 500 to 2,000 pounds each," could not be determined.

Among friends, Marsh was something of a raconteur, and he was proud of his knowledge of bones. Once, when a friend from one of his New York clubs asked him to identify a small bone that had been part of someone's dinner and then become the subject of a wager, Marsh promptly telegraphed: "Left shin bone of a big bull frog. Double your bet and let me in."

Unfortunately, despite his profound knowledge of vertebrate paleontology, Marsh failed to leave any finished manuscripts for the comprehensive monographs he intended to write. As a result, his material had to be restudied by others who did not possess his depth of understanding. Marsh, one of his colleagues later remarked, "planned his life-work on the basis that immortality is here and not in the hereafter. It seemed difficult for him to realize the limitations of human existence and worldly accomplishment."

Marsh zealously defended his prerogatives, particularly when it came to what he considered his own special reserves. One colleague who became his bitter rival for the prehistoric boneyards of the West was Edward Drinker Cope, a veteran of the Wheeler and Hayden surveys. Born nine years apart, Marsh and Cope died within two years of each other at the turn of the century, having dominated the field of vertebrate paleontology for nearly 40 years. Both men were wealthy and able to pursue

Yale University professor and paleontologist Othniel Charles Marsh led many fossil-seeking expeditions into the West, including four staffed by Yale students between 1870 and 1873. Marsh, top row center, poses at left with well-armed members of the 1872 Yale expedition. Although a tireless champion of Indian rights, Marsh had many army friends and secured cavalry escorts for his journeys at no cost. Opposite, in Night Halt of the Cavalry, by Frederic Remington, tired troopers and their mounts catch a few moments' rest in a scene that Marsh and his young fossil-hunters might have witnessed.

their careers without worrying about the cost of funding and outfitting their expeditions. They were among the last of the great field collectors of the American West, and their prominence, due to both family connections and academic ties, attracted assistance from all quarters, from frontier adventurers and prospectors to eastern university professionals.

Their competition, always intense, erupted in 1877 into a poisonous vendetta that reshaped the course of paleontological exploration and research. That spring, two Colorado schoolteachers, each with a keen interest in natural history and each unaware of the other, were roaming about in search of specimens. Less than 100 miles apart, they both made exciting discoveries of dinosaur bones. As fate would have it, one sent word of his find to Marsh in New Haven; the other alerted Cope in Philadelphia. The news set off a series of cloak-and-dagger intrigues by the two paleontologists. Each tried to bar the other from access to the bones; each enlisted armies of diggers and raced to excavate and publish. The two initial sites—near what

today are Morrison and Cañon City, Colorado—were rich, and a third site west of Laramie, Wyoming, was later characterized as "the greatest dinosaur field in the world." Inevitably, however, the acrimonious strife between Marsh and Cope robbed their work of some of its scientific importance.

Not altogether different, as we have seen, was the rivalry between government agencies that finally forced Congress to grapple with the larger question of how to control the overlapping and competing surveys and expeditions of the 1870s. The army was sponsoring two major geological surveying expeditions under Wheeler and King, the Department of the Interior was sponsoring the Hayden Survey, and the Department of the Treasury the Coast and Geodetic Survey. Even the General Land Office had parties in the field determining how land should be parceled out to settlers. Only the Powell Survey of the Colorado and of the Plateau Province enjoyed for at least a few years a certain detachment from the political turmoil, because an error by a Congressional authorization committee had placed Powell and

his work under the administration of the Smithsonian Institution.

While Congressional appropriations and the money that flowed to each survey helped define the influence and importance of its leader, the area within which each survey was mandated to operate was equally important. Each of the great surveys had several divisions with many teams operating in the field simultaneously. It was thus probably inevitable that parties of the Wheeler and Hayden surveys would find themselves camped next to each other in July of 1873 in what is today the Twin Lakes region of Colorado, bringing to public attention the fact that government exploration in the West was resulting in wasteful duplication. Although the rival Hayden and Wheeler groups were each working in an officially assigned area, the bad feelings engendered by their chance meeting sparked a Congressional investigation by the Townsend Committee in 1874.

During the hearings, Hayden bitterly accused Wheeler of invading his assigned area, while Powell observed that Wheeler had surveyed some 26,000 square miles already covered by Powell's field crews. Real and perceived encroachments on the work of others by the Wheeler survey cast an unfortunate shadow over its noteworthy accomplishments. But despite considerable testimony, much of it from Powell, Congress failed to consolidate and unify the western surveys.

Yet the seeds of reform had been sown. Of particular interest had been the question of whether the survey authority should rest with civilians or the military. When, in 1877, President Rutherford B. Hayes appointed conservationist Carl Schurz as Secretary of the Interior, the balance shifted in favor of civilian authority, a change much favored by the scientific community.

In 1878, Powell, Hayden, and Wheeler were asked to submit reports summarizing the work of their surveys to the House Appropriations Committee. The committee then asked the National Academy of Sciences to review the current status of western surveys and present Congress with its recommendations. Since the president of the academy, Joseph Henry, died before he could appoint a committee to consider the request, this task fell to the organization's vice president, who happened to be Othniel Marsh.

Othniel Marsh and his colleagues discovered an astonishing number of significant fossils, including Hesperornis regalis, *far left, a great flightless bird— with teeth—that had inhabited the shores of a shallow sea in the middle of North America about 70 million years ago. His collection of dinosaur fossils was unprecedented in its time; some are exhibited today in the Smithsonian's National Museum of Natural History, opposite. On an 1874 fossil-hunting trip near the Black Hills of today's South Dakota, Marsh ignored Sioux leaders' warnings to stay away from their territory and narrowly escaped capture by angry Sioux pursuers. Nonetheless, appalled at the corruption he found among government agents at the Sioux Red Cloud Agency, Marsh took up their cause with such effect that the ensuing uproar led to the resignation of President Ulysses S. Grant's Secretary of the Interior. In 1883 Sioux chief Red Cloud visited Marsh in New Haven, where this photograph was taken.*

Sacred to the Sioux and ceded to them by treaty, the Black Hills of South Dakota contained gold as well as fossils. In 1874, surveyors escorted by elements of the Seventh Cavalry under the command of Lieutenant Colonel George A. Custer penetrated the area, reigniting hostilities with the Sioux and other plains tribes that would cost Custer and a third of the Seventh their lives on the Little Bighorn River two years later.

Amid accusations from Cope that Marsh had stacked the deck against the military and Hayden (with whom Cope was on comfortable terms), the academy committee endorsed a Powell report that recommended a new public lands policy for the arid West and the creation of the United States Geological Survey. When western Congressmen, who feared the policy would exclude settlers, succeeded in blocking the original bill (largely drafted by Powell), a modified version was attached to the Sundry Civil Expenses Bill of 1879 and passed both houses of Congress. As a result, with the U.S.G.S. under civilian control, the death knell was struck for Wheeler and the military, and the surveys then in the field were abolished.

One member of the academy committee who must have taken special interest in the questions before it was James Dwight Dana. In appointing his mentor and colleague from Yale to the committee, Marsh recognized Dana's "long experience as a geologist and naturalist of the Wilkes Exploring Expedition," claiming that his "subsequent residence in Washington, while preparing his report, had especially fitted him to advise on government work." Marsh might well have added that Dana, a veteran of an expedition captained by a dictatorial and exacting military officer, would certainly have voted in favor of civilian control. Wilkes, after all, as Dana later wrote, "failed in never praising his officers but always finding fault with them and often unjustly; especially when he had prejudices the screws came down rather severely."

Of the several groups lobbying to influence the Congressional decision, the alliance formed by Marsh, Powell, and Clarence King clearly prevailed. King was appointed the first director of the new U.S.G.S., edging out Hayden, who had campaigned vigorously for the job. King served in the post for only a year, but in that time he established an administrative structure that stressed the importance of economic geology and the need to inventory the nation's mineral resources. Hayden was retained as one of the principal geologists with the Survey.

Powell, who succeeded King as director, shifted the emphasis of the new agency toward ethnology, paleontology, and the compilation of a national topographic map. True to his earlier writings, he also sought to reform the distribution of land according to the availability of water. His approach, predictably, irritated western politicians, and the manner in which he handled the Irrigation Survey by withdrawing public lands from settlement cost him support in Congress. Accused of being a poor planner, Powell eventually found himself and his agency politically isolated. The Secretary of the Interior, working behind the scenes, forced Powell to resign in 1894, though he remained director of the Bureau of American Ethnology until his death almost a decade later.

Charles D. Walcott, one of Powell's able lieutenants, succeeded him as director of the U.S.G.S. When he joined the Survey in 1879, Walcott had already published several papers on trilobites, and in 1884 he published *The Cambrian Faunas of North America*. According to G. K. Gilbert, Powell's top geologic assistant, Walcott transformed the Survey into "a great engine of research."

Another Powell assistant of note was geologist and poet Clarence Dutton, whose *Tertiary History of the Grand Cañon District*, illustrated by W. H. Holmes and published in 1882, still stands as a monument to his literary and scientific talent. Dutton volunteered for the army in 1862, two years after graduating from Yale at the age of 19. Stationed early on at Watervliet Armory near Albany, New York, Dutton was drawn to James Hall's paleontology museum, and his interest in geology and paleontology grew apace. A later posting to Washington brought him to Powell's attention, and, with Joseph Henry's assistance, Dutton was detailed from the Ordnance Corps to the Geological Survey. Working in the Plateau Province for the next 15 years, Dutton produced lyrical monographs that supported and extended the original Powell thesis—that the high plateaus of Utah, northern Arizona, and the Grand Canyon were the result of erosion, not catastrophe.

G. K. Gilbert was the perfect professional complement for his friend Dutton. Classically educated and then trained by John Strong Newberry, Gilbert honed his skills as a working member of the Wheeler and Powell surveys. He took on some of the major physiographic questions raised by the Powell survey, and revealed his analytical brilliance in his *Report on the Geology of the Henry Mountains* and his monograph on Lake Bonneville. Gilbert was a geologist's geologist, his research and contributions as admired in his own time as they are today. In 1879 he was appointed senior geologist of the U.S.G.S., and in 1889 became its chief geologist. An excellent administrator and editor, Gilbert gave loyal aid and comfort to Powell. But his removal from the field represented a great loss of his talent as a research geologist. His scientific work declined in Washington, and he sympathized with Dutton's complaints about "more clerks, more rules, more red tape, less freedom of movement, less discretion on the part of the geologist and less turn-out of scientific products."

But Gilbert gave his nostalgia for the field a comic twist and turned it to good account. He and several other former field men, now desk-bound bureaucrats, began meeting for picnic lunches in the Survey office. They called themselves the Great Basin Mess and sometimes went so far as to pretend they were back in Utah, bringing in camp gear and sitting on packs. The fare became more and more elaborate, until gradually the jolly crowd that had grown out of the little group had to hire a chef. The Great Basin Mess had become a social and professional forum, an important—if unofficial—branch of the Survey.

In Charles Walcott the U.S.G.S. found a leader who could resolve many of the difficulties of politics and priorities that had mired the Survey under King and Powell. Like Marsh, Walcott was introduced to paleontology during his boyhood near the Erie Canal; like Dutton, he came into the orbit of James Hall. He served in the field and in the office under both King and Powell, and he learned his lessons well.

Walcott became a consummate bureaucrat, so accomplished politically that Congress regularly increased Survey appropriations above the amounts he requested. He was destined to direct the U.S.G.S. for 13 years and then, beginning in 1907, to cap his distinguished scientific and administrative career by serving for two decades as Secretary of the Smithsonian Institution. Thus did one individual personify the intricate web of relationships between the federal government, the scientific community, and the Smithsonian first woven by Joseph Henry and Spencer Baird 60 years earlier.

Exploration of the American West had come full circle as well. The 19th century had opened with a dramatic crossing of the continent by two great captains of discovery, Meriwether Lewis and William Clark. It closed with another expedition of discovery, this one led by the great captain of industry, railroad tycoon Edward Henry Harriman. One measure of difference, however, is especially striking. The first transcontinental trek took the better part of two years; in 1899 Harriman reached the Pacific in less than a week. The millionaire capitalist purportedly harbored visions of digging a tunnel under the Bering Strait, thereby linking American Alaska with Russian Siberia as part of a globe-girdling railroad. It was a dream that would have brought smiles of recognition from the likes of John Ledyard, Thomas Jefferson, Thomas Hart Benton, and John Jacob Astor. Whether Harriman seriously considered such a plan is open to question, but it is possible. His business was finance, not exploration.

In any event, the Harriman Alaska Expedition was peculiarly a product of the Gilded Age. It began with advice from Harriman's physician to take a vacation—a restful week or two hunting, perhaps in Alaska. Harriman elaborated his doctor's recommendation into a full-blown expedition, promising its members the opportunity to collect specimens and data along the way. What exactly his motivation was has never been clear, but Harriman managed to assemble one of the most unusual expeditions of the 19th century. In addition to 14 members of his family, the expedition included 25 of the nation's most prestigious scientists, as well as artists, photographers, and taxidermists. Even a chaplain came along.

Everyone traveled first class. Riding aboard the Union Pacific Railroad—for which Harriman served as Chairman of the Board—the group left New York City on May 23, 1899, crossing the continent in six days. Upon reaching Seattle, they boarded an ancient iron steamship, the *George W. Elder,* and began a leisurely two-month cruise along the Alaskan coast.

Lending legitimacy to this cruise as a scientific expedition

William Henry Holmes's illustrations for the United States Geological Survey's Tertiary History of the Grand Cañon District *distinguished it as perhaps the most beautiful work of its kind ever published. Undertaken by Clarence Dutton under the direction of Survey chief John Wesley Powell,* *it included this view of the valley of the Virgin River. Named for a fancied resemblance to the Institution's "Castle," Smithsonian Butte is in the background.*

were such men as William Dall, John Burroughs, John Muir, C. Hart Merriam, and half a dozen other botanists, geologists, and naturalists. Getting the cooperation of this eminent group had proven relatively simple, thanks to Merriam, who was chief of the Biological Survey of the Department of Agriculture and the expedition's unofficial scientific organizer. With the promise that Harriman would bear all costs—including the salaries of those scientists unable to afford a leave of absence from their posts—Merriam managed to assemble the impressive entourage even though most of the participants must have realized that the two-month trip would hardly permit much serious research. The scientists who accepted the offer of an all-expenses-paid junket must have done so simply for the opportunity to see Alaska, for only two of them, Dall and Muir, could claim any familiarity with the terrain, and Muir joined on the strength of assurances that the expedition would go farther into Alaska than he had already gone.

The unlikely assemblage of personnel and the trip's opulent accommodations must have caused some of the veteran explorers to ask themselves the same questions that naturalist John Burroughs, uprooted from his Hudson River retreat by Harriman's invitation, jotted in his journal: "Have I made a mistake in joining this crowd for so long a trip? Can I see nature under such conditions?"

For most of the explorers, the ease and comfort in which they now crossed the continent awakened memories of more arduous trips. As their special train passed through Green River Station

Obeying doctor's orders to take time off from business, railroad tycoon Edward H. Harriman, opposite, organized a scientific voyage to Alaska in 1899. Opposite bottom, a ferry carrying members of the Harriman party crosses the Snake River in Idaho—a side trip on the way to Seattle to meet their steamer, the George W. Elder, *below, and set off for Alaska.*

in Wyoming, artist Frederick Dellenbaugh peered through the windows of the smoking car "Utopia" and was certain he spotted the cove from which he had embarked as a teenager with John Wesley Powell's second Colorado River expedition almost three decades earlier. Anthropologist George Bird Grinnell reminisced about the days in 1874 when he accompanied the flamboyant Lieutenant Colonel George Custer as naturalist on the infamous Black Hills Expedition, which discovered gold and thereby sealed the fate of the Sioux for whom those sacred hills had been reserved "forever."

Indeed, quite a few members of the Harriman group were veterans of the great surveys. Merriam saw to it, for example, that invitations went to chief geographer for the U.S. Geological Survey Henry Gannett, ornithologist Robert Ridgway, now curator of birds at the Smithsonian, and artist Robert Swain Gifford. All had been his trail companions when he visited the Yellowstone country with Hayden in 1872. Ridgway's experiences went back even further: in the late 1860s, at the age of 16, he had been a member of Clarence King's Fortieth Parallel Survey. Still another veteran explorer was 71-year-old Yale professor William H. Brewer, who had worked with King in the California state survey during the Civil War.

Not all the members of the group had already established their professional reputations, however. One whose name was soon to eclipse all the others was Edward Curtis, at the time a society portrait photographer from Seattle. Merriam had met Curtis while climbing Mount Rainier and invited him along to

Included in Harriman's party were 14 members of his family, 25 of the nation's leading scientists, naturalist-writers John Muir and John Burroughs, and assistants and crew—126 souls in all. Entirely financed by Harriman, the two-month voyage was one of the first great scientific surveys of Alaska, and perhaps the most remarkable private scientific expedition of all time. The three men who prepared the illuminated chart, right, of the voyage exemplify the character of the party: Henry Gannett, Chief Geographer, U.S. Geological Survey; Frederick S. Dellenbaugh, an artist who had accompanied John Wesley Powell on one of his trips down the Colorado River; and Louis Agassiz Fuertes, who would become perhaps the greatest of all painters of birds.

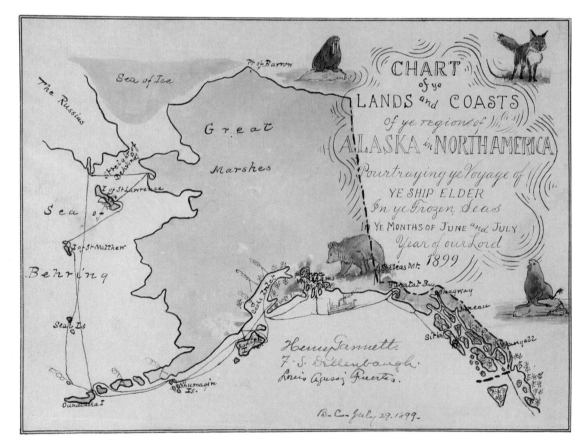

Eskimos eager to sell handi-crafts, left, often met the George W. Elder; *crowding their umiaks, or hide-covered boats, these Eskimos were encountered at Port Clarence, on the Seward Peninsula of Alaska. Walrus hides and whale bones served as construction materials for Eskimo hunters at Plover Bay, in Siberia, below, when the Harriman expedition briefly stopped in Asia.*

Harriman expedition members Frederick S. Dellenbaugh (left) and Daniel G. Elliot examine a totem pole at Wrangell, in southeastern Alaska. Russian influence was still strong in Alaska in 1899, when Harriman party member G. K. Gilbert photographed this church and hotel in Sitka, right.

serve as the Harriman expedition's official cameraman. Before many years were to pass, Curtis would establish himself as the premier photographer of the American Indian.

For two months the Harriman expedition proceeded up the Alaskan coast, stopping frequently for day-long excursions into the interior, where the explorers observed Indians and Eskimos and met with those few pioneers who had established a life for themselves in this vast frontier. Sometimes little parties of scientists, hungering for a closer, more leisurely look at some point of professional curiosity, were given the opportunity to wander off alone for a few days. At other times, they must have felt some of Edward Drinker Cope's frustration as he tried to conduct scientific research in the atmosphere of Wheeler's military survey. "It is absurd," he had written in 1874, "to order stops here, where there are no fossils, and marches there, where fossils abound!"

With so many scientists and so little opportunity to collect, ruffled feelings and frustration were often the order of the day. Writing about the expedition half a century later, Thomas Kearney, a scientist with the Department of Agriculture, recalled one of the botanists coming back to camp at night and spotting what he took to be clumps of "cotton grass" in a marsh. As the delighted botanist began collecting the grass, one of the ornithologists came rushing out of his tent. "Hey, you damn old fool," he shouted, "what do you think you are doing?" The cotton grass turned out to be markers for bird traps. Kearney

Amateur photographer as well as geologist, G. K. Gilbert captured images of pack ice at Glacier Bay, opposite below, in southeastern Alaska, and Columbia Glacier, in Prince William Sound, left. Salmonberries collected by naturalist-writer John Burroughs for his lunch were illustrated, above left, in the 13-volume report of the Harriman expedition, published in 1902. Despite initial misgivings, famed conservationists John Burroughs (in boots) and John Muir, opposite top right, delighted in the Harriman expedition, entertaining other members with poems and sprightly country dances recollected from youth. Young Louis Agassiz Fuertes, painter of the harlequin ducks, opposite above left, also regarded the trip as one of the most memorable interludes of his life.

Official photographer for the Harriman expedition Edward S. Curtis, later to become famous for his images of Indians, photographed members of the group at a deserted Indian village south of Juneau, Alaska, near the end of the voyage. Below right, his photograph of the symbol-covered front of a chief's house.

also recalled that Burroughs used to grumble at all the bird-shooting and egg-taking by the ornithologists. They had the last laugh at "Uncle John," however, when he returned from an excursion bearing a clutch of fox sparrow eggs.

Despite the difficulties of conducting research under such conditions, a few milestones were recorded. Some deserve recognition; some are better forgotten. G. K. Gilbert managed best, producing a monograph entitled *Glaciers and Glaciation* that is still consulted today. Harriman hired Merriam to edit the scientific results of the expedition to make sure that they would not be forgotten, but although 12 of the projected 13 volumes were eventually published, they did little to excite the academic community. Less laudable an achievement was the plundering of Indian villages. At one site, the explorers removed a number of massive totem poles, which were later distributed to various American museums.

In the end, some critics dismissed the Harriman expedition as more an indulgence than an exploration. But Muir was more kindly disposed. "Nearly all my life I wandered and studied alone," he later wrote. "On the *Elder,* I found not only the fields I liked best to study, but a hotel, a club, and a home, together with a floating university in which I enjoyed the instruction and companionship of a lot of the best fellows imaginable, culled and arranged like a well-balanced bouquet, or like a band of glaciers flowing smoothly together, each in its own channel, or perhaps at times like a lot of round boulders merrily swirling and chaffing against each other in a glacier pothole."

As for Harriman, his expedition proved personally satisfying. He shot a Kodiak bear, which had been his goal from the outset, and his wife succeeded in setting foot in Russian Siberia (at Plover Bay), which had been her goal. The whole family, including five-year-old Roland and eight-year-old Averell, had rubbed shoulders with some of the most eminent scientific figures of the day. Eventually, however, the expedition proved too much of a good thing for the restless financier. One evening near the end of the voyage, as Harriman sat on deck staring out to sea, one of the scientists hurried over and urged him to look towards shore at some glorious scenery. Harriman, who by now only wanted to get back to his business interests, growled, "I don't give a damn if I never see any more scenery!"

TOWARD A NEW SENSIBILITY

I n 1899, when Edward Harriman and his "explorers" set sail for Alaska, the American West had already entered a new era. Indeed, the eminent historian Frederick Jackson Turner had proclaimed the end of the frontier a decade earlier. Bonds of rail and wire now joined East with West, and the process of mythologizing the frontier was well under way. By 1890, when Turner made his portentous announcement, William F. "Buffalo Bill" Cody was mesmerizing eastern audiences with visions of a West that never was, while the bison, or buffalo, once seemingly numberless—and whose slaughter had earned Cody his early fame—was on the brink of extinction. Equally endangered was the Plains Indian, the other great symbol of the American West. That year saw the last of the Indian wars, when troopers of the Seventh Cavalry slaughtered a band of starving and freezing Sioux at Wounded Knee, an isolated wasteland in a far corner of the Pine Ridge Indian reservation.

The conquest of the Plains Indian and the destruction of the buffalo were merely the more visible manifestations of a reckless over-exploitation that threatened to deplete all the resources of the Far West. Timber, mining, railroading, and ranching interests dominated local and national legislatures, while prophets such as John Wesley Powell, who sought to persuade westerners that arid lands should not be settled beyond their capacity, were by and large ignored. Instead, all too many Americans chose to believe the "rain-follows-the-plow" credo of the land speculators, and as a result, by the end of the 19th century, with the ravaging of range land and forest continuing apace, the stage was set for the disastrous dust bowls of the 1920s and '30s.

Fortunately, the new era also witnessed the growth of a new sensibility toward the West, and a realization that its resources were no more infinite than the land itself—or the buffalo. Pioneer American conservationists included George Bird Grinnell, Gifford Pinchot, John Muir, and John Burroughs. They were joined by a host of realists and romantics, perhaps some of them disciples of the transcendentalists, who added their voices to the chorus begun by Hayden, Moran, and other preservationists to save some of the West's most scenic spots for posterity. Thanks to their efforts, Yellowstone National Park was soon joined by Yosemite, Grand Canyon, Bryce Canyon, Zion, and a score of other magnificent national parks across the country.

No longer vanishing, and in fact representing a powerful

Clearing Winter Storm (1944) *and other photographs of the valley of the Yosemite by Ansel Adams gave conservationists powerful ammunition in their struggle to convince Americans that the West's spectacular scenery was a resource in itself, intimately bound up in our national self-image.*

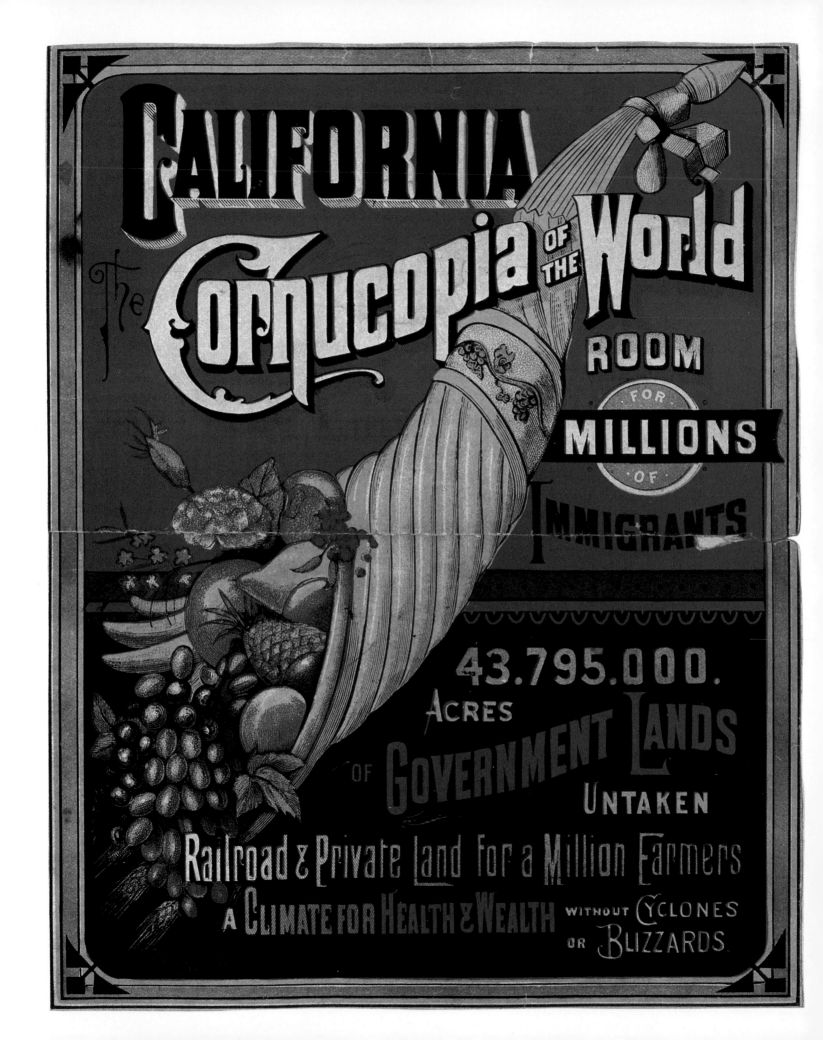

As the seemingly inexhaustible spaces and resources of the West began to be developed, the epic American myth of the "Winning of the West" flourished, reaching full bloom even before the end of the frontier.

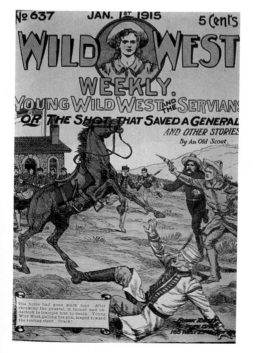

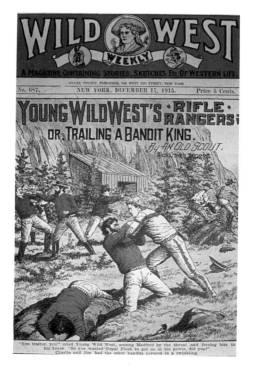

Youngsters—and, secretly, their parents—thrilled to "dime-novel" tales of heroes who faced death in a hundred frontier forms. Stampedes, besieged wagon trains, cavalry charges, and ruthless highwaymen beguiled away many a 19th-century afternoon. In the meantime, publicists for rail-roads and land companies seduced native-born easterners and immigrants alike with broadsides extolling the limitless virtues of the West.

Although the action-packed realism of Frederic Remington, Charles Russell, and others never lost favor with western art lovers, innovative painters like Maynard Dixon brought new styles to such big-sky works as Open Range (1942), above. Other artists found inspiration among the Indians of the West, most of whom had been defeated and confined to reservations. Taos, New Mexico, attracted a group of artists whose influence still colors western art: opposite top, Victor Higgins's Pueblo of Taos (before 1927), and opposite, Joseph Henry Sharp's Pipe Song (1923).

Overleaf: Angered by the needless slaughter of 150 Sioux at Wounded Knee, South Dakota, on December 29, 1890, some 4,000 Indians gathered in White Clay Valley near the Pine Ridge reservation. Quickly surrounded by 3,000 soldiers, they surrendered, and the wars between the whites and the Indians came to an end.

advocacy for a heritage to which they can lay particular claim, the American Indians have also been heavily involved in the conservation story of the 20th century. One of their most important allies in their struggle to preserve their cultures as well as the western landscape has been the Smithsonian Institution. Thanks to Spencer Baird and his legion of collectors, the National Museum of Natural History is now in the position of helping the western tribes reestablish their once proud cultures and languages.

This is probably one benefit of Baird's collecting mania that even he had not anticipated. And not only Indians, of course, but scholars and museum goers the world over are indebted to his foresight and vision, for his collections—specimens, journals, photographs, paintings, letters—are used constantly for research, publications, and exhibitions.

It was research for an exhibition based on those collections, in fact, that inspired this book. In November 1985, the National Museum of Natural History opened an exhibition entitled "Magnificent Voyagers: The U.S. Exploring Expedition, 1838–1842." Little did the team of curators working on that exhibition realize that it would lead, explorer-like, into areas of American history that few others had penetrated. Here was a handful of nameless sailors on six small ships daring to carry the American flag into remote corners of the world. Before returning to the welcome waters of the United States, they had challenged icebergs and confronted cannibals, losing both ships and shipmates in their quest for glory and knowledge. In the process they

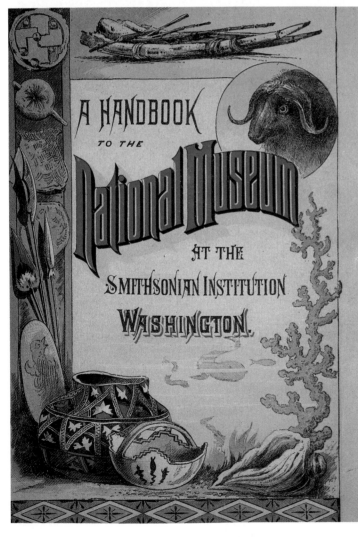

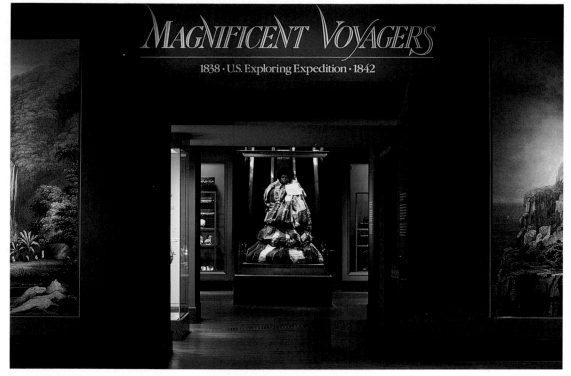

"He defined the Cambrian," said a contemporary of geologist and paleontologist Charles Doolittle Walcott, left. Director of the United States Geological Survey before he became the fourth Secretary of the Smithsonian, Walcott embodied the symbiotic relationship of the two institutions. By 1886, when the Smithsonian handbook, opposite, was published, the Institution's collections contained some two million specimens. Today they comprise about 100 million objects of every description, including the Zuni bowl, opposite above, collected by James Stevenson in the mid-1880s.

The Smithsonian's 1985 exhibit "Magnificent Voyagers," top, featured many specimens collected during the Wilkes expedition of over a century before, and brought American natural history and the Smithsonian full circle. One of 483 specimens collected by James D. Dana during the Wilkes voyage, the coral, above, can still be studied today, along with millions of other objects in the Smithsonian.

discovered a continent and carved a niche for themselves in the history of exploration. Yet, a century later, in their country's history books, their exploits were passed over with a sentence or two. Even less attention was given to the young naturalists and artists who accompanied them. Few but scholars remembered their contributions, and yet, without their selfless sacrifices, their willingness to share the dangers and privations of their shipmates, the Smithsonian Institution might well have taken a different course.

The discovery of such a great breadth of information about the Wilkes expedition, its personnel and collections, quite naturally led to the question, if so much material existed for that expedition, what about those that preceded—or followed—it? The answer is partly to be found in this book, which has attempted to rescue from oblivion some of the scientists, artists, and collectors, both civilians and soldiers, whose efforts contributed so much to our understanding and appreciation of the American West.

The desire to collect, or even explicit instructions to do so, did not necessarily presume a method of preservation or a place for such collections to be displayed. Indeed, as we have seen, much was lost by the early explorers, including most of the flora and fauna gathered by Lewis and Clark. Still, even for that expedition, bits and pieces remain.

And as we have also seen, the record for collections improved dramatically after the Smithsonian was established. Thus it is possible today to see and study the collections made by the U.S. Exploring Expedition around the world; the voluminous gatherings of naturalist-collector John Xantus from the sandy shores of Baja California; the samplings lifted from many a western outcrop by Ferdinand V. Hayden, John Wesley Powell, G. K. Gilbert, and their hundreds of coworkers. All of these vast collections, so painfully gathered during the 19th-century heyday of western exploration, today serve as priceless benchmarks by which change can be measured. They also serve as a solemn reminder that to preserve the American West we must become ever wiser in our stewardship of its resources. Begun by Jefferson as an inventory of national possibilities, the exploration of the West continues, and the materials collected by today's researchers will be preserved in the Smithsonian for the education and enjoyment of those of the 21st century.

For many Americans, Albert Bierstadt's The Oregon Trail, *painted in 1869, captures the romance of the westering movement. Through the golden haze of his sunset, we sense the courage of the thousands, now nameless, who braved dangers impossible to imagine today to find a new life beyond the Mississippi. Their courage was exceeded only by that of the soldiers and scientists who had opened the West for all who would follow.*

INDEX

Illustrations and caption references appear in *italic*.

ACKNOWLEDGMENTS

The Editors of Smithsonian Books would like to thank the following people for their assistance in the preparation of this book:

Mary Kay Davies, Ed Johnson, Ruth Schallert, and Ellen Wells, Smithsonian Institution Libraries; Felicia Pickering, Department of Anthropology, National Museum of Natural History/SI; Mary Ellen McCaffrey, Office of Printing and Photographic Services/SI; William A. Deiss, Smithsonian Archives; Harry Hunter, Division of Armed Forces, National Museum of American History/SI; June G. Armstrong; Elizabeth McLean; Marjorie Eyre; Ed Castle; Sarah E. Boehme, Whitney Gallery of Art, Buffalo Bill Historical Center; George Miles, Beinecke Rare Book and Manuscript Library, Yale University; Duane Sneddeker, Missouri Historical Society; A. D. Mastroguiseppe, Denver Public Library; John Hoover, St. Louis Mercantile Library Association; Carol Edwards, United States Geological Survey, Denver; Jonathan Heller, National Archives; Eric Paddock, Colorado Historical Society; Jeff Hunt, Museum of Western Art; Elizabeth Cunningham, The Anschutz Collection; Ann Morland, The Thomas Gilcrease Institute of American History and Art; David Hunt, Joslyn Art Museum; The Huntington Library; Carolyn McIntyre and Julie Schieber, Phil Jordan and Associates; Sidney P. Marland III, Donnelley Cartographic Services; Ronald Harlowe and Steve Smith, Harlowe Typography, Inc.; Bruce Cunningham, Stan Jenkins, and Harry Knapman, The Lanman Companies; Jerry Benitez and Sam Nutwell, Stanford Paper Company; Steve True, Lindenmeyr Paper Corporation; Rick Busick, ICG Incorporated; Ed Watters and Pete Jurgaitis, The Lehigh Press, Inc.; Gerald C. Pustorino and Walter Thompson, W.A. Krueger Company.

This book would not have been possible without the assistance of Pat Eames and Jan S. Danis. Indeed, they fully deserve to have their names on the title page with me, for they were a vital part of this effort from concept to completion. Pat not only coordinated the work of a corps of volunteers who assembled a monumental amount of material, but also she found time to research numerous topics for me and to draft sections of the manuscript itself. In this she was assisted by her husband Bill, who did biographical profiles of many of the key but obscure figures in the exploration story, thereby greatly simplifying the chore before me. Jan was not only my editor, but also a seemingly endless source of pithy statements and colorful quotations. Whenever stumped as to the direction I should take with a particular topic or in closing or opening a chapter, Jan invariably came up with the best solution.

I am also very grateful to the many volunteers and colleagues who contributed their time, talents, and energy to this project. Those who deserve special mention are Jean Admire, Howard Bennett, Fred Dalzell, Ralph Ehrenberg, William Kane, Jason Lunday, Martha Neebes, Howard Oiseth, June Robinson, Diane Schulz, Eleanor Schwartz, Cynda Wilcox, and Betty Youssef.

Working with the staff of Smithsonian Books was a real pleasure. I especially wish to thank Alex Doster, Patricia Gallagher, Amy Donovan, Nancy Strader, Patricia Upchurch, Jenny Takacs, Carrie Bruns, Bryan Kennedy, Anne Naruta, John Ross, and Louisa Woodville.

Finally, I wish to thank my wife, Susan, and my sons, Joe, Paul, and Peter, who had to listen to all my exploration stories.

Herman J. Viola

PICTURE CREDITS

Legend: B Bottom; C Center; L Left; R Right; T Top.

The following are abbreviations used to identify Smithsonian Institution museums and other collections.

SI Smithsonian Institution; NMAA National Museum of American Art; NMAH National Museum of American History; NMNH National Museum of Natural History; NPG National Portrait Gallery, SIA Smithsonian Institution Archives, SIL Smithsonian Institution Libraries.

APSL American Philosophical Society Library, Philadelphia; ANSP The Academy of Natural Sciences of Philadelphia; DPL Denver Public Library, Western History Division; ENRON/JAM Enron Art Foundation/Joslyn Art Museum, Omaha; INHPC Independence National Historical Park Collection, St. Louis; JAM Joslyn Art Museum, Omaha; LC Library of Congress; MHS Missouri Historical Society; NA National Archives; NYPL The New York Public Library; TGI The Thomas Gilcrease Institute of American History and Art, Tulsa; USGS U.S. Geological Survey, Denver.

Front Matter: p. 1 Alfred Jacob Miller, "Louis–Rocky Mountain Trapper," courtesy Buffalo Bill Historical Center, Cody, WY; 2–3 David Muench; 4–5 Tom Bledsoe/DRK Photo; 6–7 John Mix Stanley, "Encampment in the Teton Country," 1860, TGI; 8 art by Titian Ramsey Peale, APSL; 10–11 from William Henry Holmes, *Random Records of a Lifetime,* v. III, 1872, NMAA/NPG Library; 12 David Muench.

Jefferson's Vision: pp. 14–15 Leon Pomarede, "View of St. Louis," 1832, photo by Fernand Bourges, LIFE Magazine © 1950 Time Inc., courtesy Arthur Ziern; 16T art by Caleb Boyle, 1801, Kirby Collection of Historical Paintings, Lafayette College; 16B from Herman J. Viola, *The National Archives of the United States,* NY, 1984, Harry N. Abrams, Inc.; 16–17 Kenneth Garrett; 18 from Patrick Gass, *Journal of the voyages and travels of a corps of discovery, under the command of Capt. Lewis and Captain Clarke of the army of the United States,* Philadephia, 1811, SIL, photos by Ed Castle; 19T art by Charles Willson Peale, INHPC; 19B NMAH/SI, photo by Kim Nielsen; 20 art by Alfred Russell, The Bettmann Archive; 21 David Muench; 22 NMNH/SI, photo by Victor Krantz; 23T Peabody Museum, Harvard University, photo by Hillel Burger; 23B NMAH/SI, photos by Charles Rand; 24 Gary Braasch; 25 map art, courtesy R.R. Donnelley Cartographic Services, cartography, Julie Schieber, Washington, DC; 26 art by Charles Willson Peale, INHPC; 27T art by Frederic Remington for *Colliers Illustrated Weekly,* June 16, 1906, LC, photo by Ed Castle; 27B from Zebulon Montgomery Pike, *An account of expeditions to the sources of the Mississippi, and through the western parts of Louisiana,* Philadelphia, 1810, SIL, photo by Ed Castle; 28–29 George Rockwin/Bruce Coleman, Inc.; 30 art by Charles Willson Peale, INHPC; 31T Samuel Seymour, "Pawnee Council," Yale Collection of Western Americana, Beinecke Rare Book and Manuscript Library; 31B art by Titian Ramsey Peale, APSL; 32T Titian Ramsey Peale, "Bulls," APSL; 32B NA, photo by Ed Castle; 33L Yale Collection of Western Americana, Beinecke Rare Book and Manuscript Library; 33R Titian Ramsey Peale, "American Antelope," APSL; 34–35 Glenn Van Nimwegen; 36–37 Alfred Jacob Miller, "Jim Bridger in Armor at Green River," Walters Art Gallery; 38L from St. Louis Enquirer, 25 January 1823, MHS, neg.# L/A 13; 38R MHS, neg.# L-55A; 39T St. Louis Mercantile Library; 39B ENRON/JAM; 40T courtesy of John Clymer; 40BL Kansas State Historical Society; 40BR courtesy Colorado Historical Society; 41T Walters Art Gallery; 41BL courtesy Colorado Historical Society; 41BR courtesy Museum of New Mexico,

neg.# 13307; 43TL, 43TR art by George Catlin, TGI; 43B George Catlin, "View in the Grand Detour," TGI; 44 ANSP, photo by George Fistrovich; 45T John James Audubon, "American Beaver," MHS, neg.# L/A 5232; 45B art by John Woodhouse Audubon, American Museum of Natural History, neg.# 1498; 46 JAM; 47 ENRON/JAM; 48T Titian Ramsey Peale, "Missouri Bear," APS; 48B from Thomas Nuttall, *The North American Sylva,* v.3, Philadelphia, 1849, SIL, photo by Ed Castle; 49 Charles Willson Peale, "The Artist in his Museum," courtesy The Pennsylvania Academy of Fine Arts, Joseph and Sarah Harrison Collection.

From Sea to Shining Sea: pp. 50–51 courtesy Peabody Museum of Salem, photo by Chip Clark; 50T art by Thomas Sully, courtesy US Naval Academy Museum, private collection, photo by Chip Clark; 52T NMAH/SI, photo by Chip Clark; 52BL from *Thulia,* James C. Palmer, NY, 1843, photo by Chip Clark; 52BR courtesy ANSP, photo by Ed Castle; 53 from Herman J. Viola, *The National Archives of the United States,* NY, 1984, Harry N. Abrams, Inc.; 54T Philadelphia Museum of Art, photo by Chip Clark; 54B NMAH/SI, photo by Ed Castle; 55 art by Daniel Huntington, Yale University Art Gallery, bequest of Edward Salisbury Dana, photo by Chip Clark; 56T NMNH/SI, photo by Ed Castle; 56B from the Alfred T. Agate collection, courtesy Naval Historical Foundation, photo by Chip Clark; 57T Bernice Pauahi Bishop Museum, Honolulu; 57B, 58, 59T NMNH/SI, photos by Chip Clark; 59B engraving after Joseph Drayton drawing, Rare Books and Manuscripts Division, NYPL, Astor, Lenox and Tilden Foundations; 60L Oregon Historical Society; 60–61 Keith Gunnar/Bruce Coleman, Inc.; 62 LC; 63L courtesy The National Museum of Denmark, Dept. of Ethnography, photo by Chip Clark; 63R NMNH/SI, photo by Chip Clark; 64 NMNH/SI, photo by Charles H. Phillips; 65T SIA; 65B NMAH/SI, photo by Chip Clark; 66L Bass Otis, "Portrait of John Charles Frémont," 1856, NPG/SI on loan from The University of Michigan Museum of Art, bequest of Henry C. Lewis; 66R art by T. Buchanan Read, courtesy Southwest Museum, Los Angeles, photo by V. Tagland; 67 E. Anthony, 1855, MHS, neg.# B-122; 68 from John Charles Frémont, *Memoirs of My Life, a Retrospective of Fifty Years,* v.I, Chicago & New York, 1886, SIL, photo by Henry Eastwood; 69T map art, courtesy R.R. Donnelley Cartographic Services, cartography, Julie Schieber, Washington, DC; 69B NMAH/SI; 70 Glenn Van Nimwegen; 71 David Muench; 72–73 Alfred Jacob Miller, "Fort Laramie or Sublette's Fort," ENRON/JAM; 74–75 adapted from *The Expeditions of John Charles Frémont,*

University of Illinois Press, 1970, photo by Ed Castle; 76-77 Stark Museum of Art, Orange, TX; 78 from John Charles Frémont, *Memoirs of My Life*, v.I, Chicago & New York, 1886, SIL, photo by Ed Castle; 79T David Muench; 79B from Charles Preuss, *Exploring with Frémont: The Private Diaries of Charles Preuss, Cartographer for John C. Frémont on His First, Second and Fourth Expeditions to the Far West*, translated and edited by Erwin G. and Elisabeth K. Gudde, 1958, University of Oklahoma Press, Norman, photo by Ed Castle; 80 John Hovey, "Sutter's Fort, CA," courtesy The Huntington Library; 81 courtesy The Bancroft Library; 82, 83 art by John Torrey from John Charles Frémont, *Report of the Exploring Expedition to the Rocky Mountains, 1842, and Oregon and North California, 1843-44*, 1845, SIL, photo by Ed Castle; 84-85 mural study, NMAA/SI, bequest of Sara Carr Upton.

The Great Reconnaissance: pp. 86-87, 87R NMAH/SI, photos by Ed Castle; 88T NMNH/SI, photo by Ed Castle; 88B from Howard Stansbury, *Exploration and Survey of the Valley of the Great Salt Lake of Utah, including a Reconnoissance of a New Route through the Rocky Mountains*, Philadelphia, 1852, SIL, photo by Ed Castle; 89 map art, courtesy R.R. Donnelley Cartographic Services, cartography, Julie Schieber, Washington, DC; 90TL from W.H. Emory, *Notes of a Military Reconnoissance, from Fort Leavenworth in Missouri to San Diego*, Washington, DC, 1848, SIL, photo by Ed Castle; 90TR from proof plates of William H. Emory, *Report on the United States and Mexican Boundary Survey*, vol.II, *Reptiles of the Boundary*, Washington, DC, 1859, SIL, photo by Ed Castle; 90B NPG/SI; 91T from William H. Emory, op. cit., v.I, Washington, DC, 1857, SIL, photo by Ed Castle; 91B from proof plates of William H. Emory, op. cit., vol.II, Washington, D.C., 1859, SIL, photo by Ed Castle; 92T NMAH/SI, photo by Ed Castle; 92B, 93B from George Horatio Derby, *Phoenixiana or Sketches and Burlesques*, New York, 1903, from the collection of Pat Eames, photos by Ed Castle; 93T from *Regulations for the Uniform and Dress of the Army of the US, June 1851* (US War Department), SIL, photo by Ed Castle; 94L, 95L, 95R from *Report upon the Colorado River of the West explored in 1857 and 1858 by Lieutenant Joseph C. Ives*, Washington, DC, 1861, SIL, photo by Ed Castle; 96-97 Melinda Berge/Photographers Aspen; 98L, 98R ANSP; 99 David Muench; 100T courtesy Museum of Northern Arizona; 100B from Captain L. Sitgreaves, *Report of an Expedition down the Zuni and Colorado Rivers*, Washington, DC, 1854, SIL, photo by Ed Castle; 101T courtesy Museum of Northern Arizona; 101B, 102, 103 from Captain L. Sitgreaves, op. cit., Washington, DC, 1854, SIL, photos by Ed Castle; 104, 105 from Howard Stansbury, *Exploration and Survey of the Valley of the Great Salt Lake of Utah, including a Reconnaissance of a New Route through the Rocky Mountains*, Philadelphia, 1852, SIL, photos by Ed Castle; 106T lithograph by Francis D'Avignon after a photograph by Mathew Brady, NPG/SI; 106B from Thomas E. Breckenridge, "The Story of a Famous Expedition," *Cosmopolitan*, August 1896, LC, photo by Ed Castle; 107TL art by Edward Kern, courtesy The Huntington Library; 107TR Edward or Richard Kern, "Natural Obelisks," courtesy The Huntington Library; 107B from *Frémont's Fourth Expedition, 1848-49*, edited by LeRoy & Ann Hafen, Glendale, CA: The Arthur H. Clark Co., 1960; 108-109, 108B from *Reports of Explorations and Surveys, to Ascertain the Most Practicable and Economical Route for a Railroad from the Mississippi River to the Pacific Ocean*, v. XII, Washington, DC, 1860, SIL, photo by Ed Castle; 110T Ibid., v. II, Washington, DC, 1855, SIL, photo by Ed Castle; 110-111B Ibid., v. XI, Washington, DC, 1861, SIL, photo by Ed Castle; 112T, 112C Ibid., v. II, Washington, DC, 1855, SIL, photos by Ed Castle; 112-113, 113R from H.B. Möllhausen, *Diary of a Journey from the Mississippi to the Coasts of the Pacific with a United States Government Expedition*, SIL, translated by Mrs. Percy Sinnett, v. II, London, 1858, photos by Ed Castle; 114T from *Reports of Explorations and Surveys*, v. II, Washington, DC, 1855, SIL, photo by Ed Castle; 114B NA, R.G.# 48, photo by Ed Castle; 115 LC; 116TL from *Reports of Explorations and Surveys*, v. XII, Washington, DC, 1860, SIL, photo by Ed Castle; 116TR Ibid., v. II, Washington, DC, 1855, SIL, photo by Ed Castle; 116BL Ibid., v. XII, Washington, DC, 1860, SIL, photo by Ed Castle; 116BC, 116BR from Lieutenant R.S. Williamson, *Report of Explorations in California for Railroad Routes, to connect with the Routes Near the 35th and 32d Parallels of North Latitude*, 1853, SIL, photos by Ed Castle; 117T from *Reports of Explorations and Surveys*, v. II, Washington, DC, 1855, SIL, photo by Ed Castle; 117BL, BR from Spencer F. Baird, *Catalogue of North American Mammals*, 1857, SIL, photos by Ed Castle; 118-119 from *Reports of Explorations and Surveys*, v. XII, Washington, DC, 1860, SIL, photo by Ed Castle.

"*arsenic and directions*": pp. 120-121 SIA; 121R NMNH/SI, photo by Ed Castle; 122T Richard Kern, "Smithsonian Institute," 1852, Amon Carter Museum; 122B art by Thomas LeClear, 1877, NPG/SI; 123T NPG/SI; 123B art by John James Audubon, from Alice Ford, *Audubon, by Himself*, Garden City, NY, 1969, Natural History Press, photo by Ed Castle; 124 NMNH/SI, photo by Ed Castle; 125 from *Harpers Weekly*, June 1, 1878, after original sketches and photographs by Henry W. Elliott; 126 map art, courtesy R.R. Donnelley Cartographic Services, cartography, Julie Schieber, Washington, DC; 127 Nicholas Devore III/Photographers Aspen; 128 art by F.W.von Egloffstein, *Reports of Explorations and Surveys, to ascertain the most Practicable and Economical Route for a Railroad from the Mississippi River to the Pacific Ocean*, v. XI, Washington, DC, 1861, SIL, photo by Ed Castle; 129TL, 129BL from Howard Stansbury, *Exploration and Surveys of the Valley of the Great Salt Lake of Utah, including a reconnoissance of a new route through the Rocky Mountains*, Philadelphia, 1852, SIL, photos by Ed Castle; 129TR from Captain L. Sitgreaves, *Report of an Expedition down the Zuni and Colorado Rivers*, Washington, DC, 1854, SIL, photo by Ed Castle; 129BR from *Reports of Explorations and Surveys*, v.II, Washington, DC, 1855, SIL, photo by Ed Castle; 130 from William H. Emory, *Report on the United States and Mexican Boundary Survey*, v. I, Washington, DC, 1857, SIL, photo by Ed Castle; 131T NMNH/SI, photo by Victor Krantz; 131B, 132T from proof plates of William H. Emory, *Report on the United States and Mexican Boundary Survey*, v.II, *Reptiles of the Boundary*, Washington, D.C., 1859, SIL, photos by Ed Castle; 132B from Spencer F. Baird, *Catalogue of North American Mammals*, 1857, photo by Ed Castle; 133L from proof plates of William H.Emory, *Report on the United States and Mexican Boundary Survey*, v.II, *Mammals of the Boundary*, Washington, DC, 1859, SIL, photo by Ed Castle; 133R Ibid., v.II, *Reptiles of the Boundary*, Washington, DC, 1859, SIL, photo by Ed Castle; 135T, 135B NMNH/SI, photos by Ed Castle; 136 NA, R.G.# 77, photo by Ed Castle; 137T Alfred Jacob Miller, "Snake and Sioux on the Warpath," TGI; 137B LC; 138, 139 NMNH/SI, photos by Ed Castle; 140 NA, R.G.# 77, photos by Ed Castle; 141 Fred J. Maroon; 142T Frederick Behman, "Fort Pierre Dakota Territory," NA; 142B Antoin Schonborn, "Canyon of Rapid Creek," Yale Collection of Western Americana, Beinecke Rare Book and Manuscript Library; 143 J. Hudson Snowden, "Bugcatching," NA, R.G.# 77, photo by Ed Castle; 144, 144-145 from J.L. Leidy, *The Extinct Mammalian Fauna of Dakota and Nebraska together with a synopsis of the Mammalian remains of North America*, by F.V. Hayden, Philadelphia, 1869, SIL, photos by Ed Castle.

Megatheria at Large: pp. 146-147 William Henry Jackson, neg.# 526 USGS; 148T, 148B SIA; 149 Chas. Bierstadt, ca. 1880, SIA, collection of Susan Myers; 150 map art, courtesy R.R. Donnelley Cartographic Services, cartography, Julie Schieber, Washington, DC; 151T NA; 151B NMAH/SI, photo by Ed Castle; 152 William Henry Jackson, 1873, courtesy American Heritage Center, University of Wyoming; 153T from William Henry Holmes, *Random Records of a Lifetime*, v. III, 1846-1931, NMAA/NPG Library; 153B SIA; 154-155 David Muench; 155B Wyoming Fish & Game Preserve, photo by LuRay Parker; 156TL NA; 156TR from William Henry Holmes, *Random Records of a Lifetime*, v. III, 1846-1931, NMAA/NPG Library; 156B NMAH/SI, photo by Jeff Tinsley; 157 William Henry Jackson, DPL; 158 NA; 159T DPL; 159B NA; 160-161 Thomas Moran, "The Grand Canyon of the Yellowstone," 1872, NMAA/SI, lent by the U.S. Department of the Interior; 162 William Henry Jackson, 1873, neg.# 1276, USGS; 163 from F.V. Hayden, *The Yellowstone National Park and the Mountain Regions of Portions of Idaho, Nevada, Colorado and Utah*, Boston, 1876, SIL, photo by Ed Castle; 164-165 SIL, photo by Ed Castle; 166 courtesy The Bancroft Library; 167T "U.S. Geological Exploration of the 40th Parallel (King Survey)", plate 100, USGS; 167B Ibid., plate 9, USGS; 168 Ibid., plate 80, USGS; 169T Ibid., plate 13, USGS; 169B Ibid., plate 35, USGS; 170-171 David Muench; 172 Timothy H. O'Sullivan, "U.S. Geological Exploration of the 100th Meridian", plate 15, USGS; 173T Timothy O'Sullivan, 1873, courtesy Amon Carter Museum; 173B Neg.# 181, USGS; 174 John K. Hillers, ca. 1879, DPL; 175L NA; 175R John K. Hillers, 1872, Neg.# 445, USGS; 176 John K. Hillers, ca. 1872, Earthquake Information Bulletin 295, USGS; 177 Nicholas Devore III/Photographers Aspen.

The Last Frontier: pp. 178-179 Nancy Simmerman/Alaska Photo; 179 from Lucien M. Turner, *Contributions to the Natural History of Alaska*, no.II, Washington, DC, 1886, SIL, photo by Ed Castle; 180 map art, courtesy R.R. Donnelley Cartographic Services, cartography, Julie Schieber, Washington, DC; 181T Emanuel Leutze, "Signing the Treaty for the Purchase of Alaska," 1867, The Bettmann Archive; 181B The Bettmann Archive; 182 from H.M. Robinson, *The Great Fur Land or Sketches of Life in the Hudson's Bay Territory*, NY, 1879, G.P. Putnam's Sons, SIL, photo by Ed Castle; 183 SIA; 184 Stephen J. Krasemann/DRK Photo; 185T art by Frederick Whymper, NYPL; 185B art by John Webber for Captain Cook's Atlas, 1788, Special Collections Division, University of Washington Libraries, neg.# UW 6714; 186, 187 NMNH/SI, photo by Ed Castle; 188 from Frederick Whymper, *Travel and Adventure in the Territory of Alaska*, London, 1868, SIL, photo by Ed Castle; 189 from William H. Dall, *Alaska and its Resources*, Boston, 1870, SIL, photo by Ed Castle; 190 from Frederick Whymper, *Travel and Adventure in the Territory of Alaska*, London, 1868, SIL, photo by Ed Castle; 191TL courtesy The Bancroft Library; 191TR NMAH/SI, photo by Jeff Tinsley; 191B SIA, photo by Ed Castle; 192 William H. Dall, "Oxygyrus, plate I," 1866, SIA, photo by Ed Castle; 193 William H. Dall, "Clio, plate VIII," 1866, SIA, photo by Ed Castle; 194-195 Earth & Sky Creations/Jack Schick; 196 NPG/SI; 197T Edward William Nelson, SIA; 197B SIA; 198, 199 from Edward William Nelson, *Report upon Natural History Collections made in Alaska between the years 1877 and 1881*, no. III, Washington, DC, 1887, SIL, photos by Ed Castle; 200T NMNH/SI; 200B Edward William Nelson, SIA; 201L NMNH/SI; 201R from Philip Kopper, *The National Museum of Natural History*, NY, 1982, Harry N. Abrams, Inc., photo by Chip Clark; 202T NMNH/SI, photo by Ed Castle; 202B, 203 from Lucien M. Turner, *Contributions to the Natural History of Alaska*, no.II, Washington, DC, 1886, photo by Ed Castle; 204-205 Tom Bean/Alaska Photo; 206L John Johnson; 206R Alaska State Library, Neg.# 01-1094; 207 Kim Heacox.

End of an Era: pp. 208-209 LC; 209 NMAH/SI, photo by Kim Nielsen; 210 from John Wesley Powell, *Report on the Lands of the Arid Region of the United States*, 2nd ed., Washington, DC, 1879, SIL, photo by Ed Castle; 211 from Aaron Arrowsmith and Samuel Lewis, *A New and Elegant General Atlas, Comprising all the New Discoveries, to the Present Time*, Philadelphia, 1804, courtesy of the Harvard College Library; 212L NAA/SI; 212R NMNH/SI, photo by Ed Castle; 213L NAA/SI; 213R SIA; 214 NMAH/SI, photo by Ross Chapple; 214-215 Southern Pacific Transportation Company; 216-217 A.J. Russell, courtesy Oakland Museum, History Department; 218T Forest Service Collection, National Agricultural Library; 218C Western History Collections, University of Oklahoma; 218B Erwin E. Smith, LC; 219T Solomon D. Butcher Collection, Nebraska State Historical Society; 219BL John C.H. Grabill, 1889, LC; 219BR LC; 220 Peabody Museum of Natural History, Yale University; 221 Frederic Remington, Museum of Western Art, Denver; 222 NMNH/SI, photo by Charles H. Phillips; 223L from O.C. Marsh, *Odontornithes: A Monograph on Extinct Birds of North America*, Washington, DC, 1880, SIL, photo by Ed Castle; 223R Peabody Museum of Natural History, Yale University; 224-225 Shelly Grossman/Woodfin Camp & Associates; 226 SIL, photo by Ed Castle; 228T Harriman Estate/reprinted from *Audubon*, September 1982, The National Audubon Society; 228B G.K. Gilbert, #201, USGS; 229T Private collection; 229B Harriman Estate/reprinted from *Audubon*, September 1982, The National Audubon Society; 230T G.K. Gilbert, #437, USGS; 230B Harriman Estate/reprinted from *Audubon*, September 1982, The National Audubon Society; 231R G.K. Gilbert, #228, USGS; 231B G.K. Gilbert, #250, USGS; 232R Frederick A. Walpole, 1902, Harriman Estate/ reprinted from *Audubon*, September 1982, The National Audubon Society; 232B G.K. Gilbert, #343, USGS; 233TL art by Louis A. Fuertes, photo by Harold D. Walters, Neg. 2365, American Museum of Natural History; 233TR private collection; 233B G.K. Gilbert, #285, USGS; 234-235 Edward S. Curtis, private collection; 235 Edward S. Curtis, SIA.

Toward a New Sensibility: pp. 236-237 courtesy The Ansel Adams Publishing Trust; 238 courtesy The New York Historical Society; 239T NMAH/SI; 239BL, 239 BR The Bettmann Archive; 240 courtesy Museum of Western Art, Denver, photo by James O. Milmoe; 241T courtesy The Anschutz Collection, Denver; 241B courtesy Museum of Western Art, Denver, photo by James O. Milmoe; 242-243 John C.H. Grabill, LC; 244T NMNH, photo by Abrams Photo/ Graphics; 244B SI, photo by Joe A. Goulait; 244-245 SIA; 245T NMNH, photo by Chip Clark; 245B NMNH, photo by Kjell B. Sandved; 246-247 The Butler Institute of American Art, Youngstown, OH.